SELFHOOD
AND
AUTHENTICITY

SELFHOOD
AND
AUTHENTICITY

COREY ANTON

State University
of New York
Press

Published by
State University of New York Press, Albany

Production by Susan Geraghty
Marketing by Patrick Durocher

Printed in the United States of America

For information, address State University of New York Press,
90 State Street, Suite 700, Albany, NY 12207

Library of Congress Cataloging-in-Publication Data

Anton, Corey.
  Selfhood and authenticity / by Corey Anton.
    p. cm.
  Includes bibliographical references and index.
  ISBN 0-7914-4899-1 (alk. paper) — ISBN 0-7914-4900-9 (pbk. : alk. paper)
    1. Self (Philosophy) I. Title.
  BD438.5 .A68 2001
  126—dc21

                                                    00-040017

10 9 8 7 6 5 4 3 2 1

For their care
and for the person I have become
I dedicate this work to my parents,
Ron and Sue

CONTENTS

ACKNOWLEDGMENTS

This work is indebted to many persons. Most broadly, I want to thank my colleagues at Purdue and Grand Valley. I also thank the Purdue Research Foundation for a summer grant which greatly facilitated the early drafts of this work.

I must thank William K. Rawlins for all of his passion and open encouragement regarding my project. Without his continuing support, and especially his early guidance into Taylor's work, the project that generated this book would not have happened. I need to thank Calvin O. Schrag for his interest and many trenchant directives to the content of the manuscript. I particularly wish to express thanks for his quick perusals, immediate feedback, and many useful suggestions. I want to thank Mary Keehner for her many useful criticisms and suggestions for future research into rhetorical applications. And, finally, I also wish to express thanks to Jacqueline Martinez for her insightful concerns and suggestions regarding the political and scholarly implications of the project.

I want to express a deep thanks to a circle of intimate friends: Brenda, Scott and Tara, Tom and Amy, Steve and Betsy, Bryan and Joy, Laural and Jeff, and Laurie and Jonathan. I additionally want to acknowledge Abe, Mathias, Henry, Barry, Phil, and Bryan for many stimulating discussions, and also, I want to thank Stephanie for helping me through the final chapters. It was all of these people who have encouragingly endured and deeply enriched my seemingly endless—and sometimes exasperating—talk. Innumerable hours of our rangy conversations facilitated, shaped, and settled the present manuscript; more than I ever have explicitly stated and certainly more than I could express adequately. I also need to express a special thanks to Thomas S. Wright, Robert Mayberry, and Jermaine Martinez for their assistance in proofreading and editing the work during its final stages.

I must thank my family, especially my parents, for all they have done to enable this project. Without their loving support and understanding, I would not have made it this far. Also, I need to acknowledge that, in many ways, my concern regarding authenticity and the changing character of selfhood was inspired by and grounded in my parents' many lessons about meaning and existence.

Finally, I cannot not give a sounding acknowledgment to someone without whom I most likely would not have studied communication, to say nothing of entertaining the idea of graduate studies. Perhaps, only those who have been fortunate enough to have learned from him personally will know how much of the present work is indebted to Lee Thayer. In many ways, it was Thayer who convinced me to believe, to know passionately, that "as we communicate, so shall we be."

PART I

The Culture
of Authenticity

CHAPTER 1

The Culture of Authenticity

Charles Taylor's little work, *The Ethics of Authenticity* (1991), describes the distinguishing marks of modernity by addressing a moral ideal which informs numerous practices and beliefs in contemporary American and Western cultures. This ideal, that of authenticity, most broadly refers to the modern "quest" for self-fulfillment, self-realization, or personal development. For example, somewhere, individuals pursue with zeal and passion what they want to be when they grow up. Elsewhere, persons feel vaguely dissatisfied with their inability to get it all together or their indecision regarding what they want to do with their lives. Many people currently are entering the bond of marriage, seeking dreams of personal fulfillment and long-lasting happiness, i.e., a "happily-ever-after." Others are leaving a long-term marriage which, for at least one partner, was no longer self-fulfilling, no longer worth it. Such doings—and many more could be offered—seem to make sense to most of us. Indeed, many people in our culture feel themselves called to be true to themselves, called to pursue personal quests for development and fulfillment. In a word, many people today feel that it is their right to live personally meaningful lives.

SOME BACKGROUND ON AUTHENTICITY

This is not to say that individuals at other times and places did not also seek something like self-fulfillment (Campbell, 1949). Rather, as Taylor (1991) suggests, "the point is that today many people feel called to do this, feel they ought to do this, feel their lives would be somehow wasted or unfulfilled if they didn't do it" (p. 17). Further describing the centrality of this odyssey in modern cultures (e.g., the United States), Taylor argues:

> It is hard to find anyone we would consider being in the mainstream of our Western societies who, faced with their own life choices, about career or relationships, gives no weight at all to something they would identify as fulfillment, or self-development, or realizing their potential, or for which they would find some other term from the range that has served to articulate this ideal. (1991, p. 75)

3

The overarching point is that modernity has ushered in something like what Taylor calls a "culture of authenticity." We can find this ideal throughout the culture and can register its weight on many scales. But even if we grant that drives for personal fulfillment characterize the mainstream of modern cultures, whether this is a bane or boon remains open to debate.

In fact, to the debate about the culture of authenticity we most likely find ourselves as latecomers. Both "boosters" and "knockers," as Taylor terms them, have emerged already. The boosters, commonly siding with the intellectual left, celebrate the modern individual's sense of freedom and right to "do their own thing." An individual's prerogative to decide for him- or herself basic life issues is advocated and furthered. Said otherwise, the boosters, often continuing a neo-Nietzschean spirit, want to advance individual's "poetic license" for composing and accomplishing their own lives and the sense of meaning for them. Indeed, boosters valorize the spirit of artists and poets, and suggest that one's life is an accomplishment won away from the leveling indifference of mass society. Thinkers from this camp even claim that more individualization is necessary, that even further deconstruction of mass morals or meanings is warranted.

The knockers, on the other hand, generally believe that the culture of authenticity reflects a moral laxity, and hence, in actuality, is no ethical ideal at all. Rather, it is an unfortunate relativizing of ethics, a license for moral sloth. That is, because the background premise to the ideal of authenticity is that one must realize a potentiality which is properly one's own, some thinkers suggest that this kind of thinking leads people into degraded, absurd, or trivialized modes of existence, if not socially irresponsible ones. The individualization of human life, and an increasing ego-centeredness, can "flatten and narrow" life's moral and ethical significance. Hence, although some aspects of the world and its order are open to the individual's poetic appropriations, they are not completely self-determined, and so individuals, according to the knockers, may have mistaken an epistemological insight of relativity for a practical or ethical maxim.

Attempting to eke out some space for his position, Taylor argues that both the knockers and the boosters are somewhat off the target. The knockers, he states, fail to acknowledge that, regardless of how weak and distorted its expression might be, a powerful moral ideal is at work in the culture of authenticity. Counter to the knockers, Taylor maintains, and I think rightfully so, that "Once we try to explain this simply as a kind of egoism, or a species of moral laxity, a self-indulgence with regard to a tougher, more exigent earlier age, we are already off the track" (1991, p. 16). The boosters, on the other hand, fail to recognize the requirement of horizons of significance as well as the dialogical nature of self.[1] I shall return to these two issues in the next section, but for now, a few additional issues must be addressed before advancing any further.

First, social scientific research can be seen as slowly embodying and taking on many of the characteristics of this ideal of authenticity. For example, challenges to traditional notions of representation and representability, and more localized accounts of social interaction, (e.g., more individualistic research strategies such as ethnography, autoethnography, personal narrative analysis, etc.) are becoming common place (Bochner, 1985; Bochner, Cissna, and Garko, 1991; and Gergen, Gulerce, Lock, and Misra, 1996; Goffman, 1963a, 1967, and 1971). Within social scientific research practices we can discern a movement against traditional conventionalized means of doing research and an increasing concern over the extent to which accounts are generalizable or applicable to diverse populations (Gergen, Gulerce, Lock, and Misra, 1996).

Additionally, social scientific explanations tend to deny, or fail to address, the moral force of our cultural ideas (Hudson, 1972; Schumacher, 1977). In fact, in "the normal fashion of social science explanation . . . what are invoked are motivations that are non-moral . . . social science seems to be telling us that to understand such phenomena as the contemporary culture of authenticity, we shouldn't have recourse in explanation to such things as moral ideals" (Taylor, 1991, pp. 19–21). Social scientific explanations, hence, remain somewhat silent regarding the extent to which people are morally moved, if not empowered, through articulated cultural ideals.

Second, Taylor points out that an "inarticulacy" rides throughout the debate. This inarticulacy mainly arises from the culture of authenticity itself; it is carried along in the notion that "Everybody has his or her own values, and about these it is impossible to argue" (1991, p. 13). The fact that persons have their own values thus easily leads them to think that values are not open to reasonable debate; they are simply based upon each individual's choices. That is, people commonly believe that they cannot give valid reasons for some good being qualitatively better than another because such preferences ultimately rest upon subjective appraisals. Elsewhere Taylor describes this as, "modern skepticism," referring to "the widespread belief . . . that moral differences can't be arbitrated by reason, that when it comes to moral values, we all just ultimately have to plump for ones which feel best to us" (1995, p. 34). This further means that while critics of contemporary culture are free to disparage authenticity as an ideal, the boosters are often "pushed into inarticulacy about it by their own outlook" (Taylor, 1991, p. 21). Hence, the boosters apparently fail to recognize the importance of being able to talk reasonably about moral choices with others.

Taylor's Admonishments

The present discussion raises some interesting questions: First, how should we regard and understand this culture of authenticity? Second, is it to be scorned or celebrated?

Taylor, as already suggested, argues against both the knockers and the boosters. Even more specifically, he argues that what we need is to "show that modes that opt for self-fulfillment without regard (a) to the demands of our ties with others or (b) to demands of any kind emanating from something more or other than human desires or aspirations are self-defeating, that they destroy the conditions for realizing authenticity itself" (1991, p. 35). Let me carefully unpack what is at issue here.

First, self-centered modes of authenticity tend to direct the idea of fulfillment toward the individual. This, in turn, can make personal affiliations seem to be purely instrumental. Taylor argues that some proponents of these debased modes of authenticity, "tend to see fulfillment as just of the self, neglecting or delegitimating the demands that come from beyond our own desires or aspirations" (1991, p. 58). Relations with others can seem expendable according to the individual's interests, and such a degraded understanding of authenticity seems to overlook that we cannot separate ourselves from others. Supporters of this mode of authenticity seem to believe that self can be individually or "monologically" generated, and so, they may underassess the extent to which we discover and negotiate selfhood through dialogue, whether that dialogue be overt or internalized. Taylor's articulation of the ideal of authenticity, then, argues that interpersonal relationships which are exclusively instrumental to personal interests are self-stultifying.

Second, a difficulty encountered in the notion of "authenticity" is that it commonly travels with the idea of originality, poetic and artistic creation serving as obvious exemplars. As such, this ideal often demands a revolt against social convention; authenticity is a personal achievement in the fullest sense of the word. "Indeed," Taylor writes, "the very idea of originality, and the associated notion that the enemy of authenticity can be social conformity, forces on us the idea that authenticity will have to struggle against some externally imposed rules" (1991, p. 63). In addition to this general context of creative opposition, the search for authenticity is commonly pitted against traditional moral orders. These are to be, in Nietzsche's terms, "transvalued." Moreover, some individuals on the quest for authenticity may believe that they can go all the way down to self-determining freedom. They may overlook the necessarily horizontal nature of human life. They may overlook the fact that meaning is always accomplished from within already existing horizons of significance.

Finally, there is always a "background" of intelligibility.[2] This means that our poetic improvisations, our acts of individual originality, make sense only against (and/or within) traditions and backdrops of significance. Taylor argues, "We have to share also some standards of value on which the identities concerned check out as equal. . . . Recognizing difference, like self-choosing, requires a horizon of significance, in this case a shared one" (1991, p. 52). This communal backdrop implies that choice for the sake of choice is not a defensible position. People must reckon with a horizon of "important questions" if they, in seeking significance in life, are to define themselves meaningfully. In the end, "To shut out demands emanating beyond the self" Taylor argues, "is precisely to suppress the conditions of significance and hence to court trivialization" (1991, p. 40).

To review what is at stake here, let me rehearse Taylor's important distinction between the necessarily self-referential orientation of authenticity and the actual content of the pursuit of authenticity, which need not be self-referential. He argues that,

> Only if I exist in a world in which history, or the demands of nature, or the needs of my fellow human beings, or the duties of citizenship, or the call of God, or something else of this order matters critically, can I define an identity for myself that is not trivial. Authenticity is not the enemy of demands that emanate from beyond the self; it supposes such demands. (1991, pp. 40–41)

This distinction stresses that people are, in a sense, perpetually outside of themselves, actively caught up attending to and caring for the things that matter to them. People dwell in the things into which they meaningfully weave their lives. Said otherwise, to achieve personal fulfillment, persons need not explicitly focus upon themselves, as if self were best taken care of in such a direct, literal manner. In a word, self-fulfillment need not specifically focus upon self per se. I believe that Taylor is correct in his position, and yet, we might still want to know why this is the case. The present project is partially motivated to show why and how such a conclusion is warranted.

I conclude this section with a dense summary by Taylor. He offers a rough outline regarding the character and nature of authenticity as an ideal:

> Briefly, we can say that Authenticity (A) involves (i) creation and construction as well as discovery, (ii) originality, and frequently (iii) opposition to the rules of society and even potentially to what we recognize as morality. But it is also true, as we saw, that it (B) requires (i) openness to the horizons of significance (for otherwise the creation loses the background that can save it from insignificance) and (ii) a self-definition in dialogue. (1991, p. 66)

In the end, Taylor encourages us to join in the unending struggle to articulate and enable the higher and richer modes of authenticity while cutting off or at least curtailing the lower and shallower forms.

Prospects and Aspirations

Compared to this exceedingly brief and rough sketch, the concrete issues at stake seem so vast and the constellations of difficulties so nettlesome that "a solution" appears on the distant horizon, if at all. Nonetheless, I believe Taylor is quite correct when he claims that

> instead of dismissing this culture altogether, or just endorsing it as it is, we ought to attempt to raise its practice by making more palpable to its participants what the ethic they subscribe to really involves. . . . What we ought to be doing is fighting over the meaning of authenticity . . . we ought to be trying to persuade people that self-fulfillment, so far from excluding unconditional relationships and moral demands beyond the self, actually requires these in some form. The struggle ought not to be *over* authenticity, for or against, but *about* it, defining its proper meaning. We ought to be trying to lift the culture back up, closer to its motivating ideal. (1991, pp. 72–73)

The culture of authenticity, I maintain, does reflect in part an ethical aspiration, but one which demands an effective safeguard against the self-defeating ego-centered varieties. Therefore, authenticity, as a quest for self-fulfillment, requires or demands an adequate comprehension of the selfhood that is to be fulfilled. And yet, such a comprehension is sorely lacking. We seem to be without an adequate grasp on the nature and constitution of the human self, and moreover, it is only through such a comprehension that the quest for authenticity may be fruitfully enabled.

The present project will undertake the task of thematically delineating an adequate conception of self for the culture of authenticity. I take as my point of departure advice suggested in Taylor's concluding remarks. In my judgment, his closing words propose a project that needs to be taken up, and he further indicates some necessary considerations. He writes, "We are embodied agents, living in dialogical conditions, inhabiting time in a specifically human way, that is, making sense of our lives as a story that connects the past from which we have come to our future projects. That means (b) that if we are properly to treat a human being, we have to respect this embodied, dialogical, temporal nature" (1991, pp. 105–106). It is, thus, these three issues which need further careful consideration, as does, a highly related one to all three, the role of human symbolicity.

Accordingly, this book addresses two primary questions: (1) What is the basic character of selfhood? (2) How are we to understand selfhood so as to effectively further the quest for authenticity? Moreover, my inquiry shall be focused further through several guiding questions: What is the specifically embodied character of selfhood? What is the specifically social character of selfhood? What is the specifically symbolic character of selfhood? What is the specifically temporal character of selfhood? How are these characters related to each other?

To provide compelling responses to these questions, I shall engage in an extended phenomenology of selfhood and authenticity, addressing how these four dimensions (i.e., embodiment, sociality, symbolicity, and temporality) are fundamentally interrelated ontological conditions of the human self. Moreover, I attempt to carve out a space for a different mode of scholarly research, one which focally works from and for the ideal of authenticity. My overall project draws heavily from writings in existential phenomenology, and it gives continued focus to the drive for authenticity and the role of selfhood in this quest. At this juncture, and before advancing further, I think some additional considerations are warranted.

As I have already argued, the culture of authenticity, if it is to cultivate higher forms, needs to articulate an adequate comprehension of selfhood. This means that many of the current difficulties, in some way or other, tie back to contemporary understandings of selfhood. Given that self comes to the fore in the quest for authenticity, I must briefly review some of the dominant contemporary stances toward self and preview some prospects for advancement.

The Self in Question

Of the self so much already has been said. Why should we want to add to the sea of paper on this issue? Is there not already an adequate understanding of self? Or perhaps, on the other side, is not questioning about selfhood misguided and doomed from the very start? I begin with the latter challenge.

In the later part of the twentieth century, the integrity of selfhood has come under a great deal of scrutiny. Some schools of inquiry (e.g., structuralisms) suggest that questions regarding selfhood are simply misguided. The structuralism of Levi-Strauss and the early neostructuralism of Foucault are cases in point. Schrag well summarizes this issue where he writes, "The dissolution of the human subject is a theme that appears and reappears throughout the structuralist literature. Indeed, it may well be designated the central motif of structuralism" (1980, p 42). In some form or other, structuralisms, including varieties of social constructionism and constructivism, leave open many critical questions regarding human selfhood: Are there any free spaces for the existing individual? Is the notion of the individual simply an illusion, a trite cliché worn by contemporary Americans?[3] Is "socialization" necessarily distinct from "growing up?"

(Goodman, 1957). Whether or not the "death of the subject" has been declared prematurely, the point remaining in force is that the existing self is easily lost (if not intentionally negated) in numerous structuralist accounts.

Even more radical assaults on selfhood come from various schools of postmodern thought. Here, thinkers seek to deconstruct self and show how it is a fleeting and eluding phenomenon. Scholars following thinkers such as Derrida and Lyotard have placed not only the "presence" of self into radical question, they also have challenged movement toward meaningful dialogue and solidarity. Thus as selfhood is dismantled, so too is the ideal of community.

But perhaps we are past both the grip of structuralism and the jostle of postmodernity. Perhaps self is known quite clearly, that is, all too well. That the human self is socially constructed through various communicative practices is pretty much standard fare to many contemporary scholars. Indeed, in some shape or variety this thesis informs perhaps the bulk of contemporary theorizing. Still, what most needs correction is the meaning of the words "socially" and "constructed." Commonly, the fact that sociality is already phenomenologically constituted seems to pass without due address. Relatedly and likewise, we can find an underappreciation of how central embodiment and temporality are to meaning construction. I can summarize these issues this way: Social constructionist thought, which has shaped a good deal of contemporary social theorizing, picked up many phenomenological insights through the works of Alfred Schutz,[4] who rather uncritically appropriated certain aspects of Husserl's work.[5] Other second generation phenomenologists such as Heidegger, Sartre, and Merleau-Ponty, although undeniably learning much from Husserl, were much more critical in their appropriations. And more specifically, they explicated the many passed over existential issues. In a word, much social constructionist thought seems to have missed the "existential turn" in phenomenology. The fundamental importance of temporality and embodiment have been largely pushed to a blurry periphery as focus has been primarily on sociality and symbolicity. But, this is not to imply that human symbolicity is now adequately comprehended.

The turn toward linguistics, textuality, and most generally symbolicity, has been exceedingly rewarding and insightful, and yet, it is not without limitations. Therefore, given that human existence often is addressed in terms of symbolicity, a third and highly related difficulty with current conceptualizations of self is that a great deal of contemporary theorizing is based on mechanistic metaphors, models of the human as an information processing machine. The self's fundamental relations to and with speech are underemphasized, and speech is reduced to a tool for thought. Indeed, the contemporary human sciences are dominated by materialistic and mechanistic understandings of both self and information. Many scholars' theorizing on the self and language not only base their theories upon computers, but they view human speech and interaction basically as acts of processing "bits" of information (Greene, 1984). But to suggest that the human is simply a complicated machine is not to state a fact. It is to exemplify, as Nietzsche (1979) points out, how metaphors can deaden, becoming forgotten as the metaphors they are.

Thinkers such as Heidegger, Merleau-Ponty, and Dreyfus, have astutely critiqued these information processing models. Likewise Taylor, in his *Human Agency and Language* (1985, p. 1), offers a sustained and thorough criticism of "the understanding of human life and action implicit in an influential family of theories in the human sciences," giving specific attention to weaknesses and shortcomings within cognitive psychologies. The notion of "information" as bits, as well as the idea that context is some "thing" that can be quantitatively measured—analytically parceled out in full—must be critically assessed (Thayer, 1987; 1997). Overly analytical approaches thus easily overlook (i.e., undersee) the largely holistic and tacit nature of our comprehensions and capacities. Given the predominance of such atomistic and analytical models of self, further discussion is needed which focuses on thinkers like Heidegger and Merleau-Ponty, whose works are driven by a recognition of the implicit character of sense making and the tacit nature of intelligibility.

As a final note, it is rather interesting that communication scholars have said so little about the concept of authenticity. Perhaps it is in part because the notion seems to cut against various schools of social constructionist thought. Indeed, some scholars might want to suggest that socialization is so thorough that individual choice is always an illusion; it cannot help but be an expression of socialization. Thus the current project attempts to challenge this assumption, and more generally to break open the silence regarding the notion of authenticity. I wish to demonstrate how the notion of authenticity should be a central concept to communication studies.

Why should it be central? Because questions of selfhood (or embodiment, sociality, symbolicity, and temporality) are uniquely communicational issues. In the end, many of these questions return to Aristotle's original formula: "'zôon logon echon,' which means 'animal possessing logos'" (Taylor, 1985, p. 217). What is at issue is nothing less than an investigation into the full meaning of human logos. Unfortunately, logos has come down to us as meaning "reason." But the original notion includes such varied sedimentations as speech, language, logic, thought, discourse, and reasoned argument. This richness seems deeply lost in much contemporary social scientific thought. Whether someone's focus is upon textuality, or sociality, or perhaps even communication patterns, the profound depth of the meaning of logos seems lost in contemporary culture. We find a richer and more profound understanding of logos when we consider, for example, Heidegger's early writings. Here he tells us that "Man shows himself as the entity which talks. This does not signify that the possibility of vocal utterance is peculiar to him, but rather that he is the entity which is such as to discover the world and Dasein itself" (1962, p. 187). It is this level of profundity regarding the full significance of logos that needs to be recovered if selfhood is to be adequately addressed. The necessary interweaving of embodiment, sociality, symbolicity, and temporality seems underappreciated in a good deal of contemporary accounts of selfhood. Thematically describing these interrelationships is specifically what is needed to address the culture of authenticity sufficiently.

The notion of authenticity, I maintain, should be a central concept to general communication theory. Thus my project seeks to offer an account of selfhood that will provide correctives to these numerous difficulties. It hopes to give a compelling account of selfhood. I want to provide an articulation in which the richer and more complete modes of the quest for authenticity can come to fruition. In the end and most generally, I attempt a critical yet integrative dialogue among numerous, diverse currents of scholarship. I offer an ontological exposition of the overall constitutive structures and processes that are necessary for human selfhood. Said simply, I seek to explicate and delineate the essential features of self. By critically synthesizing diverse yet thematically related lines of scholarship, I document key relationships among embodiment, sociality, symbolicity, and temporality. Ultimately, this account of selfhood hopes to enable those persons who feel called to respond to the quest for authenticity.

PART II

Phenomenological
Dimensions
of Selfhood

What is needed here is nothing less than a series of "transcendental argu-ments" regarding the constituent dimensions of human selfhood (Taylor, 1995, pp. 20–33). Unfortunately, transcendental arguments, (i.e., meta-physical approaches), as a paradigm for inquiry, have suffered numerous critiques in the twentieth century (Rorty, 1979). In fact, we may wonder whether or not metaphysics rightfully should be called "dead." If not dead, perhaps metaphysics is irrelevant or simply not that useful. Berger and Luckmann, in their treatise on *The Social Construction of Reality*, stress an eschewal of metaphysical categories, and go so far as to state: "The philosopher is driven to decide where the quotation marks are in order and where they may safely be omitted, that is, to differentiate between valid and invalid assertions about the world. This the sociologist cannot possibly do. Logically, if not stylistically, he is stuck with the quo-tation marks" (1966, p. 2). Throughout the next four chapters, I intend to show that avoiding transcendental and/or metaphysical arguments regard-ing selfhood simply sets one up to fall prey to contradiction and incoher-ence (Taylor, 1995; Schrag, 1969).

In many ways I want to rewrite social constructionist approaches according to the insights of existential phenomenology. Unfortunately, these insights were passed over in Schutz's appropriations of Husserl (Carr, 1986, pp. 37–38). I want to demonstrate that beneath socially constructed and symbolically constituted reality, a phenomenological constitution makes any and all of this possible. We need to reconsider the possibility of a metaphysics of selfhood, even if it must be refigured and vigilantly pruned of epistemological croppings. Such a recovery concern-fully attends to the ontology of selfhood, and therefore, the issues at stake are not knowledge, truth, and reality, but rather, they are experi-ence, meaning, and existence.

In this second part of the investigation, I explore selfhood as a dynamic intersection of four dimensions: embodiment, sociality, symbolicity, and temporality. By the notion of dimensions of selfhood, I am referring to those essential characters which cannot be ignored if the portrait of selfhood is to retain any coherence. These dimensions provide an inexhaustible depth, and yet, they are best described as fundamentally "contentless." They are so deep that they are an empty or cleared ground.

Two directive comments must be made at this point. First, each dimension is transactive to the others, as all mutually intersect and support selfhood's manifestation and continuance. This means that all of these dimensions must be examined if we are to obtain a rightful view of selfhood. Second, self is thoroughly *each* dimension without any one liquidating the depth of the others. Said simply and directly, we are embodied through and through; we are social through and through; we are symbolic through and through; and finally, we are temporal through and through. Each of these vectors provides inexhaustible sources of transcendence, and respectively, a plenitude of explorable depth.

Chapter 2, the first chapter of Part II, reconsiders the embodied nature of self. Specifically, I examine the meaning of embodiment by making recourse to the body's earthly ground. I try to show that embodiment refers not to our material tangible bodies, but rather, to the fact that I always already am in-the-world. Chapter 3 addresses the social condition that pervades human selfhood and the world. I underscore the ontological sociality of selfhood, and further demonstrate that although we are thoroughly social beings, this vector does not exhaust self's resources or depths. Chapter 4 addresses a veritable hot spot of later twentieth-century theorizing regarding selfhood: the symbolic or linguistic nature of self. I argue for due recognition to a more natural and/or organic character of language (what I, following Merleau-Ponty [1968], will be calling "sonorousness"). Even more generally, I elucidate how selfhood is thoroughly symbolic (i.e., sonorous through and through), and yet is not exhausted by this dimension. Chapter 5, the final chapter of Part II, addresses the temporal constitution of selfhood. Unlike sociality and symbolicity, temporality's role in the ongoing odyssey of selfhood has been largely unaccounted for. I attempt, therefore, to elucidate how we are time, not so much subjectively (i.e., internally or idiosyncratically), but rather, we, as lived bodies, are temporal clearings through whom world *and* self come to concrete existence.

My method is to integrate each chapter's insights into the following chapter, systematically showing the interdependent character of the dimensions.

CHAPTER 2

The Embodied Self:
Earthly Worldings

Three basic and deeply interrelated sets of questions regarding embodiment must be asked: First, what does it mean to say that self is always embodied? What does it mean to be a body? Does it mean that self, or some I, is enclosed in a sack of skin as a body rides in a vessel? Does it mean that the human is thingly and therefore one thing among other things? Second, what is meant by the word "world"? Is the world an objectively present entity? It is a thing? Is it the totality of extant entities collected and inductively unified into a whole? And finally, what is the relationship of embodiment to the phenomena of the world? Does the world, in any way, continue or cease, without lived-bodies? My examination broadly considers these questions by engaging in an extended phenomenology of embodied experience.

Some rather obvious difficulties for a full recovery of self's bodily character need explicit acknowledgment. Schrag, in his astute discussion of *The Self after Postmodernity* (1997), states,

> The assumption appears to be that everybody in the philosophical neighborhood knows what it means to be a human body, leaving the central task of getting things straight on the peculiar marks of the mental. . . . It is precisely the taken for granted concept that the human body as simply a thing among other things, an object among other objects, an extension of material substance in general, that needs to be problematized. (p. 47)

His point is that we, using common sense, might try to understand our own body as we understand another's body. It then could seem to be a thing that has punctuated boundaries and outlines, some thing wholly located "in" space and time. We may even assume, as Levin states, that "we are nothing but 'encapsulated bodies' standing and moving in a space to be defined by Euclidean geometry and Newtonian physics" (1985, p. 137). These commonly entrenched beliefs regarding the bodily basis of selfhood must be kept in check as our investigation continues.

In addition to the difficulties of what it means to be a body, we also find that, within contemporary theorizing, the concept of "world" needs clearer elucidation. The meaning of the word "world" has admittedly

15

received provocative reexamination (Blumer, 1969; Deetz, 1973; Stewart, 1994; Shotter, 1995; Thayer, 1987). The beginnings of a conceptual renaissance are already present within the humanistic disciplines. Granting this, we can still find overly linguistic/symbolic as well as overly social accounts of world. As a result, contemporary reconsiderations of the meaning of world can be instructively advanced and fortified by carefully elucidating the bodily and temporal constitution of world-experience.

A final and more general difficulty, already hinted at, is that today we live in a world haunted by specters of linguistic relativism, a world tending toward linguistically based social idealisms. Postmodern thought, in its many flavors, displays a tendency to overtextualize world-experience (Derrida, 1974; Baudrillard, 1983). It is no doubt true that "world" is a word, as is any other we speak, and moreover, I would grant that we may not know precisely what we mean by it. But, these initial insights do not relieve us from our duty to recover the fullness of its meaning. Stated quite otherwise, the remarkably profound impact of discourse and sociality should not be underassessed, but on the other hand, we must be cautious not to engage in "semiological reductionisms" (Dillon, 1988; 1995).

This investigation attempt to alleviate some of these difficulties. We must pay close attention to our own experiences and carefully describe what makes its appearance.

INITIAL SKETCH

To examine the meaning of human embodiment in its *fullest attenuation*, I begin by sketching a kind of mythological backdrop. Hans Jonas's powerful and provocative "Immortality and the Modern Temper" provides words so well phrased that I would like to claim them as a useful context for the present exploration. He writes, "If, as one sometimes cannot resist doing, I permit myself the license of ignorance, which in these matters is our lot, and the vehicle of myth or likely imagination, which Plato allowed for, I am tempted to thoughts like these" (Jonas, 1966, p. 275). The ground meaning of embodiment can be recovered when we understand that to be a body is to be thrown-out-from-and-yet-indigenous-to Earth. A living body is a site of transcendence and of worlding. It is part of a much larger, though in-itself uneventful, eventing of Earth.

Earth as Earth is a nonexisting event. It can be grasped only through a living imagination which attempts to regard the abstractions of Space and Time devoid of any experiencer. "Time" and "Space," as used here, refer to the uneventful eventfulness of Earth which, strictly speaking, does not and could not exist.

Earth as Earth, I am suggesting, is inevitably derealized if it lacks an existential center, and so, nothingness infects Earth and therein opens spaces for localized and meaningful participations in the otherwise uneventful eventing of Space and Time. Human embodiment, always implying a nothingness effecting various existential decompressions, is, fundamentally, a "making-room-for," a choreographing of figures, backgrounds, and selves. By making room, the uneventful eventing of Space and Time is existingly transformed; it is decompressed and valuatively articulated along spatial and temporal lived-horizons. It is worlded.

"World," manifest in and through Earth's internal negations and corresponding existential decompressions, opens and tarries along the concrete and unfolding lived-horizons of spatiality and temporality. "Temporality" and "spatiality," as used here, are the lived-through horizons for the ecstatical eventfulness of world, and therefore, world is not simply a perspective on, or an abstracted representation of, an independently existing Earth. World is always worlded earth; it is the existing, the "significance," of self-negating Earth (Heidegger, 1962).

The lived-body, therefore, is not simply a thing among other things, a type of the world's furniture. Rather, it exists as the localized site of Earth's internal negations and which, articulates and choreographs Earth's existential decompressions by way of a multidimensional nexus of intentional powers. To exist as a lived-body is always already to be-in-the-world; it is to be cast out from nonexistent Earth; it is to be a worlding. In a word, to be embodied is to be outside one's flesh both in space and time; it is to be more than a *here and now*.

But this beginning mythological backdrop is highly abstract, and, most obviously, it requires much more elucidation. Let me develop this a bit further, and then, in the rest of this chapter, provide key assumptions, terminology, and implications.

Earth, World, Self

I can clarify the ontological ground of the lived-body this way: "Earth," as I mean the word here, is a limit concept by which we, in our imaginations, try to grasp the ungraspable. It, "Earth," feebly refers to that which wholly and completely is what it is (Burke, 1966, p. 419). As always and only what it is, it can never be "a was" or a "will be." And, certainly, it cannot ever be the "will-have-been" (Heidegger, 1992). In a word, it is unable to possess any limits or delimitation on its infinite and intractable density to itself. It can go nowhere because it is always already there. Not in any way can it be at any distance from itself. And yet, most paradoxically, being so full of itself—so inseparably thick—Earth, we can say, does not exist. There is, and perhaps not surprisingly, an old philosophical riddle which claims that only one thing cannot exist. This is said to be so because there must be "something" that is not the one thing in order to register the one thing's outline or boundaries. This is the state, the problem, of Earth as Earth. As so full of itself, it exists not. Again, Earth, without sites for decompression (and somewhat similar to Sartre's Being-in-itself), "does not exist either as a totality (in the sense of 'the world,' 'the universe') or with differentiated parts. . . . It is simply undifferentiated, meaningless massivity" (1956, p. xx). Therefore, any attempt to speak of Earth per se, for example, the notion of Nature In-Itself, is more of a "de-worlding of the world" than a rendering of Earth as Earth (Heidegger, 1962). Said otherwise, if we dare attempt to grasp the ungraspable (Earth as Earth), we should not turn to some notion of "Nature In-itself." Instead, we should appeal to the nonexperience that is sleeping without dreaming. When our bodies dreamlessly sleep, having absolutely no differentiation, being without temporal orientation and in utter meaninglessness (Straus, 1966), they come closer to the spirit of Earth as Earth than does the wide-awake concept of "Nature." Earth as Earth, again, is but a limit concept by which we imaginatively try to grasp the ungraspable.

As a nonexistent, uneventful plenitude, Earth, if it is to fall into existence, requires events of existential decompression. It requires localized and meaningful events of releasement and appropriation to choreograph its concrete existence. The word "choreograph" is employed here and not by chance. It obliquely underscores the notion of chora. In his recent discussion of the relationships among world, emptiness, and nothingness, Klaus Held writes of the chora:

> This feature of the world's space-giving, to my knowledge, has been broached only once in the long Western tradition of thought: In the "Timaeus" Plato introduces the *chora* as the most primordial, barely conceivable, precondition for the beautiful ordering of appearance, hence of the *kosmos*. . . . Chora actually means "place." The word goes together with choreo: one could paraphrase the meaning of this verb as: "to give place by withdrawing and becoming an embracing space." (1997, p. 159)

The notion of chora recently has received more attention. We find it in Kristeva, Derrida, and in fact, Heidegger also has made use of "chora." In his *Introduction to Metaphysics*, Heidegger suggestively writes, "Might chora not mean: that which abstracts itself from every particular, that which withdraws, and in such a way precisely admits and 'makes place' for something else?" (1961, p. 55). Earth then, as chora, tries to gain a distance from itself, to take a perspective on itself, to somehow and in some way, go away from itself so that it may first come to itself. In a word, it tries to found itself. But this attempt fundamentally fails, for Earth eternally falls unable to gain itself as itself. Earth, properly speaking, degenerates and loses itself. It flees from itself only to return and haunt itself as an Other: it obliviously forsakes itself into the disclosed and unfolding spectacle of cosmos.

This implies that although Earth cannot found itself, it can found its own nothingness (Sartre, 1956). Earth, therefore, contains within its fullness the possibility of perpetual internal negation. Special choreographic potentials are harbored in Earth, flowering movements which perpetually secrete the nothingness by which it first gains the distance to come to itself.[6] An embodied self is Earth's way of taking flight from its fullness and first coming to itself, though now fundamentally caught within the throes of finitude. Humans, as embodied beings, are self-surpassing, transcending activities of Earth; they are sites of perpetual decompression into lived-through world-experience. Embodiment refers back to a localized unfolding, a once-occurrent eventing of world [and] self which meaningfully surpasses the total and absolute uneventful event of Earth. The lived-body is thus not a thing among other things within a pre-given world (i.e., yet another thing). Embodiment is a special activity within and of Earth by which world, objects, and selves come to be. To be a body, I shall try to make clear in this chapter, is to articulate and choreograph Earth's existential decompression along the ecstatically unfolding horizons of spatiality and temporality, and so, it is to inscribe a once-occurrent and meaningful event of world [and] self into an otherwise nonexisting Earth. Humans are not simply things on the Earth; we are something it is doing. Earth continually negates its nonexistence and so gains world by forgetfully doing bodies. Said more strictly, in its timelessly original attempts to first gain itself, Earth primarily loses itself by forgetfully "bodying" itself (i.e., throwing itself into the contingencies of living finitude), and only thereby, does it gain world.

Earth's perpetual degeneration and conditional renunciations are the very upsurging and eventing of world [and] self as existential correlates. In summary, the original and continual upsurge of lived-through world-experience (i.e., the co-disclosed, co-given correlation of world [and] self) is founded upon and within ontological negations. That is, lived-through world-experience is ontologically funded by internal negation—that of Earth negating itself as Earth, losing itself so that it may first come to itself as world [and] self. But, I must explicitly stress that, as already suggested, it would be a conceptual mistake to think that we, as living individuals, are Earth coming back to itself. Earth as Earth never comes to itself. That is impossible. Earth, in a most fundamental and primordial way, loses itself. In the strictest sense, in its internal negations, Earth does not regain the intentional correlates of self [and] world. Rather, Earth as Earth, even though non-yet-existent, is that which nevertheless is lost in the continual upsurging of lived-through world-experience.

Nothing Separating

Let me try to elucidate these claims further by reentering through a single claim: "Nothing separates my body from the world." This claim can be misunderstood easily, and so, I need to stroll down some obvious corridors of interpretation. At a first read, one might take this as a sort of ecological or holistic assertion. It perhaps suggests that humans are intricately suspended within a physically closed system. We might take this claim to mean that body and world are inseparable. We might offer physiological evidence and scientific data which demonstrate the skin's open and porous boundaries, or we might show the molecular intermingling and interpenetrating of air and the skin. Someone might point out that we can bamboozle ourselves by employing reified language: Because "air" is one word—naming one thing—and "lungs" is another word—naming something else—we may come to believe "them" to be "separate things," and so, perhaps against such common sense, one could claim, "Nothing separates my body from the world." But the claim means much more than this. Indeed, it is because of this first and rather obvious meaning, the fact that I am not separate, that we need to grasp its deeper and seemingly opposing implication.

"Nothing separates my body from the world" primarily means that internal negation perpetually infects Earth; spindly fissures of nothingness serve as localized cracks of "space making." The claim that "nothing separates my body from the world" basically points us back to the earthy origin of embodiment. It addresses how the human is not so much in space as of it and how, being of it, the lived-body maintains its indigenous density with world while nevertheless maintaining a distance from it (Merleau-Ponty, 1962). Said otherwise, we, as bodies, are beings at a distance from the world, and yet, we are able to experience the world because we are ontologically indigenous inhabitants: my body is of it and is as indigenous to it as it is to itself. Therefore, to say that "nothing separates my body from the world" is basically a different way of getting at the fact that world [and] self are existential correlates of the intentional threads that are decompressed out of Earth's continuous internal negations.

In quite parallel fashion to the claim that "nothing separates my body from the world," we also might suggest that: "Nothing separates any phenomenal object from its background." This, again, does not mean that they are inseparable but rather that one is *not* the other: nothing separates them! To note and identify an object is to select *i* background, to isolate "it" from what is not it. Without ness, there would be no room, no space, for such a localized deͨᴏͷᴜͷ sion and we could not even begin to isolate, identify, and sustain a figure or ground. The difference between the figure and the background is neither in the figure nor in the background; it is nothing (Bateson, 1979, pp. 100–107; Wilden, 1972, pp. 155–195).

More Than Here

To gain a better understanding of Earth's internal negations, the term "decompress" requires more elucidation. To decompress is to manifest various phenomenal fields, each of which opens along spatial and temporal horizons. That is, to speak of decompression is to address the conditional renunciations in which Earth's utter fullness, its infinite and nondelimited totality, is presenced within particular evaluative configurations having spatial and temporal horizons. Spatiality and temporality refer to the primary connective tissues along which this expanding destructuring of Earth (and structuring of world) proceeds and continues. Temporality will receive more extended and focused address in Chapter 5. For now, I must stress that neither spatiality nor temporality are simply categories of thought. They are not merely concepts; they cannot be reduced to theoretical sense content (i.e., typifications). Hence, the words "spatiality" and "temporality," more primordially, refer to the depth and endurance which characterizes all lived-through world-experience.

My actual living body is at a unique—a nonrepeatable and noninterchangeable—moment and place of Space/Time. Indeed, I am not simply in space but am of it, and this means that my body has always already made room for itself (Merleau-Ponty, 1962). But this does not limit my body to its physical extension over certain Space/Time coordinates. Not by any means is this the meaning of each person's unique position and moment. In fact, human embodiment is deeply misunderstood if it is approached as physical extending over spatial coordinates specified within an abstract grid of representation. Such an understanding is but a derealized abstraction, a rendering of the body as it is only for others—the body as a totalized, whole object. Therefore, the "room-making" furnished in and through Earth's internal negations, makes room for much more than the area of my body. My body, then, does not simply "extend" in space as a thing does, but rather, it occupies and inhabits it (Merleau-Ponty, 1962).

My body is spatial as an ecstatical and valuative connective tissue of world-experience. To speak of occupying and inhabiting one's place and moment is already to speak of radiations emanating outward from my body into the decompressing event-horizon in its localized unfolding.

Bakhtin (1990) makes a significant contribution where he notes that I, regarding my own body, cannot perceive its spatial boundaries; I cannot see the whole of my body. That is, in my everyday experience, the spatial boundaries of my lived-body remain ungiven to me. On the other hand, I might, upon looking in a full-length mirror, attempt to disclose my body's boundaries, seeing my own body somewhat as I see others' bodies. (Or as they see mine). Yet what is disclosed in the mirror is not the whole me, even though I now first gain access to the "whole" of my body. Why? Because to be a body, a self, is to be-in-a-world; it is to be an ecstatical flight of transcendence beyond the boundaries of the skin (Csikszentmihalyi and Rochberg-Halton, 1981). As a body, (i.e., as a site of Earth's internal negation), I am continuously given over to, directed toward, and fundamentally copresent with world.

As it is lived through, my body is always outside and past its fleshy boundaries. In fact, my body as I live through it, not as it is merely "for-others," can instructively be described as a faceless, or headless body.[7] That is, the world laid out before me is made manifest through that strange "empty-yet-filled-hole" where my face should be. D. E. Harding well describes this profound insight where he recounts the "best day" in his life as the day when, atop the Himalayan mountains, he realized that he "had no head." He states,

> It took me no time at all to notice that this nothing, this hole where my head should have been, was no ordinary vacancy, no mere nothing. On the contrary, it was very much occupied. It was a vast emptiness vastly filled, a nothing that found room for everything—room for grass, trees, shadowy distant hills, and far above them snow-peaks like a row of angular clouds riding the blue sky. I had lost a head and gained a world. (Harding, 1981, p. 24)

Thus, aspects of the world, even though at a distance, can nevertheless be "present" where my face/head strangely is not.

Again, to be a body is to be spatial, that spatiality referring not to the three-dimensional area over which it extends. Spatiality always refers to the choreographed incorporation of space, to the unfolding disclosedness of some "there" which is not simply the spatial coordinates specifying the "here" of my body's fleshy boundaries. Our bodies are indeed of space rather than simply in it, and yet, we are not of space in the way an ashtray is. We are of it in such a manner (i.e., by way of internal negation) that we always are out and beyond the here and now of the flesh.

If I am awake, a "there" (i.e., a situation) is concernfully disclosed along with the "here" of my body. This is precisely what is underscored in Heidegger's word choice of "Da-sein" for the human. To be human, qua Dasein, is to be, to exist as, the "there-here." Heidegger, in *Being and*

Time, stresses this point where he states, "Da-sein is its disclosure . . . the existential statement that 'Da-sein is its disclosure' means at the same time that the being about which these beings are concerned in their being is to be their 'there'" (1962, p. 125). This highly enigmatic sentence basically means that a concern over world—a concernful regard for the world—is inherent in our nature as the ecstatical transcendens (i.e., as the lumen naturale). To *be* a body, then, is to be outside one's flesh; it is to participate in the flesh of world (Merleau-Ponty, 1968). It is to be fundamentally near things, tending to them in a host of practices, projects, and engagements. Heidegger's recently released early lectures make this most explicit:

> We say that the Dasein does not need to turn backward to itself as though, keeping itself behind its own back, it were at first standing in front of things and staring rigidly at them. Instead, it never finds itself otherwise than in the things themselves, and in fact those things that daily surround it. It finds *itself* primarily and constantly in things because, tending them, distressed by them, it always in some way or other rests in things. Each one of us is what he pursues and cares for. In everyday terms, we understand ourselves and our existence by way of the activities we pursue and the things we take care of. We understand ourselves by starting from them because Dasein finds itself primarily in things. The Dasein does not need a special kind of observation, nor does it need to conduct a sort of espionage on the ego in order to have a self; rather, as the Dasein gives itself over immediately and passionately to the world itself, its own self is reflected to it from the things. (1982, p. 159)

The main point here is that as lived-bodies, we are not simply nor exclusively concerned with or for own bodies per se. We care over ourselves by concerning ourselves with those things which are co-dislosed with and by our bodies.

To be a body is to disclose and draw near to things which are "not us," and yet, which nevertheless "critically matter to us" (Taylor, 1995). To be a body is to be valuatively implicated with the disclosedness of the "there."[8] These evaluations are not simply the outcome of the psychic sphere of the subject, but they are manifested in things themselves (i.e., in the things disclosed and made manifest in the upsurging event of world [and] self). Thus, given that my body occupies an existential center, entities light up with valuative meanings in terms of my once-occurrent participation in existence. Regardless of cultural variations regarding the ultimate objects of concern as well as differing levels of evaluation, to be human, at all, is already to evaluate, to be concerned over and reckon with the disclosed world. I will return to this issue in Chapter 6.

In summary so far, the very fact of world—that it is—is part and parcel of Earth's internal negations and various intentional activities. The human, qua existing, is not a thing inside another thing called "the world." On the contrary, we are the continuous eventing, the worlding of that world (Heidegger, 1962; 1985). Said otherwise, the lived-body is primarily, as Leder states, *The Absent Body*, a body which "is never just an object in the world but that very medium whereby our world comes into being" (1990, p. 5). As living bodies who ecstatically transcend their own surfaces, we are perpetually caught up with and concerned over that which we find around us (Csikszentmihalyi and Rochberg-Halton, 1981). Fundamentally directed toward the unfolding event-horizon, we care for and concern ourselves with that which we find around us (i.e., that which is disclosed and made-manifest given the localized decompression of Earth).

More must be said regarding that which the lived-body discloses. That is, given that the lived-body is outside itself, articulating and choreographing Earth's existential decompression, what needs more clarification is the specific nature and character of the "there." The "there" can be addressed more fully by considering phenomenological notions of intentionality and phenomenal fields. I begin with the latter, tracing them back to their grounding in the former.

Phenomenal Fields

Various phenomenal fields (i.e., world-experience profiles) are made possible given Earth's internal negations: fields of action, fields of perception, fields of emotion, fields of imagination, fields of speech, fields of thought. In all of these fields, we find that which matters to us, entities and events over which we are concerned.

Of both the fields and objects which become manifest, three main points need address. First, the specific term, "phenomenal fields" refers us to the fact that any figure is always decompressed out of and stands against a background. As I sit here at my chair and look at the computer screen, I also see numerous objects on my desk. There is a ballpoint pen, a mechanical pencil, several books, and a stack of note cards. There is an arm-swivel lamp secured to the edge of my desk, and there is a plastic mat beneath my computer chair. Each of these objects finds its place in the room, which finds its place in the house, which finds its place in a city, etc. Objects, as manifesting themselves in fields, therefore always have moving and open-ended fringes, giving them a horizonal feature. The limit toward which the different fields unfold, that which unifies the differing horizons, that which is always already taken-for-granted, is world. "World" then is not merely, and certainly not primordially, something cosmologically given (i.e., "objectively there") and to which the human comes later as an add-on; nor is world derived or deduced by simply adding up a subject's different fields (i.e., it is not "subjectively constituted"). World is the a priori in which all the fields, as implicated in intentional relations, are implicitly grounded. Heidegger states:

> World is not something subsequent that we calculate as a result from the sum total of beings. . . . The world is not the sum total of extant entities. It is, quite generally, not an extant at all. It is a determination of being-in-the-world, a moment in the structure of the Dasein's mode of being. The world is something Dasein-ish. It is not extant like things but it is da, there-here, like the Dasein, the being-da which we ourselves are: that is to say, it exists. (1982, pp. 165, 166)

The world, as the ultimate and a priori space-making, exists. It, most generally then, is that wherein there are things to be done, that wherein things that matter to us can be found.

Second, each phenomenal object has a lived-through or "a provable depth," to use Husserl's term. Disclosed objects are not atomistic, granular, and completed. They are not final, exhausted objects. Rather, the "there," which is locally disclosed and made manifest along with the "here" of the lived-body, is a decompression and therefore refers back to the indefatigable depth of world-experience. Entities are disclosed while retaining hidden depths and unexplored regions. Moreover, as will be addressed more fully as I proceed, objects manifest themselves in phenomenal fields, and so, they can seemingly change their manifestness when apprehended in and by different intentional threads. For example, I look at the pen on my desk. I pick it up and rotate it, noting that I am unable to see all of its adumbrations at once. The plenitude of the pen refers to the unending exploration it will endure, how it unfolds itself across its adumbrations, and to the fact that there is more to come even though I hold it itself in my hand. I can even close my eyes and simply touch the pen, explicitly thematizing the way it feels on my finger tips. Also, I can simply imagine the pen. I may arrive at school, and while looking in my backpack, I find that it is not there. That is, I can, by imagination, intend it as "not being there" and this is one way the pen itself can become manifest. All of these different ways of intending the object give it an enduring richness and an explorable depth.

Third, a common character can be found throughout the different phenomenal fields: all phenomenal objects and their fields are characterized by intentionality. The term "intentionality" was employed several times already, and yet, it may still lack due explanation. That is, the concept of "intentionality," which was only obliquely referred to so far, may need much more critical discussion. This third point, in fact, introduces a more nuanced vocabulary for recovering the meaning of human embodiment. Taken generally, intentional vectors refer to those concrete connective tissues by and in which world [and] self are configured within lived-horizons of temporality and spatiality. The various modes and activities of intentionality meaningfully disclose (existentially re-relate) what has been separated by fissures of nothing. They are the positive or constitutive fibers by which Earth "returns" to haunt itself as an Other. In a certain way then, the various modes of intentionality are the inverse of Earth's internal negations: they refer not to the destructuring of Earth, but more fundamentally, to the various correlative constituting of selves experiencing phenomenal objects within fields (Schrag, 1969).

My body is never not here, just as a "there," if I am awake, is never not co-disclosed along with it. We, as lived-bodies, are always implicated as the correlates to the various objects within phenomenal fields. But as a word of caution: Just because all lived world-experience requires and implicates an experiencer, this does not, in any way, reduce world to an experiencer's concept of it. World, phenomenal fields, and objects, are not simply projections or representations, something an epistemological or transcendental subject manufactures or produces. Heidegger offers suggestive direction where he states, "Intentionality is neither objective nor subjective in the usual sense, although it is certainly both, but in a much more original sense" (1982, p. 65). Both the experiencer and the various phenomenal objects and fields are emergent and upsurging correlates; they are made possible through Earth's internal negations. In fact, in the "characterization of intentionality as an extant relation between two things extant, a psychical subject and a physical object, the nature as well as the mode of being of intentionality is completely missed" (Heidegger, 1982, p. 60). Thus, two fallacies to be challenged throughout this entire phenomenology of selfhood are the fallacy of naturalism (i.e., of reified objects) and the fallacy of constructed objects (i.e., of total constitution by the subject). And so, the underlying motive of the Initial Sketch was to discuss, loosely, how "world" can be manifest without simply subscribing to an idealism, or a realism, nor even a relativism. But, obviously, this is not even close to fleshed out adequately; this first section was but a sketchy approximation of what needs to be opened in order to enter strategically our interrogation into the meaning of human embodiment.

THE LIVED-BODY AS AN INTENTIONAL NEXUS

Phenomenological notions of intentionality must be centerpieces for any rigorous account of embodiment. "Intentionality" allows us to undercut numerous dichotomies which plague a good deal of modern thought, and, it is the "misplaced concreteness," as Whitehead would say, of the subject/object split which the phenomenological notion of intentionality attempts to radically challenge. Madison sums up well the enormous importance of this concept, suggesting that by it, "phenomenology effectively overcomes the most fundamental of modern dichotomies, that of mind versus world" (1996, p. 79). This implies that, as already suggested, there is never an independent world "out there" to which I might, occasionally, attempt to direct myself. This also means that world, in its various profiles, is always already manifest according to the multiple and diverse intentional threads underlying our various comportments. Schrag well clarifies this where he states,

> Every occasion of experience 'takes over' or appropriates its content, not by internalizing it but rather by determining the content as content for me in my lived world. . . . Experienced objects, events, and persons are objects, events, and persons as meant. Meaning is always for an experiencer even though the conditions for meaning are not all supplied by the experiencer. An object or event 'in-and-for-itself' remains a theoretical limit. Such an object remains outside the intentional structure and never enters the fabric of world experience. (1969, pp. 85–86)

Intentionality, then, refers us to the multifarious means humans have been granted for comporting themselves and so of worlding the world. Ultimately, it underlies and accomplishes the meaningful and significant particularizing of Earth's existential decompression into spatialized and temporalized world-experience.

Vectors of Intentionality

Intentionality, I already suggested, globally refers to the various powers the lived-body maintains for worlding the world. To elucidate the phenomenological notion of intentionality, I consider various vectors (motility, sense perception, emotion, and imagination). Before specifically addressing these diverse intentional threads and the peculiar modes of making-manifest granted to each, four general introductory points must be made. These four points, it should be remembered, apply to all of the following discussion on embodiment.

1. First, Heidegger offers some guidance where he states that the term "intentionality," comes from intentio, which most broadly means "directing-itself-toward" (1985, pp. 29–131). As living beings we are always already directing-ourselves-toward aspects of the world. Stating this more explicitly, Heidegger observes, "Intentionality comprises both moments, the intentio and the intentum, within its unity. . . . The two moments are different in each comportment; diversity of intentio or of

intentum constitutes precisely the diversity of the modes of comportment. They differ each in regard to its own peculiar intentionality" (1985,
p. 58). Thus, the different intentional tissues by which we inhere in the
world can be characterized as lines of force manifesting two poles or
ends: the intentio and intentum. For example, there are acts of touching
(intentio) and objects touched (intentum), activities of thinking (intentio)
and things thought about (intentum), activities of seeing (intentio) and
things seen (intentum), etc. In general, various intentional activities,
according to their mode of operation, manifest particular world profiles
of their intended objects.

   This discussion of "directing-itself-toward" should not lead us to
assume overly subjectivistic or overly objectivistic notions of intentionality, as if world were a concept or something that the subject simply pro-
duces/manufactures, or as if the world were fundamentally pregiven and
the subject, already detached, merely "discovers" it. In general, I must
stress, as Schrag, states, that, "intentionality, generically understood as the
pervasive vectorial connections within experience that occasion the emergence of meaning or sense, carries with it neither a doctrine of a timeless
ego nor a doctrine of intended eternal essences" (1969, p. 83). To help
further Schrag's point here (i.e., to counter tendencies toward overly subjective and overly objective accounts), we might, as does Heidegger in his
early lectures, trisect intentionality. To each of the various intentional
activities and their correlative intended objects belongs a peculiar proper
regarding the specific "intendableness" of the intentum. This "intendableness" of the intentum is neither subjectively constituted, nor is it
objectively present. Said otherwise, there is the perceiving, the perceived,
and also the very perceivedness, and, this perceivedness cannot be reductively located in either the subject or the object. We find, then, a dialogic or transactive nature to the intentio and the intentum. And thus,
"intentionality," in Schrag's apt terms, "is centripetal as well as cen-
trifugal. It reaches 'back' to a centered experiencer as it reaches 'out'
toward figure and background" (1969, p. 86). Consider again our moods,
our skillful movements, our use of tools, and our perceptions. We find
within all an intentional character. They are intentional tissues by which
world-experience is concernfully manifest and managed. In each case, a
line of existential decompression—a line of force—centripetally moves
back toward the embodied self while also and simultaneously moving
centrifugally toward the particular figure-background configurations.

   2. The second point is that every intentional thread, regardless of its
peculiar mode, accomplishes an understanding of world [and] self, even if
only prethematically. Said otherwise, these diverse intentional vectors
are similar in that each thread accomplishes a specific understanding, a

particular means of making manifest or articulating contact. For example, when we encounter some object in the room, say a chair, we are not concerned with "the object itself," but with the object in the how of its "intendedness."[9] We are interested in the chair according to its disclosedness through and by the different ways we can meaningfully take it under concern (e.g., sitting on it, calculating about it, dreaming about it, drawing it, looking at it, etc.). This intentional relatedness implies that any perceived entity is an entity in its perceivedness. Clarifying this point Heidegger states:

> The expression the perceived as such now refers, (not to the perceived entity in itself but), to this entity in the way and manner of its being-perceived. . . . We thus have an inherent affinity between the way something is intended, the intentio, and the intentum, whereby the intentum, the intended, is to be understood in the sense just developed, not the perceived as an entity, but the entity in the how of its being-perceived, the intentum in the how of its being-intended. (1985, pp. 40–45)

When Heidegger states that the perceived as such refers to "the intentum in the how of its being-intended," he is basically elucidating a point he makes elsewhere: "to every intentional comportment belongs an understanding of the being of the being to which this comportment relates" (1982, p. 158). Each of the various manners of intending—of concernfully relating to—given objects, events, or persons disclose those entities according to its own understanding-of-being (e.g., in being-acted-upon, or in being-perceived, or in being-feared, or in being-talked about, or in being-judged) and according to an object's intendableness.

Not only does each intentional vector have its own specific manner of understanding entities, also, each vector implicates an experiencer. The different ways the chair manifests itself thereby implicate differently comporting selves (i.e., a sitting self, a calculating self, a dreaming self, a speaking self, etc.). In general, Heidegger nicely sums up the present discussion where he writes, "to intentionality belongs, not only a self-directing-toward and not only an understanding of the being of the being toward which it is directed, but also the associated unveiling of the self which is comporting itself here" (1982, p. 158). Any phenomenal object emerges out from Earth's existential decompression and so leads back to the embodied subject's intentional comportments—not as its source but as its correlate; self is always at least implicated in any intended object.

3. The third point, somewhat following from the second, is that although Earth's existential decompressions manifest correlates of figures-in-fields-with-experiencers, I again need to undercut proclivities toward epistemological accounts of intentionality. For the most part, in

our everyday lives, the objects over which we concern ourselves are not explicitly and thematically "present-at-hand," (Heidegger, 1962) nor is self explicitly and thematically given to itself. We are not walking about reflectively and consciously thinking about all of the various activities and involvements in which we engage. Our understandings are largely tacit or nonexplicit or nonthematic in character, and this pertains both to the disclosed objects-in-fields and to the comportments lived-bodies are able to maintain (Polanyi, 1962; 1966).

To explain this important issue further, I must clarify a key distinction between "reflective" and "pre- or nonreflective" modes of intentionality. Merleau-Ponty's *Phenomenology of Perception* (1962) suggestively distinguishes between what he terms "operative intentionality" (also 'pre-thetic' intentionality) and the "intentionality of act" (also 'thetic' intentionality). He states, "we found beneath the intentionality of acts, or thetic intentionality, another kind which is the condition of the former's possibility: namely an operative intentionality already at work before any positing or any judgment" (1962, p. 429). His point is that beneath reflective moments of judgment, before acts of detached staring at objects, and prior to attempts at adjudicatively predicating present-at-hand entities, there are prereflective or operative modes of intentionality which display a more holistic and nonanalytical character. That is, before—as well as underlying—any categorical thought (e.g., asserted "beliefs" about the world), there is a playful absorptive character to our understandings.

The operative threads binding the intentio and intentum are taut threads. This means they are lived-through as a transubstantiation, a fusing of both ends, the former receding from awareness as the manifestation—the showing itself—of the intentum is maintained. Again, pre-thetic intentionality operates prior to any explicit, thematic, or analytic division between the intentio and the intentum. This lived-through unity congeals and displays itself within our everyday comportments (ways of moving, manipulating entities, perception, emotions, gesturing, and speaking) and so produces "the natural and antepredicative unity of the world and of our life" (1962, p. xviii). Operative intentionality yields what Schrag (1986) has called, "expressive meaning," referring to the layers of participations whereby individuals act and are inscribed into their world involvements. Such intentionality refers to all those modes of pre-predicative understanding which antedate the explicit and reflective division between inner and outer as well as the separation between an intentional activity and its intended meaning. By and large, we are transparently caught up and absorbed in that over which we care. We commonly "find ourselves," to use Gurwitch's terms "in a situation and are interwoven with it, encompassed by it, indeed, just 'absorbed' into it" (1979, p. 67).

Thus nontheoretical absorption characterizes the modes and moments of pre-thetic intentionality, and, they are well described in Stewart's terms as "mindless everyday coping" (1996, p. 33; also see Dreyfus, 1991).

But we, as the beings we are, do not lack resources for reflectively and analytically sorting out our pre-thetic comprehensions. In fact, the notion of "thetic intentionality" or "judgment" specifically accounts for the manner in which operative intentionalities can become objects for critical and thematic interrogation. Admittedly, within phenomenology, especially the Husserlean tradition, the "intentionality of act," as assertions predicating essences, has received a good deal of criticism. As Schrag states, "To be sure, many of the postmodern critiques of classical phenomenology are on target, and this includes the postmodern assault on 'act intentionality' as a transcendental structure of consciousness" (1997, p. 57). Granting that the notion of essence needs to be radically refigured, the human, although primarily operating by pre-thetic intentionalities, has the indigenous ability to reflectively surpass its absolute facticity toward idealities of repeatability and essence. So how are we to describe our powers for critical reflection without appealing to transcendental consciousness or eternal noemata? We again can make recourse to Merleau-Ponty (1962), noting specifically his refiguring of "intentionality of act." Something like a Husserlean quest for essences, Merleau-Ponty maintains, can be pursued if those essences are radically refigured as horizons of idealized possibilities emerging from and returning to the antepredicative unity of pre-thetic intentionalities. A similarly refigured notion of thetic intentionality, of judgment, is well formulated by Schrag where he writes:

> We have encountered the requirement to move beyond expressive meaning so as to provide a posture of critical understanding and reflective assessment of the facticity of our involvement. This move beyond expressive meaning we have named the move to meaning in the mode of signification, attended by a new emphasis on the hermeneutical functioning of the 'sign' as a mediator between the retentionality and protentionality of historical experience. The mantle of idealities in signitive meaning allows for the repeatability of meanings that issue from expressive discourse and action and in turn legitimates talk of their sameness within the history of communicative praxis. (1986, p. 67)

Again, and in agreement with postmodern assaults on Husserlean essences, we must observe that, in reflective moments, what is being assessed is not some independently existing reality.

"Reflection," Merleau-Ponty instructively states, "does not withdraw from the world toward the unity of consciousness as the world's basis . . . it slackens the intentional threads which attach us to the world and thus brings them to our notice" (1962, p. xiii). By a "slackening of intentional threads" he refers to moments of reflection, not back toward oneself, but rather, toward various intentio/ intentum correlates. Said otherwise, thetic intentionality operates by slackening the intentional threads themselves, making both ends explicit; both the intentional activity and the intentional object are explicitly and reflectively assessed. Therefore, "acts of judgment" do not furnish epistemological security regarding some independently existing reality. As moments of signitive meaning, they reflectively appropriate what was previously manifest only in our pre-predicative (i.e., pre-thetic) involvements. This insight can be clarified even further by considering Heidegger's claim that,

> in reflection . . . I am thematically focused upon the perception and not upon the perceived. I can of course make the perception itself the theme such that the perceived, what the perception perceives, its object, is itself co-apprehended, but in such a way that I do not live directly in the perception, say, of the chair, rather live thematically in the apprehension of the perceptual act and of what is perceived in it. This way of considering the act and its object is not a transcendent apprehension of the thing itself. (1985, p. 99)

We have discovered that reflection, and "the intentionality of act," is not a turning back to an "independent" or sovereign constituting subject nor an attempt to "mirror" an independently preexisting world, but rather, it is the explicit and analytic presencing of the intentional threads themselves. And so, we have both nonexplicit powers of comprehension as well as specific powers for critical and reflective interrogation. Said in phenomenological terminology, the different intentional threads, which "anchor us in and to the world," (Merleau-Ponty, 1962) display various levels of thetic and pre-thetic comprehension.

4. Fourth and finally, of the diverse modes of intentionality, all are unified through their comprehensions of lived-through horizons of spatiality and temporality. Said even more strongly, each vector of intentionality spatializes spatiality and temporalizes temporality in its own peculiar manner. The specifically temporal character of intentionality can be mentioned here only lightly; I must delay a fuller address until Chapters 4 and 5. In general, the diverse intentional threads are different modes by which world and self are temporalized in certain configurations, and likewise, are modes in which entities are spatialized in a certain manifestness. Still, I must underscore that the various intentional threads do not, by any means, operate either independently or separately. They all interact, transact, and inform each other; the lived-body, as incorporating spatiality and temporality, ecstatically unifies the various fields and their objects. Normally, in our everyday dealings, we do not reflectively parcel

out the contributions of each vector. More generally, lived-through world-experience is shot through with various profiles of various intensities according to different intentional activities and involvements. The phenomenological notion of intentionality refers to bodily powers that manifest world-experience profiles according to acts of existential decompression and that allow the lived-body to gather up and organize, to care over, more than the here and now of its own flesh. In the end, the phenomenological notion of intentionality depicts the human as "a project of the world, meant for a world, which it neither embraces nor possesses, but toward which it is perpetually directed" (Merleau-Ponty, 1962, p. xvii). I now explore four different and yet highly interrelated intentional tissues, showing how they articulate and choreograph (i.e., spatialize and temporalize) the existential contact we maintain with the world. I briefly examine the intentionality of movement and action, perceptual intentionality (e.g., different sensorimotor powers), the intentionality of affects or emotions, and finally, imaginative intentionality.

Motility and Action   My body is always touching something it is not, always. Never am I simply isolated or not in various forms of contact, whether I stand on the ground, sit in a chair, ride in a car, or even jump through the air. We touch world. We dwell in contact with more than our own bodies. This may not, in itself, seem all that important; the ubiquity of touch is perhaps trivial. Its significance can be brought out by turning our attention to the different ways that touch spatializes and temporalizes lived-through word-experience.

We, each of us, find surrounding us, at all times, a field of action, a cropping up of bodily possibilities before us. Movements operate as tissues of world-comprehension. It is by movement that that which is disclosed becomes relevantly freed up in various everyday involvements (Heidegger, 1962). There are, for example, things to do, things that need to be taken care of, stuff that has to get done around here. In comporting ourselves toward these everyday tasks, we free entities up, making them "available for" and "relevant to" various projects and dealings (Heidegger, 1962). I open doors, type on keyboards, write with pens and chalk. I use silverware (and often chopsticks), and I drink from the glass I place before me. I open small and large bottles, turn faucets as well as light switches on and off, and I open and close numerous drawers and cabinets. I put on clothing, and I take it off, and sometimes, I fold, stack, and put clothes in closets. I open windows, wipe counters, sweep floors, and generally clean things up. In summary, by making physical contact through touch, the lived-body comports an understanding of worldly objects. It meaningfully discloses them according to the various projects for which they have been freed as available and relevant.

Heidegger, in *Being and Time*, provides a penetrating discussion of human powers of spatiality and further offers two major modes of world-comprehension: "directionality" and "de-distancing." To see how thoroughly directional the lived-body is, consider again that the most fundamental, most primordial spatial relations, as already alluded to, are "here" [and] "there." These are existential locations, not simply givens of abstracted and geometric space and time. They are part of the lived-body's powers for disclosedness. The lived-body's spatial being means that the disclosedness of space and the presence of the "there" moves along with my body. Our bodies thus never escape the fact of having a forward; the "there" in which objects of concern are disclosed is the world's face, for we fundamentally must face it.[10] As Schrag states, "In working we face the front, for it is there that our project lies" (1969, p. 62). Our bodies are geared toward the entities which, as we bring them near, seem to face us.

The lived-body, I have suggested, is a site of Earth's existential decompression, and moreover, it articulates and choreographs this spatial decompression in terms of its forword orientation, that is, by its always facing its involvements. To this facing, there also belongs "de-distancing." "De-distancing," Heidegger tells us, "means making distance disappear, making the being at a distance of something disappear, bringing it near" (1962, p. 97). I, as my body, exist in the mode of "de-distancing" objects so as to free them for various encounters and involvements. I take care of things by bringing them near. I tend to them by occupying myself with them, and so, in taking them under concern, I implicate and so tend to my own self. That our bodies de-distance means that our movements are connective tissues of world-comprehension.

The directionality and de-distancing of our being-in-the-world is easily found in our wide range of movements both functional and artistic—articulate gesticulations and delicate hand movements. We gather and dwell in the spatiality that is opened through our movements which are thus flights beyond themselves.[11] In general, lived-bodies care for phenomenal objects through movements that culminate in acts of touching, and even more specifically, activities of handling.

A vital intentional organ of the human's lived-body, therefore, is the hand. I do not mean to address hands as they gestures for-others, not hands as vehicles for interaction and communication. Hands, as I address them here, are primarily absent hands. They are haptic intentionalities which "focally disappear" (Leder, 1990) as they make concern over entities and various projects possible. Merleau-Ponty tells us,

> The subject, when put in front of his scissors, needle and familiar tasks, does not need to look for his hands or his fingers, because they are not

objects to be discovered in objective space: bones, muscles, and nerves, but potentialities already mobilized by the perception of scissors or needle, the central end of those "intentional threads" which link him to the objects given. (1962, p. 106)

This absence is also evident in psychological studies which have shown that nine out of ten people cannot recognize (i.e., accurately pick out) pictures of their own hands from a set of ten pictures of others' hands (Leder, 1990, p. 1). This demonstrates not so much that people are forgetful or unobservant; it emphasizes that hands, most often, are not objects of explicit attention. Our hands, on the contrary, are concernful flights of transcendence; we attend to the possibilities opened and maintained according to their powers. In general, the innumerable hand movements the lived-body accomplishes in an average day bear and release meaning in terms of the specific projects toward-which objects become relevant, even if this remains prethematic, tacit, or simply operative.

Heidegger, in *What is Called Thinking?* (1968), provocatively states,

> The hand is infinitely different from all grasping organs—paws, claws, or fangs—different by an abyss of essence. Only a being who can speak, that is, *think*, can be handy in achieving works of handicraft. But the craft of the hand is richer than we commonly imagine. The hand does not only grasp and catch or push and pull. The hand reaches and extends, receives and welcomes—and not just things: the hand extends itself, and receives its own welcome in the hands of others. The hand holds. The hand carries. The hand designs. (p. 16)

Hands are, perhaps, the prime exemplar of the lived-body's intentional powers for occupying space and of how it choreographs and articulates intentional objects. It is through hands that "the worldhood of the world" comes to be. Interestingly, Heidegger's early writings characterize the Being of non-Dasein entities as either "readiness-to-hand"(e.g., tools and utensils) or "presence-at-hand" (e.g., objects assessed as "objectively present"). Not by any accident (yet with no explicit address), his terms for the manner in which beings disclose themselves refer back to hands. This underscores their intentional nature and the fact that their comportments "intend" worldly entities. Obviously, touch demands a nearness, a "physical contact" which sight, hearing, or even smell, seem not to demand. These latter sensorimotor powers are "distance senses" (Leder, 1990), vectors of relatedness over greater distances; they manifest entities as present-yet-at-a-distance. Touch, as a means of physical manipulation, allows for transformations of the world, and so, this fundamentally offers modifications to our temporal dwelling. Said otherwise, sight and hearing are modes of contact that cannot, by the sheer power of their own office, leave a created artifact in their wake. When we touch things, changing them and/or using them, we gather and organize spatiality and temporality.

We are haptic creatures, lived-bodies who move toward beings by acts of hands, and so, the human world upsurges in and through handicrafts. We produce all forms of artifacts, both practical and artistic: buildings, vehicles, roads, monuments, textiles, utensils, crafts, etc. Right now I look around the room. Not only does everything, absolutely everything, tie back to being—in some way or other—the product of human hands, but also, many objects solicit and require further hand manipulation. It is filled, one might say, with objects made by hands for hands.[12] Consider the positions and configurations hands have of comporting toward entities, and consider the way entities can be freed up, made available and relevant, in those diverse comportings: Musical instruments, tools, and everyday objects of all kinds, are opened by the way they are given to the ontological structure of the hand.[13] Said more rigidly, the specific intendableness of entities is released and appropriated by the comportments our hands are able to maintain with regard to them.

In summary, one of our basic means of intending and caring for objects is by handling them. Through touch, most commonly with the hands, we direct ourselves toward the world and intend it. We release and appropriate entities according to their touchableness and their relevance in our projects and dealings. The lived-body, through pre-thetic motor intentionalities, comprehends entities according to the comportments it maintains toward them. This implies that bodily and handy movements, as they are lived-through, are not simply or merely behavior. Rather, a nontheoretical comprehension is woven into them. To move is to inscribe the world with meaning and significance. In reaching, grasping, holding, in running toward or running away, in lifting up and over, or in bringing intimately near, a lived-through comprehension, a choreographing of nontheoretical significance is accomplished (Polanyi, 1966; Thayer, 1997).

The operative intentionality of our handling is indeed central to human world-building, but physical touch is only one mode of contact, one tissue by which the disclosedness of "the there" is manifest, one manner by which world [and] self emerge. And, I should not underaddress our other, more subtle, intentional vectors. In fact the lived-body's motor movements and handling, more often than not, are guided by and enabled through other modes of existential decompression. Most commonly, we handle something only after having made other forms of intentional contact.

The Senses   As lived-bodies, we continually bring entities near and dwell in nearness. We face objects, events, and persons, and often, as I already suggested, we handle things. But there are many ways of bringing near, numerous powers by which Earth's internal negations are surpassed in "articulate contact" (Stewart, 1995; 1996). By simply looking at something, we meaningfully choreograph Earth's existential decompression; this is already to *be* "the there-here." As Heidegger provocatively states, "When I go toward the door of the lecture hall, I am already there, and I could not go to it at all if I were not such that I am there. I am never here only, as this encapsulated body; rather I am there, that is, I already pervade the room, and only thus can I go through it" (1971, p. 157). Recall again that all intentional relations are existential: they are not external, are not simply categorical. As the world's manifest and internal correlate, the lived-body is "in contact" in many ways. Said otherwise, I may de-distance something by actually moving through space, bringing it near to me so as to free it for relevant hand manipulations. But, I also can bring something near—taking care of it—by simply looking at, or by listening to it, or by tasting it. Indeed, the lived-body's sensorimotor powers are intentional vectors through which "the there" is released and appropriated.

What does it mean to say that the lived-body's sensorimotor powers are characterized by intentionality? It means there is never an intentional activity in-itself without its intended field. To see, at all, is to see something, to hear is to hear something, to smell is to smell something, and to taste is to taste something. Never is there a visual field without eyes, an audible field without ears, a gustatory field without the taste buds, etc. Nor is there ever an eye, an ear, a nose, or a tongue simply in itself, for the being (i.e., the existence) of each releases and appropriates an intended object (i.e., an object as meant by the intentional activity).

The intentionality of the sensory powers is well elucidated in Leder's (1990) use of Polanyi's distinction between "from" and "to," the two end poles of intentional threads. Somewhat similar to Heidegger's (1982) observations regarding the intentio and intentum, Leder (1990) suggests that when we look to some object we see from our eyes and our eyes themselves do not appear in the visual field. Likewise when we listen to some sounds, we listen from our ears and our ears are not heard. He further argues, "To state a general principle: insofar as I perceive through an organ, it necessarily recedes from the perceptual field it discloses. I do not smell my nasal tissue, hear my ears, or taste my taste buds but perceive with and through such organs" (pp. 14–15). To say an organ disappears is to claim that when it is presencing a perceptual field, it is absent from that field. Stated otherwise, the knowledge that my eyes see need not, and often does not, accompany acts of seeing, and in fact, I routinely become oblivious to the fact that my eyes are seeing. Well in line with Harding's notion of "having no head," Leder (1990) describes the lived-body as primarily an absent body, claiming that the natural and routine functioning of the sensory powers leads them to disappear. The senses, therefore, are modes of absence which are the revealing presence of worldly aspects.[14]

None of the intentional powers, as already suggested, presence total or completed entities. Instead, they manifest fields having open horizons and a basic inexhaustibility. The world presenced through my sensori-motor powers is a world that cannot be thoroughly depleted; it is never complete; it is always, always, with more on-the-way. Merleau-Ponty thoughtfully addresses this when he states, "Things perceived would not be evident for us and present in flesh and blood if they were not inexhaustible, never fully givens. They would not have the air of eternity we find in them unless they were open to inspection that no time could terminate" (1973, p. 37). This is part and parcel of the lived-body's once-occurrent position and moment, of the finitude to its powers (i.e., that it always decompresses along particular spatial and temporal horizons). As a common example, I hold a cube in my hand. Although I cannot see all sides of the cube at once and must rotate it—exposing only three sides to my gaze at any time—I still have a whole cube in my hand. The world is a plenitude, a thickness that appresents what is not presented, and the ideal of an exhausted, isolated, and phenomonologically complete object is but a positivist dream.

Moreover, to the degree that "each organ of sense explores the object in its own way" (Merleau-Ponty, 1962, p. 223), the same objects show themselves differently according to the manner of understanding given to the intentional activities by which they are intended (say, of hearing or sight, or touch). Take, for example, the different phenomenal manifestness of the same object: consider the peculiar distinctions between someone who is earmuffed and looking at a set of stereo speakers, and, on the other hand, someone who is blindfolded and listening to the sounds pouring into the room. Consider now someone who is earmuffed *and* blindfolded, and who is running her hands along and around the speakers, haptically feeling the vibrations. In each case, peculiar ways of releasing and appropriating the varying plenitude of intendableness can be found. The peculiar proper to each intentional thread is noticed most clearly if one strictly disallows contributions from the others, as this fast and loose hypothetical consideration tries to show. But what, then, are the specific differences between seeing something, hearing something, and touching something? More will be said on this most difficult question throughout the rest of this chapter, but for now, we should acknowledge, at least, that we already experience the differences. We understand them even if we remain unable to speak clearly about them. Still, an approximate, initial response is that, roughly, differences in intendableness refer to differences in spatialization and temporalization (Straus, 1963 and Heidegger, 1962, respectively). Each of the perceptual powers and their intended objects is differentiated according to the peculiar configurations of spatialized and temporalized world-experience by which entities are disclosed.

Perhaps we should consider these phenomena for ourselves. When I touch an object, if my eyes are kept closed, the object as a whole, is slowly and seemingly additively disclosed. It is accomplished by the retentionality and protentionality of the hand's sensible movements. This apparent additiveness might even lead me to be fooled as to the whole entity, especially if I do not explore all of it (e.g., as in the oft-told Sufi story about three blind men and an elephant). Our powers of sight, on the other hand, are a quicker movement. They are lighter contact, a choreography of rapid eye movements which disclose the field of seeableness. Sight is a nonphysical caress, a mode of manifesting colorful presences-at-a-distance (Straus, 1963). In fact, one cannot see something if it is too close, and especially if it is actually touching the eyes. Nevertheless, sight is a way of intending objects themselves: "We must take literally what vision teaches us," states Merleau-Ponty, "namely that through it we come into contact with the sun and stars, that we are everywhere all at once" (1964, p. 187). Sight is an intentional activity that intends objects in their seeableness.

Sight spatializes spatiality by opening the exteriority of objects to us and to themselves (Ong, 1967). Sight manifests the world's colors and hues, spatialized in experiencable configurations. For example, colors, hues, and shades are spatialized throughout a room, seeming to be on entities themselves. Again, seeableness is a distant releasement or constitution. It refers to the manifestness of depths, spaces-at-a-distance, and ultimately, the steady appearance of whole and colored (or at least shaded) objects.

It also temporalizes temporality in its own particular way: things-as-a-whole are evident immediately. It offers me a constant setting with stable and continuously present objects. When Merleau-Ponty (1962) suggests sight is a privileged sense, he refers to the continuous spread-out all-at-onceness which it accomplishes. Where Schrag (1969) challenges this claim, suggesting that sight is too easily disembodied, he refers to the peculiar "at-a-distantness" that is necessary for seeing objects. For present purposes, I only stress that seeableness, as distinguished from touchableness or hearableness, has its own peculiar configuration of spatialized and temporalized lived-through world-experience.

So, what about the spatialized and temporalized character of hearableness? First, hearableness refers to manifestations or presences that are, like seeableness, present-yet-at-a-distance. But hearableness is not localized to objects per se, as the seeableness of colors is attached to objects themselves. Sounds seem separated from their source, and so, they fill a room in a homogenizing way (Straus, 1963; 1966). This means that hearableness is kind of spatializing in which something can "be there" without being seen or touched. Moreover, hearableness opens us to interiority as such (Ong, 1967). It is indeed a dwelling in that interiority which is distant but also intimately near.

Hearableness is also more eventful, more evanescent, than is seeableness. To release hearableness is to experience that which seems to be fleeting and fading. Said simply, hearableness is a flowing and so makes room for what must be caught in the act (i.e., in its temporal unfolding). Particular sounds rapidly fade away as others freshly arrive to take their place. This fading back and coming to, given the unity of retentionality and protentionality to the auditory intentional threads, manifests and makes apparent lacunae, periods, and rhythms. Listening to some music, I hear a rich tapestry of sounds unfolding over time, a texture which makes room for the different instruments' sounds. Moreover, sounds are often spatialized in particular bodily configurations: my entire body may be enlivened and animated, having different bodily regions ensnare by gesticulation the many beats, riffs, and rhythms (Straus, 1963).

Finally consider the intendableness called "tasteableness." No amount of looking at, listening to, or touching with the hands will ever release and appropriate the taste of food (e.g., a strawberry sundae, a piece of cheese, or a chip dipped in salsa). Tasteableness, unlike hearableness and seeableness, requires bringing something into physical contact with the body. It is, then, a kind of touching, one which is significantly different from sensible hand touch. Taste is a tonguing caress which releases a temporalized (i.e., fleeting) gustatory experience, and which spatializes entities by smearing them across the tongue's buds. It is more intimate in its spatialization and temporalization, more of a hidden releasement; it is a mode of caring for the world, and one which, most often, culminates in a mysterious communion.[15] Note also that it primarily, most commonly, includes fumed horizons and vapory pockets of olfactory presences. A given food's odor might even be included as a moment of its taste; it is that part which, though not exclusively, can be present-at-a-distance.

Tasting reveals entities in the particular intendableness of tasteableness; note that entities tasted are experienced as if they themselves have the taste within them, as if they objectively contain their taste. But this should not lead us to believe that taste is simply present in the food. It is perhaps more useful to suggest that taste is primarily a prereflective intentionality; it disappears to presence what it is not. For example, if I were to bite into a raw onion, the onion itself seems to have the taste. Although I may immediately blurt out, "Raw onions taste bad," I might, later and after reflection, suggest, "I don't like the taste of raw onions." Surely, in reflection, I may suggest that it was, in fact, my experience of the taste. But, should we conclude from this that taste is, therefore, subjective? Do the intentional activities of tasting simply create the tasteableness of something?[16] Clearly, one's tastes change over time due to physiological changes in one's gustatory organs. But still, the prereflective character intentionality as well as the dialogical nature of tasteableness must be retained.

In summary, although the various sensory powers all display a prereflective "from-to" structure, this should not be taken to imply that the world is "subjectively constituted." The phenomena of perceptual intendableness are granted neither simply by the world in-itself nor sheerly by the powers of a self-sufficient subject. Merleau-Ponty eloquently addresses this issue when he writes:

> What there is then is not things first identical with themselves, which would offer themselves to the seer, nor is there a seer who is first empty and who, afterward, would open himself to them—but something to which we could not be closer than by palpating it with our look, things we could not dream of seeing 'all naked' because the gaze itself envelops them, clothes them with its own flesh. (1968, p. 131)

Intendableness, therefore, is neither subjectively attributed nor objectively present. This notion is offered as a subtle but persistent way of attending to the fact that the intentional threads are indigenous to self-negating Earth. Sensory powers and their intended objects are gifts by which world [and] self are spatialized and temporalized in particular lived-through configurations.

Affectivity   In everyday engagements and dealings, the lived-body encounters many objects, events, and persons, and cares for them according to the affective intentional comportments maintained regarding them. This means that in addition to perceptual powers and capacities for skillful movements, the lived-body also has various emotive-volitional powers. These powers disclose an affective intendableness to entities and fields and thereby implicate an affecting lived-body. Regarding the specific character of lived-body's affective intentionalies, I discuss four general and interrelated points.

First, "feelings," Schrag states, "are bearers of intentionality; they manifest a behavior style and disclose a world" (1969, p. 92). I must stress that as a lived-body I am outside myself. Just as the body's other intentional powers do not represent an outside world, so too emotions are not something simply inside the subject; emotions and feelings are not merely psychological states which an inner self expresses outwardly. They are bodily comportments which intend a world, lighting it up according to various emotional-volitional powers. As modes of both prereflective and reflective world-comprehension, emotions include not only various intended objects and events (i.e., objects disclosed in their affective intend-ableness), but also reveal, as their existential correlates, an affectively comporting lived-body. Take, as examples, anger, fear, sorrow, hope, disgust, joy, envy, apprehension, confidence, etc. The way the lived-body is emotionally animated, the specific facial and bodily comportments it maintains, the subtle tones which intonate and resonate throughout movements, all of these manifest worldly entities in a certain emotive color and tone. Emotive intentionality, then, is a mode of world-disclo-sure, a peculiar manner of revealing how and in what ways my projects and the event-horizon toward which I move critically matter. Feelings and emotions speak to me about what matters in a nontheoretical, non-intellectual manner; they disclose a valued world [and] a valuing body. In summary, emotions are not simply inner states which I express outwardly, but rather, they are intentional tissues through which world [and] self are concernfully disclosed and tended.

Second, I must stress the importance of the distinction between reflec-tive and prereflective modes of intentionality. Our feelings and emotions are primarily, though certainly not exclusively, prereflective in character. Sartre's *The Emotions* (1948) holds his famous critique of the psycholo-gist's approach which, according to Sartre, gives a primacy to emotions as they appear in reflection. From the psychological perspective, an indi-vidual may claim that emotions are internal states which we can be and are conscious of. Sartre somewhat reverses this claim, suggesting that emotions are not simply different intentums of consciousness, but rather, are modes of intentio in their own right. "In emotion," he states, "it is the body which, directed by consciousness, changes its relations with the world in order that the world may change its qualities" (1948, p. 61). This means that a given emotion, in prereflection, is not something we attend to, but is that which allows a particular mode of attending from. The emotions, therefore, are themselves intentional bodily comportments, threads that "magically" disclose world-profiles whose manifestness is inaccessible to other intentional threads.

Third, world disclosures vary from manifesting particular value-col-ors of certain objects (e.g., as in fear or disgust) to overall existential dis-closures regarding my "being-in-the-world" (e.g., as in mood or anxi-ety). That is, affective disclosures range from the emotional-volitional tones pervading everyday entities of the world to overall revelations regarding the meaning of one's very existence. To unpack this third point, I need to stress that our bodies maintain an emotional regard for the unfolding, temporal event-horizon: the "already happened," the "not-yet" and the "will-have-been." Moreover, whenever I find myself, I find that I have always already begun (Heidegger, 1962). That is, when I come to myself, I always already have a past, a situatedness, a facticity regarding the host of involvements in which I have engaged and do engage. Affective tones of the world, then, include a nontheoretical comprehension of world experience which understands this thrownness. In my everyday encounters I am never without a mood, without a general emotional-volition level, even if the mood is boredom or leveled-indifference (Heidegger, 1995). Bakhtin argues that the "experiencing of an experience . . . means not being absolutely indifferent to it, means an affirming of it in an emotional-volitional manner" (1993, p. 34). The world, which is the a priori correlate to the lived-body's various intentional activities, is lit up by and implicated in evaluative intentionalities, even if specific emotional objects are not analytically manifest. As Bakhtin further insightfully states,

> the emotional-volitional tone cannot be isolated, separated out of the unitary and once-occurrence of a living consciousness as related only to a particular object as such. This is not a universal valuation of an object independently of that unique context in which it is given to me at the moment, but expresses the whole truth [pravda] of the entire situation as a unique moment in what constitutes an ongoing event. . . . The moment constituted by the performance of thoughts, feelings, words, practical deeds, is an actively answerable attitude that I myself assume—an emotional-volitional attitude toward a state of affairs in its entirety, in the context of actual unitary and once-occurrent life. (1993, p. 36–37)

We find, then, a particular emotional-ladeness to our everyday activities, and a seemingly unaffective dwelling is but a leveling down to an everyday mood rather than a moodlessness. This general and diffuse level of intentionality is difficult to simply point out, mainly because it is a comprehension regarding my unique once-occurrent participations. It always includes much more than the simple "here and now" of my body; it includes the world which is the current correlate to my lived-body as well as all of my "was," my "yet-to-be," and my "will-have-been."

Fourth and finally, the various affective intentionalities ecstatically modify the spatialization and temporalization of lived-through world-experience. Said otherwise, the different affective comportments and their intentional objects are spatialized and temporalized within particular configurations. The emotionableness of the human world, therefore, includes a configuration of intentional bodily comportments, especially subtle difference in bodily deportment and carriage, and further discloses the world as having certain spatial and temporal bearings.

Bodily comportments are not simply of expressions of internal feelings but are ways of "understandingly-being-toward" disclosed entities and events. In certain cases, take depression, the lived-body hangs a little more limply. It is much more heavy, more cumbersome. The face feels spatialized downward, as if gravity's pull localized all of its weight to the eye brows, lips, and chin. The head itself feels heavier, making it feel somewhat natural to "hang one's head low." Movements are slowed down, modified by and resonating with the affective intonations of list-lessness and apathy. Happiness, as a significantly different case, is a light-ness throughout the lived-body, an increased energy level tingling through its limbs. Also, a taken-for-granted confidence intonates bodily move-ments. The head seems light, and the face is lit up, showing a kind of radi-ance, as if projecting itself outward.

Again emotions are embodied, meaning they are not limited to the body's spatial area: I am outside myself, directed toward worldly entities. To be depressed is not merely to embody a depressed behavioral style. It is to discover and dwell in a depressing world; the depressiveness of the world is all-too-easily made manifest (i.e., released and appropriated). World horizons, for a depressed person, may seem to shrink, the past being severed from meaningful relation to the present, and a meaningful future appearing dismally unimaginable, absolutely unreachable. Situa-tions can look irrecoverably damaged, unfixable. It feels as if things will never get better. In general, the depressed affected body discloses a world in which time drags and space shrinks up. Likewise, sadness, as Sartre suggests, undifferentiates the structure of the world so that "we behave in such a way that the universe no longer requires anything of us" (1948, p. 65).

On the other hand, joy is the disclosure of the objects of our desires as "near and easy to possess" (Sartre, 1948, p. 69). Happiness discloses the world as a happy place. Indeed, implicating a happily affecting lived-body, someone might simply say, "The birds were singing, the sun was shining." Consider also feelings of hope. Hope is a kind "seeing," a kind of worldly comprehension which is unavailable to perceptual intention-alities. It is, in fact, a disclosure that can seem to cut against the other intentional vectors (perception or reflective judgment). About hope Schrag states, "The consistency of the lived space that surrounds hope is expan-sive rather than constrictive" (1969, p. 98). Thus, affective intentionalities disclose projects and involvements according to their own peculiar means of spatialization and temporalization.

In addition to touch and handling things, and in addition to sensory powers of sight, smell, hearing, and taste, our emotive intentionalities open a certain manifestableness, a peculiar intendableness, of world. The human world is a world in which objects, events, and persons are emo-tionally valued just as indigenously as they are looked at, touched, or heard. These are various ways that Earth, in negating itself as Earth, (i.e., losing itself in existential decompression), has of coming to itself, and so of releasing and appropriating experienceable phenomenal fields and objects, and of implicating embodied selves. All of the intentional vectors display their own logic of care-taking; through and by all of the various intentional powers, the lived-body discloses a "there" in which entities that critically matter are tended to and cared for.

Imagination   The final intentional vector needing address, at least briefly, is imagination. Imagination, I need to show, is an indigenous connective tissue through which world [and] self are concernfully manifest and taken under care. This task is not without many difficulties. A most stubborn prejudice in modern thought is that whatever is inaccessible to the body's "empirical" (i.e., sensory) powers is somehow not real, or is something fundamentally subjective. There seems to be, or at least there is said to be, a real world which is available to the senses, and also an imaginary world which is available only to one's "subjective mind." As with emotive intentionality, a common obstacle to uncovering the intentional workings of imagination is the tendency to consider images reflectively. Here one easily concludes that images are something we attend to, something we are conscious of. That is, in reflective moments, (i.e., for thetic intentionality), an image may seem not as intentional, but may instead appear as an object of consciousness. But this, I need to show, is what images are not; images are not objects I am simply conscious of. They are intentional structures. They manifest world and implicate self in their own peculiar ways (Casey, 1976).

Many entities of "the there" are presenced not merely through movement, touch, sight, hearing, smell, taste, or even affect. These objects, events, and persons, are made manifest and drawn near through imaginative intentionality; threads of imaginative intentionality offer their own manner of releasing and appropriating world-experience. Richard Kearney, in his lucid *Poetics of Imagining* (1991), discusses Husserl's view on imagination, and suggests that imagining something, as distinct from seeing that something, is a different manner of intending it. He states, "To perceive my brother and to imagine my brother are two different ways of intending the same transcendent object. The intentional percept refers to the same object—my brother—as the intentional image; but the crucial difference is that the first intends him as real, the latter as unreal" (p. 17). This is a clear and useful explanation. But we must not take it to imply that imaginative activities are limited to themselves, as if they did not interpenetrate and move in and throughout the other intentional threads (Casey, 1976). In fact, to constrict imagination this way would lead to an underestimation of its pervasiveness to lived-through world-experience.

In stricter phenomenological terms, an object of perceptive or affective intentionality may be not only an intentum, but moreover, it can be part of the intentio of imaginative intentionality (i.e., part and parcel of other intending activities). Take an example: I look to some object, say a bright red convertible Corvette. Although this object is disclosed through ocular intentionalities, it also may be laden or shot-through with affective colorings according to the emotional-volitional comportments I maintain regarding it. This object of the lived-body's perceptual threads can be an intentional structure, a flight beyond itself. The perceived car, as intended object, also can be an intentional image (i.e., an intentio intending something other than itself). This example illuminates why Sartre, in his *The Psychology of Imagination* (1991) writes,

> There is not a world of images and a world of objects. Every object, whether it is present as an external perception or appears to intimate sense, can function as a present reality or as an image, depending on what center of reference has been chosen. The two worlds, real and imaginary, are composed of the same objects: only the grouping and interpretation of these objects varies. (p. 27)

The image, as intentional, is a flight toward something it is not. It surpasses itself and is an image of something more or less than itself. Therefore, an image is an intentional power, a way of drawing near or keeping at a safe distance, a manner of taking care of entities and self.

Imaginative intentionalities, like the other bodily powers, are funded by Earth's internal negations, and yet, these tissues seem to further pursue or carry out that internal negation in a special way. That is, in imaginative threads, objects, events, and persons are concernfully tended through negativity. As Sartre suggests, "the imaginary object can be posited as non-existent, or as absent, or as existing elsewhere, or not posited as existing. We note that the common property of these four theses is that they include the entire category of negation, though at different degrees. Thus the negative act is constitutive of the image" (1991 p. 265). This negativity can be further understood by considering these different levels as peculiar and particular means of organizing spatiality and temporality. That is, the peculiar proper to the intentional threads of imagination shows itself as a unique power for particular spatialization and temporalization (also see Kearney, 1991, p. 54).

We can presence objects, people, or events that, as their way of showing themselves, are manifest as unavailable to any other senses and as forever so. This is perhaps why Husserl claimed that a "centaur," imaginatively posited as not existing, is not simply an object in the immanent sphere of the subject. The imagined centaur is presenced as something nonexisting, and hence the image makes a statement about the world. Another way something can imaginatively show itself is as absent, or more specifically, as somewhere else. Sartre's famous example in *Being and Nothingness* (1956) is of his looking in a café for his absent friend Pierre. Looking for an absent friend, I perpetually make an image of him, while also continually nihilating it before the faces disclosed as not him. He, my friend, is not simply, rawly, "not there"; the friend is continuously disclosed as absent. Sartre states, "I myself expect to see Pierre, and my expectation has caused the absence of Pierre to *happen* as a real event concerning this café. It is an objective fact at present that I have *discovered* this absence" (1956, p. 10). This is one of the ways that persons can manifest themselves. Imagination thus refers to a negativity which opens entities for particular spatialized and temporalized manifestations. This also means that imaginary objects are not simply subjective, are not merely made up by the subject. Rather, they tell us something about the world and the manners in which we care for entities.

I conclude the present discussion on imaginative intentionalities, by turning, strangely enough, to the early beginnings of the phenomenological concept, that is, to where intentionality historically began: theoretical assertions and mathematical entities. Take the simple judgment: "I walked around the parking lot, and I saw that your car was not there." This everyday kind of judgment is funded through imagination. But this does not mean it is merely subjective. It is a releasement and appropriation of something about the parking lot itself; I am stating something about "the there." And yet, because every situation positively is what it is, how can this lack of the car manifest itself? How can we "see" this absence? Clearly, the sheer lack of the car (i.e., the fully positive presence of only other cars) is not the same as the car being experienceably absent; there are many places where the car is not, and yet, it may not be manifest as "not there." The absence of the car can be manifest as an absence only because of the negativity infecting world [and] self. It is our ability to imagine it as present that manifests it as absent. Therefore, many imaginative experiences, especially of absence, cannot be analytically reduced to presences through other intentional threads.

We might also suggest that the objects of mathematics (e.g., 2, 5, 2001, etc.) are real entities, not simply subjectively constituted. In a sense numbers are imaginary, for they are not open to the empirical senses (i.e., one cannot see them), and yet, numbers are not locked up in the mind either. The basics of mathematics (e.g., natural numbers) are not relative from culture to culture. Objects, events, and persons can be intended in mathematical calculations as a way of making them manifest. Counting, then, is an imaginative intentionality which releases and appropriates various intended objects: entities and/or groups as mathematized. Things display a manifestness in terms of the terms we use to come toward them. Math is indeed a speech activity, and, in speaking about entities in terms of their mathematicableness, we release and appropriate one of the profiles by which they can be concernfully disclosed. Counting is a way of bringing near and tending over, as is seen in a shepherd who is counting his flock. Said otherwise, many entities are taken care of not by touching them, or sitting on them, or looking at them, but by speaking about them, by counting them. Again, this is a way of intending those things themselves, one of the ways in which things manifest themselves according to comportments we maintain with regard to them.

We are beings who release and appropriate world-profiles (i.e., existentially decompress the plenitude of Earth) by the intentional threads of imagination. We should not imagine that imagination is an occasional presencing of internal and fanciful images. In fact, it may be more appropriate to suggest, as Thayer (1987) does, "We need 'the facts' only where imagination fails us" (p. 121). Imaginative activities and their correlates are natural to the world; they are part of the way objects, events, and persons show themselves. In our everyday lives there is an intermingling of motor, perceptual, affective and imaginative intentions, all intermingling to presence entities and fields in their varied intendableness, and so to implicate a multifigured, embodied self.

Unifying the Differences

The lived-body is implicated in a network of varying intentional threads by and through which world-experience is concernfully lived-through. Intentionality, I maintain, underlies our motility and our skillful manipulation of handy material conditions (Heidegger, 1962; 1982; Schrag, 1969), our sensorimotor powers of perception (Merleau-Ponty, 1962; Leder, 1990), our affects and emotions (Bakhtin, 1993; Heidegger, 1995; Sartre, 1948), and our imaginations (Casey, 1976; Kearney, 1991; Sartre, 1956). In all of these diverse ways of meaningfully comporting ourselves, worldly entities are taken under care, even if only unthematically or implicitly.

When we compare seeing something, with tasting it, or dreaming about it, or acting on it, or imagining it, or even—as we shall see later in more detail—speaking about it, we basically find different manners of intending it. And yet, as already suggested, each of these different manners has its own peculiar way of releasing and appropriating. They are different manners of disclosing world and implicating self. That is, there are certain aspects of world [and] self—certain profiles or ways of experiencing—which are available to one intentional thread and not to the others. For example, imagine effectively explaining the differences between sight and hearing and touch and imagination. We undergo and endure these, and yet, we also seem unable to explain fully their differences. We should here recall Heidegger's claim that "to every intentional comportment belongs an understanding of the being of the being to which this comportment relates" (1982, p. 158). Hence, the manner and mode of the different intentional threads can remain mysteriously "dumb" to the others. Stated by way of some examples: we cannot taste an imagined object, nor can we see the hearableness of music filling into a room. We do not smell either mathematical objects or the emotion of joy. A child may enjoy playing with a chocolate sundae, but no amount of handling it, or even speaking about it, can release and appropriate its taste. And, never do we go out to listen to a lunar eclipse. The nature of embodiment is such that the lived-body holds a host of powers by which world-profiles are released and appropriated (i.e., existentially decompressed), and, these are fundamentally, that is always, dialogical. Nevertheless, the limited intercommunication between the intentional threads should not be overstated, nor should I understate the integral importance of speech/language to the human world. Differing intentional comportments commonly do interact with each other. In fact, they routinely display a prereflective interactive harmony (Merleau-Ponty, 1962).

The more general point here is that humans are suspended within an intentional nexus, and so, phenomenological differences reopen a question regarding the meaning of the hermeneutical circle. We might step into the circle here: Any and every phenomenon has its ways of showing itself. Therefore, we might curtail the quick question: Is the object in question real or not real?, and instead learn to ask the question: By what intentional powers (in what mode of intendableness) is the object under consideration to be released and appropriated? Therefore, the question regarding the disclosure or manifestness of a given entity is not, Which is subjective and which objective? It is, rather, in and through which intentional threads is the entity made manifest?

SUMMARY: SELFHOOD [AND] EMBODIMENT

This chapter explicated the meaning of human embodiment as ultimately resting in the fact that Earth, in itself, cannot exist. If Earth is to entertain existence, it must lose itself by "falling" into existential correlates of world [and] self. Earth's internal negations and ensuing upsurgings of phenomenal fields open along spatial and temporal horizons; the different threads of intentionality open world [and] self to particular configurations of spatialized and temporalized experience.

Given the inexistence of Earth as Earth, we can say that all livedthrough experience is of world [and] self. Moreover, there is neither world nor experiencer without the other as its existential correlate. Schrag well articulates the whole of these concerns:

There has been a pronounced tendency in the history of philosophy to approach the world as a cosmological issue. In such an approach the world as 'cosmos' is pictured as an external totality of entities within an objective extensive continuum of space and time. The peculiar and ironic destiny of such a world picture is that it has no place for the experiencer. . . . The world is viewed as an external totality of entities somehow presented to an internal mind, self, or consciousness. Self and world are split and separated in accordance with the dichotomies of internal and external, subject and object. The experienced world is older than this split and precedes these dichotomies. (1969, p. 44)

Said in strict terms, all intentional relations fundamentally rest upon the primordial and continuous internal negations of Earth. Embodied selves are Earth's way of losing its nonexistence to "regain" world. They, by having various objects and involvements of concern, are focal and gravitational centers—once-occurrent and living participations—by which Earth is spatially and temporally decompressed into particular world-experience configurations. This global depiction of embodiment, which radically places the body outside itself, avoids reducing existence and/or experience to the product of an embodied subject.

Phenomenological notions of embodiment are nothing so trivial as a slight critique to textualisms or social constructionisms. Such trivializations miss the ontological significance of embodiment. Being a body means being-in-the-world, that world in which we take care of things by concernfully dwelling in nearness. We are lived-bodies, meaning that we care not merely for the extended space of our flesh; we care for and concern ourselves with that which surrounds us, and so, lived-bodies understand themselves by understanding worldly entities and involvements. As Heidegger states, "World-understanding as Dasein-understanding is self-understanding. Self and world belong together in the single entity, the Dasein. Self and world are not two beings, like subject and object, or like I and thou, but self and world are the basic determination of the Dasein itself in the unity of the structure of being-in-the-world" (1982, p. 297). Numerous comprehensions and understandings precede the division of inner and outer and the reflective severance of subject and object.

The discussion of imaginative intentionality lead to two examples of speech as an intentional vector, and yet it is there, then, that I have had to stop. I am not yet ready to address this most wondrous intentional power, even if I have uncovered a bit of the truth to Thayer's claim: "To name something is to imagine where it goes when it is not in sight" (1997, p. 109). Much more address will be given to speech throughout the whole of Chapter 4. Before that, I need to address the social dimensions of selfhood.

I now turn to the sociality of world [and] self. World, as the existential correlate of self, is socialized through history and so is a structuring of intentional (i.e., existential) relations. I need to address the historical continuity of sociality and so of world, as well as the question of how the embodied self, an earthly worlding, organizes and sustains particular intentional relations with others. I have already suggested that an operative intentionality underlies our motility and manipulation of handy things, and that, by handling material conditions I can temporalize world by leaving handy items in the wake of my projects. But what now needs more clarification is how others introduced me to world.

World already has been decompressed by others' touch. Almost all of the world I experience was first, in some way or another, opened up or given over by and through others.[17] And, so much was "handed down" in a rather reified manner. Sociality, then, is a basic layer by which internal negativity and world-building infects Earth. Ultimately, other persons are mutual sites of existential decompression, lines of involvement inertia, rallying points of power, and/or currents of opposition. These meanings of sociality must be critically unpacked, showing how others carry out world-building significance by way of socially orchestrating and regulating particular spatializations and temporalizations of lived-through world-experience.

CHAPTER 3

The Self (Through, As, With, For, Against, as Not) Others

The self is social. This is no news flash for modern scholars. But this does not mean that the peculiar character of sociality is well articulated and understood. Indeed, a lack of conceptual clarity pervades a good deal of contemporary thought. Some questions needing serious address can be offered: To what does the term "sociality" refer? And also, what, exactly, does it mean to say that human selves are social selves? Am I first an individual who subsequently becomes social or who could have been not social? How are subjectivity and intersubjectivity related? Which precedes? Which follows? What are the critical differences, if any, between sociality and socialization? Are the apocryphal "feral children" somehow not social?[18] Can one have a self without being socialized? Do language, communication, and "background practices" (Dreyfus, 1991) turn human individuals into social beings? To what extent, if at all, are the social self and the existing body mutually exclusive? The present chapter addresses this rangy and complex host of questions by unpacking various insights from numerous thinkers.

A significant yet largely implicit difficulty in contemporary theorizing stems from the underaddressed question of whether or not sociality is something bestowed upon individuals.[19] To this concern John Dewey was undeniably well on track where he suggested that, "There is a peculiar absurdity in the question of how individuals become social, if the question is taken literally" (1925/1988, p. 138). The question must be: What specifically do we mean by sociality?

For starters, every person up to this point in history (2000) has come into worldly existence through other persons. All living creatures come into being through other entities like themselves. It is by others, in the plural, that any lived-body comes to exist as a living breathing entity. In this most basic sense others are the source of my existence. I therefore encounter others, as they encounter me: someone with whom a cross-fertility is maintained, and thus, we hold mysterious power to join in a bond of miraculous fecundity. Cross-fertility, in-itself, is a level of sociability etched into Earth's fateful sending of itself out from its nonexistence.

Ultimately, neither language nor communication, nor even culture bestow sociality. "Sociality, in other words, is a given of the human condition, not a product of human making" (Stewart, 1995, p. 137). But still, this sheer fact of organismic (i.e., ontological) sociality is not what most needs our attention, even though it never should be forgotten nor underassessed. Sociality is much more than natural association; it includes numerous and diverse modes by which others are meaningfully, concernfully, "there" in the world.

This chapter focuses on how others manifest and implicate themselves. In preview, first, the world itself, as that wherein things to be cared for are found, is always already socialized by predecessors and contemporaries (Schutz, 1967). Even in my solitary moments, largely anonymous others are present—if only implicitly—due to their intentional powers. Second, others are a source of self-transcendence as well as a source of self-stultification. This means that world, as already socialized, enables a real-izing of otherwise undreamt potentialities, but it also constrains the capabilities to dream otherwise. Third, three broad and general modes of concrete face-to-face engagements between consociates are considered: being-with (Heidegger, 1962; Leder, 1990; Schutz, 1967), being-alienated (Sartre, 1956), and being-consummated (Bakhtin, 1990). Fourth, I bring the scholarship of Erving Goffman into Calvin O. Schrag's work on "communicative praxis," addressing how ritual practices are orchestrated according to interpersonal particularity and thereby form the communicative microtexture in which qualities of social character are articulately stitched. Finally, the lived-body's fundamentally once-occurrent participations in existence are underscored as dimensions of sociality (Bakhtin, 1990), and thus, a vital part of the lived-body's sociality is its non-interchangeability with other persons.

WORLD AS ALREADY SOCIALIZED

Most generally, sociality is a fundamental condition by which the upsurging existential correlates of world [and] self come to historical existence. This implies that others are not simply an occasional feature of either self or world. Both I [and] others are that through which world is what it is, and also, other people are one of the conditions by which I am able to become who I am as I am one of the conditions by which others are able to become who they are. Earth, therefore, is not only existentially decompressed (i.e., worlded) according to various intentional vectors reaching back to me. Also, it already has been and is being decompressed by others' intentional powers.

The existential decompressions by which Earth loses itself to haunt itself as an Other are not only choreographed and articulated by the lived-body's various intentional threads, but are, equiprimordially, orchestrated and regulated by social inertias as well as the direct impositions of others' intentional powers. This means that sociality is that by which both world-understanding [and] self-understanding emerge and develop within lived-through world-experience. Others are part of the way world [and] self become manifest. They bear upon the lived-body's intentional powers by "orchestrating" and "regulating" its concernful being-toward. In "my" concernful being-toward various objects-in-fields, I am always already "being-with-others." To illustrate these rather abstract claims, let us consider how concrete artifacts can be instituted (i. e., spatialized and temporalized) through predecessors' and/or contemporaneous others' engagements and involvements.

Availability and Relevance

The last chapter stressed that one way the lived-body accomplishes world [and] self comprehension is by physically touching with the hands. That is, in handling things we free them up and draw them near. We make them "available for" and "relevant to" various projects and involvements, and in doing so, we invest them with meaning and significance. I furthermore suggested that touch, especially of the hands, has its own manner of spatializing and temporalizing. It is largely through handiwork that the modern world has become spatially and temporally manifest. The world is therefore socialized in that it already has been spatialized and temporalized by others' touching activities, and hence, it is discovered as already laden with artifacts by which anonymous others are implicated, even though remote in space and/or time.

Other persons construct diverse material artifacts that allow for various kinds of spatializing and temporalizing of world [and] self. This means that artifacts are discovered as already prefigured, as already available for and relevant to various projects and involvements. As an initial example, I look around the room in which I am sitting. Almost all the entities I find around me were constructed by someone else, *and* they were constructed as "available for" and "relevant to" various concrete involvements. The coffee cup I am currently drinking out of was made by the handy works of others. Moreover, the cup itself calls forth not only the kinds of projects and involvements in which it becomes meaningfully available and relevant (i.e., drinking coffee), but it also calls forth certain kinds of bodily comportments by which it is freed up (i.e., various skillful hand movements). The lived-body therefore encounters a world whose socialization requires that it is able to comport itself according to the ways world has been opened and sedimented. The lived-body, as a concernful flight of transcendence beyond itself, follows out and continues in the already decompressed lines of readiness that have been established and are maintained by others.

The world itself is socialized. Others already have decompressed it, and they have done so in such a spatialized and temporalized manner (i.e., by their touching) that it offers me many sources of self-transcendence. If one were, figuratively speaking of course, to choose projects "all by oneself," one may never imagine either having certain projects, nor might one imagine to free up particular entities as relevant to and available for such projects. In fact, the lived-body might not even learn to comport as it could be comported to achieve certain goals. Bottles, jars, and cans, door knobs, light switches, and handles, numerous kinds of tools and utensils, all were made with availability for and relevance to various purposes and involvements already in view. Others have created technologies and material conditions for the use and modification of our bodily intentional powers: clocks, books, pencils, microscopes, telescopes, loud speakers, telegraphs, telephones, tape-recorders, radios, televisions, computers. All of these technologies (i.e., these "with-whichs" of our "concernful-being-toward") have been created by others, and are available for and relevant to various involvements which extend and modify our own intentional modes of concern (McLuhan, 1964). In a word, these with-whichs offer me pre-decompressed lines of transcendence, and open me to possibilities. Consider, as a different kind of example, what is meant in contemporary North American culture by the word "food." Most of us (U.S. citizens) could not simply "go into nature" and differentiate "food" from "nonfood"; we much more commonly rely upon what can be bought from others as food (e.g. from stores, marts, and co-opts). Said simply, we rely upon others to provide us with what is food, meaning that it already has been decompressed out of Earth's plenitude and made available for and relevant to eating.

Therefore, the world the lived-body concernfully discovers is already socialized (i.e., pre-decompressed or already meaningfully spatialized and temporalized by others). Note also that handled things, once decompressed out, take on social sedimentations of meaning (i.e., become traditions or institutions); handled objects which have been freed-up and left as available for and relevant to certain involvements are invested with a social meaning. This implies that artifacts cannot be freed up simply or solely according to the availability and relevance structures of the lived-body's powers for dwelling in nearness. Instead, "appropriateness" and "acceptability" overlay social configurations of meaning which copenetrate and even annex the meanings of relevance and availability. For example, even when I am alone I never simply place food directly on a table (Henry, 1965). Rather, I eat food off of something that was made for eating food. Plates were created by others to have a use-meaning inscribed into them: they are already available for and relevant to eating engagements. Said otherwise, those very artifacts, as entities spatialized and temporalized, become slowly sanctified as those which are socially "appropriate" and "acceptable" in such eating contexts. The lived-body could use a host of different items "as a plate," but many would be inappropriate. Equally, someone might make a comb available for and relevant to acts of eating, but obviously, this is clearly inappropriate, if not highly unacceptable.

Social meanings, as is starkly evident in situational improprieties, orchestrate and regulate Earth's existential decompression and thereby implicate socially involved selves in certain meaningful manners (Goffman, 1967). The intentional comportments by which world [and] self are taken under care are socially regulated and orchestrated so that one's concernful involvements and dealing unfold and develop within already proscribed and prescribed configurations. This fact underlies Heidegger's insight that in my concernful "being-directed-toward," I am already "being-with-others." This means that handy entities, those spatialized and temporalized through others' touching projects, are to be met by certain comportments and are to be made available for and relevant to already proscribed and prescribed activities and engagements.

In general, other persons already have spatialized and temporalized the world. Consequently those entities which already have been made available and relevant are discovered and encountered as appropriate and acceptable for prescribed and proscribed involvements (i.e., not simply as available for and relevant to any project whatsoever). Said otherwise, in conjunction with the meaning accomplished via availability and relevance, our freeing up of entities in terms of their appropriateness and acceptability also operates as a mode of understanding lived-through world-experience.

Social Negativity and Intentional Vectors

The social meanings pervading Earth's existential decompressions (i.e., in the forms of appropriateness and/or acceptability) are established and maintained mainly through socially issued negativity. Others therefore orchestrate and regulate the lived-body's intentional powers by extending the negativity that infects Earth. This negativity opens world [and] self to socially meaningful comprehensions, to modes of taking care which, in some form or other, always implicate others.

Children are born into communities that issue a flurry of negativity. This negativity is present in acts of physical resistance, and just as importantly, it takes form in the "tribal thou shall nots" (Burke, 1966). We, as children, are surrounded by and inundated with numerous "hortatory dont's" (Burke, 1966), and thus, the intentional threads by which we inhere in the world are thereby ratified and sanctified by societal imposi- tions. These layers of meaning are seen clearly in early parenting, where much time is spent directing and guiding the child's exploration of worldly entities. For example, a baby sits in a living room and has an abundance of toys around her. She puts blocks in her mouth and seems to enjoy this. Still, we might say, "She does not yet know how to play with most of the toys." Her mother keeps showing her "what 'you' do with the blocks" and how "'you' ride in the car." The child seems more inter- ested in the mother's movements and sounds than in her play advice. Later, the same young couple tries to show their almost two-year-old son how to look through a kaleidoscope. The youth looks at it, and gen- erally waves it around like a dagger. "Take it out of your pocket," they say, and "Don't cover that up. You're supposed to look through it." That the kaleidoscope is something "one" looks through does not occur to him, just as his ways of freeing it, making it available and relevant have long since been forgotten by the parents. In general, children, as lived- bodies, display world [and] self comprehensions by which they make entities available for and relevant to certain projects. And yet, they are surrounded with a flurry of social negativity that serves to regulate and orchestrate the way "one" is to comport toward various entities as well as the kinds of involvements that entities (as "with-whichs") are to be avail- able for and relevant to. Thus, others shape and organize the lived-body's powers for making available and relevant (i.e., our powers for dwelling in nearness). They regulate what is appropriate and acceptable, and thereby, social meaning further infuses lived-through world-experience.

Table manners also well exemplify how our bodily intentional pow- ers are socially orchestrated and regulated. By manners, I refer not only to many subtle semiotic meanings which ride through eating practices, as Barthes's *Empire of Signs* (1970) provocatively depicts. I refer, instead, to the ways availability and relevance are socially annexed by appropriate- ness and acceptability. In general, we learn not to mix or bring together certain items. Consider an example: I sit in a small mom-and-pop diner in the Midwest. On the table are glass salt and pepper shakers, a small bot- tle of Tabasco sauce, an ashtray, a red squeeze bottle of ketchup and a yellow squeeze bottle of mustard. There is also a clear glass sugar dis- penser with a silver lid, and a clear hard plastic tray divided into four sec- tions, each section having various kinds of jellies. Thus, on the table are many artifacts, each of which could be freed up as relevant to and avail- able for highly complex sets of interactions. But the kinds of projects into which they actually are taken up do not vary that greatly, nor do the kinds of comportments taken with regard to them. Few persons, if any, will stir Tabasco or jelly into a cup of coffee. One does not dollop mustard into drinking water. No one puts mustard on a piece of apple pie, nor have I seen anyone use the ashtray as a serving dish. I never have seen anyone put ketchup in their mouth first and then apply it to their French fries. Moreover, if I were to walk into this diner and take these table condiments as available and relevant art supplies, constructing a large abstract work on the table, this would be inappropriate, and most likely, highly unacceptable.

Jules Henry also provides a wonderful example where he discusses "The Doctrines of Eating," and describes how Bobby, a mentally troubled youth, poured "milk on his ear of corn to cool it off. . . . He then had his cup filled with milk again and squeezed a lemon wedge into it and drank it" (1965, pp. 78, 89). Because this behavior breaches social sedimentations of acceptability and appropriateness (though not necessarily availability and relevance), it implicates social selfhood in terms of the lack of understanding world [and] self. The child can thus be seen as either "a psychotic child who has not been able to learn how to eat . . . [or] a child who is imaginatively experimenting with eating" (Henry, 1965, p. 89).

Finally, consider the different kinds of comportmental care-taking that are associated with food, gum, candy, and glass marbles. These four kinds of entities vary in regard to the world-profiles (i.e., the intendableness) available to the lived-body's different intentional powers. Moreover, they vary in regard to the intentional comportments and projects that are appropriate and/or acceptable for each. Children are told, "take the marble out of your mouth" and also, "stop playing with your food." "Gum," they are told, "is something you put into your mouth, but it's not something you eat." On the other hand, food is to be swallowed after chewing, and it is not to be held in the mouth for long periods of time. In general, if children walk about with food in their mouths—or if they spit food out after chewing it—parents will tell them "Stop it" and also "Don't do it again."

The lived-body's powers for manifesting world-profiles and phenomenal fields, I have tried to show, are socially orchestrated and regulated, meaning that a layer of selfhood inheres in the appropriateness and/or acceptability of certain world-experience involvements and comprehensions. Note how this is quite distinct from the sheer "unavailability" of a given world-profile to a given intentional thread. A child may desire to "touch" the moon, for example, but the moon is not available for that intentional thread. On the other hand, food is easily touched with the hands and may be fun to play with. And yet, children are strictly taught that this is inappropriate and that there are certain ways of respectfully comporting oneself toward food. In a word, our various ways of understandingly-being-toward are, already, fundamentally, forms of "being-with-others."

The embodied self is socialized through and through, becoming itself only through its emergence from a social flurry of "thou shalt nots." Indeed, not only are the manipulations of handy items socially orchestrated and regulated, as the practices of eating show. So too are all of our intentional powers. Consider some brief yet telling exemplars that illustrate the social negativity which regulates and orchestrates our powers for caring-over entities. There are many places where it is posted: "No Touching Allowed," and likewise, we are sometimes told to "Keep off the Grass." Paintings on the wall, no matter how fun they might be to touch, are mainly for viewing, and so, we often tell a child, or an adult who apparently failed to learn this lesson, "Don't Touch." There are many places and events where one is to "be quiet," and, we are not supposed to eavesdrop on conversations into which we have not been invited. One is not to enjoy smelling socks or garbage, and one is not to relish the taste of either worms or slugs, regardless of their nutritional relevance and commonplace availability. One is not, normally, to fear Coca-Cola bottles, and there are numerous "display rules" which regulate our affective comportments. We are told to not touch certain areas of the body, especially others' bodies—at least not without consent. And, one is not to kiss or have sexual congress with someone while imagining someone else. In all of these different cases (only a brief consideration of innumerable examples that could be given), the concernful freeing up of entities and thereby making them available-for and relevant-to is socially orchestrated and regulated such that social meanings of appropriateness and acceptability manifest themselves.

Regarding the concrete emergence of our actual possibilities, then, atomistic individualism is widely off the mark. The fact is that, in some form or other, the accomplishments and comprehensions of my life have been funded by, or made possible through, other people. We are immeasurably indebted to others (Ricoeur, 1992; Reynolds, 1983). In summary, although humans have various intentional powers for world [and] self comprehension, these powers are thoroughly socially orchestrated and regulated: certain modes of intentional contact are legitimated and sanctified, while others are forcefully denied and shunned. Background practices, those imposed mainly through social negativity, orchestrate and regulate the kinds of comportments and involvments that are deemed appropriate and/or acceptable.

Human-made artifacts, literally, are the presence of others in their spatialized and temporalized historical and social accomplishments. In review, we, as individuals, fall into a set of historically sedimented practices which are, by and large, enabled by and sustained through particular material conditions as well as a flurry of social negativity. To the extent that my involvements are enabled by the material conditions left by others, and to the extent that I am able to comport myself to pre-decompressed objects—making them available for and relevant to projects for which they are socially appropriate and/or acceptable—I am already a social self. Said otherwise, objects themselves enable various projects (of course assuming given modes of intentional comportability), and so, "anyone" can take them up and can thereby gain the modes of selfhood implicated therein. But the handy items themselves, as ancient cities and artifacts make amply evident, do not simply hold their social meanings. I could say it like this: "relevance" and "availability" might be deducible from the objects themselves, assuming various bodily comportments by which the objects could be freed up. Still, how items were appropriate and/or acceptable can remain a mystery, for these dimensions of meaning are much more subject to localized practices of negativity and are maintained mainly in concrete face-to-face encounters. Thus, others cannot be reduced to their implicature as existential correlates to pre-decompressed worldly entities.

ENCOUNTERING OTHERS IN THE FLESH

Others are, without a doubt, more than a regulating and orchestrating force of socialization. They are living events of existential decompression by which the lived-body, as it is for-others, is concernfully presenced (Sartre, 1956; Bakhtin, 1990). As an initial thought pump on this point, consider George Steiner's wonderful *Real Presences* (1989). He describes the presence of others by asking us to imagine a painter who, after much time and effort, has produced a work of art. The painter then becomes concerned over the possible judgments that others might make, and he can't decide how others will receive it. Then, in an attempt to safeguard it from others' appraisals, the artist destroys the painting before anyone else has a chance to look upon it. The question Steiner poses is this: Did the destruction of the painting allow him to avoid others' looks? To which we must agree with Steiner: No. The act of destruction was, in fact, an implication of others. As Steiner states, "It is because the claims of the other's presence reach so deeply into the final precincts of aloneness that a creator may, in circumstances of extremity, seek to guard for himself or for willed oblivion what are, ineluctably, acts of communication and trials of encounter" (p. 137). Others are our condition, not occasional entities in our experience. They are part and parcel of the way we see things, as is evident when relatives phone to announce an impending visit and my residence is suddenly disclosed as "a mess." But the presence here discussed is perhaps only an imagined one; I do not mean not real, but rather, only that others can manifest themselves within our imaginative powers; we can see things as we imagine they would. Still, this important point is not yet what most needs our critical address. What must be elucidated is how the concrete other—this one and not another—is encountered in the flesh.

Being-With-Being-Toward

Even when all alone, the lived-body maintains a "being-with-others-being-toward-world." It concernfully discloses and prereflectively comprehends pre-decompressed entities in terms of their appropriateness and acceptability to various projects, and not simply in terms of their availability and relevance to its own projects. In this way, "'The others' does not mean everybody else but me—those from whom I distinguish myself. They are, rather, those from whom one mostly does not distinguish oneself, those among whom one is, too" (Heidegger, 1962, p. 111). This anonymous interchangeability is funded mainly by the spatializing and temporalizing powers of others' touch (i.e., by sedimented material conditions) and also by the co-comportabilities of lived-bodies. But, as already suggested, being-with-others-being-toward-world pervades concrete face-to-face encounters (see Schrag's discussion of "concrescence" 1994, pp. 135–155), and this is what occupies our present concern.

More commonly than not, we gather with others to share in mutual "toward-whichs" of intentional concern. That is, when physically "with" others, there is almost always a "that-toward-which" we are concernfully co-comported. It may be food we eat jointly, perhaps an athletic competition that we view; we may be playing music together, or mutually attending a lecture. Perhaps we are sharing in the view of a sunset or a campfire, or, perhaps, simply watching T.V. In these events of concernful co-comporting to a mutual "toward-which," others are encountered as fellow sites of decompression. Drew Leder instructively offers the term "mutual incorporation" to characterize our concernfully being-with-others-being-toward. He stresses that the precondition for an alienating gaze or touch (i.e., an objectification of one's body) is an intersubjectivity that facilitates a common disappearance into worldly concerns. The lived-body's intersubjectivity, therefore, refers to the mutual extension of intentional powers which allows our own threads to thematize not only to others but to thematize from (i.e., with) them. As cotransparencies, we supplement each others' intentional powers; we form common intentios and concernfully share common intentums. Leder writes,

> My own subjectivity does not force the other into a position of object, nor vice versa. We are cosubjectivities, supplementing rather than trun-

cating each other's possibilities. I come to see the forest not only through my own eyes but as the other sees it . . . we supplement our embodiment through the Other. . . . In mutual incorporation, each person's capacities and interpretations find extension through the lived body of the other. . . . Our bodies stand in cotransparency, ecstatically involved with a shared world. The structure of bodily disappearance is modified but fundamentally preserved in this being-with-another. (1990, p. 95)

Co-attending to a presenced field, others extend my intentional powers, revealing more than I could reveal alone. Note that although others' perspectives can disclose previously unnoticed aspects of the world—aspects I would not or could not attend to on my own—these differences need not challenge nor deny the validity of one's or the others' existential decompressions. The intentional vectors manifest configurative fields rather than atomistic entities, and therefore, Leder's concept of "mutual incorporation" operates with a recognition of the finite nature of our intentional powers, the situatedness of embodiment.

"Being-with" particular others, those with whom I concernfully share "intentios" and "intentums," is a primary mode of sociality within lived-through world-experience. This primacy has, perhaps, been underplayed in the previously mentioned accounts of sociality as anonymity and interchangeability. In addition to Leder, Alfred Schutz provides several concepts which further aid in understanding the dynamics of interpersonal particularity (see Schutz, 1967). Although world [and] self, according to Schutz, emerge through and against the backdrop of largely anonymous others, lived-through world-experience is played out within concrete interactions between and among "consociates." Specifically delineating the events of being-with-others-being-toward-world, Schutz writes, "It is only from the face-to-face relationship, from the common lived experience of the world in the 'We,' that the intersubjective world can be constituted" (1967, p. 171). By placing a primacy on face-to-face interactions among consociates, Schutz lessens the predominance of the predecessors' and contemporaries' anonymous socialization of world. He offers the concept of "We-relationship," referring to events where we come together to share in specific being-towards. Further clarifying his notion of "We-relationship," Schutz suggests,

When I encounter you face-to-face I know you as a person in one unique moment of experience. While this We-relationship remains unbroken, we are open and accessible to each other's intentional Acts. For a little while we grow older together, experiencing each other's flow of consciousness in a kind of intimate mutual possession. (p. 181)

Thus, "we grow older together" during those moments of being-with-particular-others-being-toward-world. Moreover, given the stratification of the social world according to different relevances, different distributions of the stock body of knowledge, and different kinds of material conditions (i.e., varying availability of that with-which and toward-which we could be concernfully comported), others are thereby increasingly particularized and become less and less anonymous, less and less interchangeable. The notions of the We-relationship and of growing older together, then, further help to delineate the manner in which concrete particularity unfolds and maintains itself within lived-through world-experience.

Being-for-Others

In "being-with-others-being-toward-world," I commonly encounter particular others as concernful cotranscendences, as mutual flights toward the unfolding event-horizon to which we are concernfully co-comported. Still, this is not the only way I encounter others. I also can turn them into less than flights beyond themselves, as they, too, can disclose me as a spatialized and temporalized entity rather than a spatializing and temporalizing one. In this fundamental sense others can manifest the lived-body in ways that it cannot manifest itself. And it is here, in this deep meaning of sociality, that we must proceed slowly and with extreme caution.

Consider this: It has been suggested that only through acculturation do individuals learn about world and acquire "self-concepts" and "self-identities." Other scholars claim that humans do not have selves or even "live in a social world" until or unless they have been socialized. George Herbert Mead's (1934) early articulations on the emergence of selfhood are a case in point. He describes how we learn to take a view on ourselves according to others' reactions to us; it is by others that I gain my selfhood (i.e., my "me"). The same could be said of social constructionism and symbolic interactionism (Berger and Luckmann, 1966; Blumer, 1969, respectively). These schools of thought argue that we "internalize" the "externalized objectifications" of our social surroundings, and thereby, we come to live in "social reality." Even within phenomenological writings one can find sociality described as something that is internalized and then stands over-and-against each individual. Dreyfus, an exceedingly astute Heidegger scholar, for example, states, "Babies get socialized, but they do not Dasein [verb] until they are already socialized" (1991, p. 145). The common logic across these diverse views grasps, unfortunately, only one parameter of self, others, and sociality. These under-appraisals of our ontological sociality are subtle remnants of Cartesian prejudices and may lead us, each of us, to believe our only being is being-for-oneself. Sartre critiques this pervasive neglect of sociality as an ontological ground, stating, "In this state of blindness I concurrently ignore the Other's absolute subjectivity as the foundation of my being-in-itself and my being-for-others, in particular of my 'body for others.' . . . There are men who die without—save for brief and terrifying flashes of illumination—ever having suspected what the Other is" (1956, p. 381). What needs to be made much more evident is that the lived-body is always social. As always already social, the lived-body holds a depth of selfhood before, after, and even beyond, what it is in its "being-for-me."

We must not collapse the being of others to our view of them. This means that part of the lived-body flees away from itself according to others' intentional powers. Sartre's great contribution, as already alluded to, was recognizing that an essential part of the lived-body is its "being-for-others." I, as a lived-body, am both being-for-me and being-for-others, and hence, neither of us (self or other) is a transcendental ego or a monad locked inside a private psychic prison. There is not a real self somehow inside the body, meaning that I am no more accessible to myself than the other is to me.[20] Said most generally, both I and the other can be intentums for different intentional threads, as well as tacitly held implicates to various intended objects. What must be emphasized, if only briefly, is that aspects of my own body come to manifestation only through others. First, for example, I arrive in the world already social; I "am someone" long before I have been "socialized" into my community's world. That is, I exist "for-others" before I exist "for-myself." I might have been planned and even named before my conception. Second, various social identifiers apply to me such as a name, a social security card, a birth certificate, as well as various legal rights, all even though I do not yet "know" that I exist. Here it is enough if others recognize me. Finally, others, after my death, can disclose me as a cadaver, revealing me, exclusively, in my being-for-others. Note that this aspect of my selfhood is not simply other's subjective view of me, it is me; it is part of the body's for-others. In general, all of these being-for-others aspects of my body are me, even though they flee away from my lived-through experience.

Much of the chapter on embodiment (Chapter 2) stressed that I, for-me, am an "absent body" (Leder, 1990), meaning that the lived-body exists as a concernful flight toward a there beyond the here of its spatial boundaries. I suggested that, as it is lived-through, the lived-body is a headless body, a pocket of emptiness which makes room for what it is not. But I equally could have said that my seeable face is not for-me but is for-others. My face, as it is for-me, is not an object I am directed toward, but rather, it is part of the lived-body's means of being-toward. It maintains a wide range of physiognomic comportments toward the there to which it is concernfully directed (Sartre, 1966). Again, a face is part of the lived-body's comportmental directedness, part of the intentio the body maintains toward objects, persons, and events. This also means that faces, as being-for-others, are equally expressive fields by which we, as outside ourselves, are present for others' viewing. In fact, a face, as an intentio, commonly shows its intended object. We can "see" objects of concern "on" the faces of others.

It is perhaps well known that in many cultures, specifically those without mirrors, others decorate one's face. That is, one's face is literally "put on" by other people. This should not be surprising: it actually makes good sense given that I do not see my face, only others do. My face, as it is for-me, is an intentional absence, yet it is that absence by which others' faces come to seeable existence. As D. E. Harding suggestively states, "When I see you your face is all, mine nothing. You are the end of me" (1981, p. 30). This can be said simply as, I can see everyone's face but my own, and my face, as for-others, flees from me. Said more playfully, I don't have a face; other people have mine and I have theirs. The real point to be underscored is that the seeableness of my face exists only through other people; it depends upon others for its releasement and appropriation, even if this flees from me.

The problem of atomistic individualism thus reappears: the seeableness of my face is manifest only by the intentionalities of someone who is not me. Others are the source of an objective presence of myself in the mode of not being me. Likewise, I exist as not being others even though vital aspects of them exist only through and by me. Rigid boundaries between others and self need to be loosened because part of me is manifest only through others. Said simply: nothing separates me from others.

Alienation   Although I, for-myself, am there in addition to the here of my body's physical dimensions, others, who too are outside themselves, are able to reduce and truncate my ecstatical flight. As already suggested, they can collapse me to my body's boundaries, and thus, I can be objectified, disclosed to others as nothing but a self-contained mass. During such encounters I not only see them seeing me, but also, they can see me seeing them see me.[21] Here I look to their faces as concernful comportments toward me as their intended object, (i.e., me in my being-for-others). The other's face, therefore, can be viewed as an intentio whereby my lived-body (in its being-for-others) is the intentum; my body is disclosed in correlation to the other's intentional comportments toward me. As commonly conceived, such objectification refers to the conditions by which struggles against alienation, struggles between the looker and the looked-at, are played out.

The themes of objectification and alienation pervade accounts of encounters with others. Characterizing the predominance of negativity in contemporary thought, James Edie states, "Alienation has been taken to be one of the most, if not the most, important characteristics of human experience" (1965, p. 211). For many thinkers, encountering others is a kind of "trial," including meanings such as "judgment," "guilty," and perhaps even "sentencing." Almost exclusively emphasizing the negative aspects of concrete relations with others, Sartre's *Being and Nothingness* (1956) powerfully shows how I become an object before myself in the gaze (i.e., "le regarde") of the Other. He also discusses the phenomena of shame and guilt, as well as highlights the sadistic and masochistic tendencies within concrete relations with others. In fact, what becomes increasingly evident in his hellish account (see 1955) is that others' abilities to locate me "amidst-the-things-of-the-world" easily transforms me into either a tool for their possibilities or an object for their possession.

Indubitably, the themes of objectification, alienation, estrangement, and domination have bled heavily into modern considerations of self/other relations. Said otherwise, contemporary thought readily acknowledges the negative characteristics of being-with-others. Who would want to deny that encounters with others always hold possibilities for confrontation or that activities of being-with always provide potential sites of struggle? But must we not also agree that this tells only part of the story?

Aesthetic Consummation   What needs to be shown is that these moments in which others render my lived-body an object, a completed whole, are not necessarily alienating nor estranging to my selfhood. More than anyone else, perhaps, Mikhail Bakhtin forcefully has shown how others are necessary for aesthetizing lived-through world-experience. Stressing others' outside relation to my own lived-body, he states, "I am not capable of experiencing the emotionally consolidated time that encompasses me, just as I am not capable of experiencing the space that encompasses me" (1990, p. 106). Bakhtin's point, then, is that only others can render me as a whole. In a word, others "consummate me," and this provides the conditions in which my selfhood can be artistically manifest and experienced by others. This mode of objectification or totalization is not an act of sucking me into the orbit of their projects; it is not simply the other seeing me in the horizon of their concerns or placing me, to use Sartre's terms, admist-the-things-of-the-world (Sartre, 1956). Moreover, neither is this, as Leder (1990) has observed, a "co-transparency" by which I concernfully co-attend to that which the other attends. Rather, others "consummate me" in that they maintain a "surplus of seeing" which comes from their "outsidedness" to me.

To flesh out further this overly neglected insight, we need to recall Bakhtin's *Art and Answerability* (1990) where he makes a distinction between "horizon" and "environment." He writes:

> From within lived experience, life is neither tragic nor comic, neither beautiful nor sublime, for the one who objectively experiences it himself

and for anyone who purely co-experiences with him. A soul living and experiencing its own life will light up for me with a tragic light or will assume a comical expression or will become beautiful and sublime—only insofar as I step beyond the bounds of that soul, assume a definite position outside it, actively clothe it in externally valid bodiliness, and surround it with values that are transgredient to its own object directedness (i.e. provide it with a background or setting as its environment and not with a field of action—as its horizon). (p. 70)

The point in this quite dense passage is that the outsidedness of self and other to each other provides the conditions through which human actions and engagements are aesthetisized. The environment is the backdrop in which my spatial and temporal boundaries become evident to others. Thus, as a lived-body I face various horizons which often include seeing others. In doing so, I provide, through my surplus of seeing, the environment by which I comprehend others in terms of their horizon and yet also in terms of their body as limned by the environmental light of my transgredience. The there toward which I am meaningfully comported includes others as concernful flights toward a horizon, and moreover, it also adds the transgredience of my environmental contextualizing, consummating their existence into an aesthetic whole.

In summary, then, I may attend to others not by merely co-attending to their there, nor by reducing them to my circle of projects and concerns. On the contrary, I attend to them aesthetically: I concernfully regard the there to which they are directed (i.e., their unfolding and not-yet horizon) in terms of the environmental context in which I place them due to my "surplus of seeing." Thus the aesthetisizing of lived-through world-experience, Bakhtin shows us, first becomes possible only where and when we look "from" *and* "to" others. Said otherwise, from within our own lives we are not aesthetic for ourselves. It is only by others that my life is rendered aesthetic, and likewise, only others, those whose projects I cloak with my outsidedness, can be aesthetic for me.

Given that part of my being is being-for-others, I have unveiled both negative and positive modes. The other can be a force of alienation and objectification. Still, others are also the condition of aesthetic consummations. What now needs further consideration is how the three examined dimensions, being-with-particular-others, and looking-at (both positively and negatively) are orchestrated and regulated in our microlevel, face-to-face encounters. Notice that this chapter began with the abstract interchangeability of persons made possible through material conditions and descended to address concrete relations with particular others. Now, I further descend the level of investigation to address specific ritual practices that manifest and disclose character. I examine face-to-face interactions as ritually laminated with many nuanced ceremonial shows, varied microevents of communicative praxis which dialogically implicate a "sacredness" to selfhood.

Ritual Inscriptions of Social Character

Given that humans dwell in concernfully being-near, we should not be surprised to find a complex host of subtle displays that sanctify the concern of humans and their dealings. Additionally, because we are the face of others in the mode of "not being them," it is not surprising that persons often exercise care and concern when concretely encountering others. Many taboos and ritual practices regulate and orchestrate the appropriate treatment of another's face, name, and body (Goffman, 1967; Frazer, 1909; Levi-Bruhl, 1975). Again, when interacting with other persons, living entities who are fundamentally characterized by an existential concern over world [and] self, we take great care to give proper respect (i.e., appropriate ceremonial regard) for their "theres" and their selfhood.

The delicate fabric of selfhood requires an adequate spatial and temporal domain if character is to be accomplished and instantiated. And, in fact, Schrag (1986) has shown how the space of subjectivity is a texture of communicative praxis. That is, communicative praxis, as an amalgam of expressive and signitive discourse and action, is the fabric in which selfhood is hermeneutically stitched. Selfhood, as negotiated in immediate encounters with others, is fundamentally inseparable from the intentional comportments and material practices that are opened for self inscription. Schrag's perspicacious account effectively challenges the postmodern and largely wholesale rejection of subjectivity, and so offers a viable refigured notion of the subject, one which eschews epistemological prejudices. Still, his account could benefit from more exploration into the concrete activities, the specific manners and modes of communicative praxis, which stitch together the overall fabric of selfhood. A more mircolevel account of "hermeneutical implicature of self-with-other" (1986, p. 136) would further illuminate how the lived-body's involvements and comportments are orchestrated and regulated by historically sedimented and socially sanctioned practices.

The works of Erving Goffman provide much detailed support for Schrag's general thesis (see 1959, 1967, 1963a, 1971). Goffman's research on the micro-order of face-to-face involvements delineates the ritual habits and practices which serve no purpose save that of opening a texture for the accomplishment of selfhood. Said more simply, when someone is claimed to *be* sincere, honorable, dignified, tactful, witty, intelligent, rude, ostentatious, deceitful, or incompetent, etc., these are not internal qualities of an epistemological subject. Rather, historically sedimented practices, which issue an appropriateness and acceptability to certain embodied comportments to others and their involvements, are the very substance—the spatialized and temporalized texture—of these qualities. Ultimately, it is in and through such embodied comportments that social dimensions of character are negotiated and experienced (e.g., aspects of identity such as generosity, dignity, petulance, virtue, being cool, etc.). As Goffman instructively tells us, "A status, a position, a social place is not a material thing to be possessed and then displayed; it is a pattern of appropriate conduct, coherent, embellished, and well articulated" (1959, p. 75). Qualities of character are issued and maintained within interpersonal encounters according to one's manners of complying with or forgoing various traditions and institutions regarding the appropriateness and/or acceptibility of treating others, self, and most generally, objects or events of human concern.

When individuals come face-to-face, they sustain a viable position and generate a "dramaturgical" gloss relative to those around them. This ritual care is often prereflectively undergone, becoming part of the tacitly operative background practices by which the lived-body comprehends its world (1967, pp. 113–136). Throughout routine everyday dealings we find many "brief rituals one individual performs for and to another, attesting to civility and good will on the performer's part and to the recipient's possession of a small patrimony of sacredness" (Goffman, 1971, p. 63). Again, the experienced sacredness of face-to-face-involvements is generated according to our compliance with or our neglect of the traditions that self be treated with appropriate ritual care and be presented properly to others.

Three Laminations   Social character is achieved through various communicative practices and is implicated according to what is appropriate and acceptable (both of which continually undergo slight modifications). In general, three main domains interactively bear upon appropriateness and acceptability. First, interactants display some level of appropriate regard for the situation; they properly enact respect for the main involvement of the gathering. This means that in our being-with-others-being-toward-world, we commonly maintain an appropriate ceremonial lamination to our various comportments. We specifically signify regard for and attention to that toward-and-around-which we have been gathered and/or to those with whom we are co-comported. This includes subtle physiognomic shows of respect for self, for the assumed hosts or sponsors of the occasion, as well as for bystanders, onlookers, and generalized others who are not ratified within a given involvement. Thus, the first ritual tradition refers to those communicative practices that display an appropriate "attachment to, and respectful regard for, the situation's participants and the encompassing social occasion" (Goffman, 1963a, p. 25).

Second, face-to-face interactants, in terms of their particularity, concernfully comport themselves so as to give appropriate regard to particular "ratified" participants. These rituals express and signify both the broad social statuses of the others *and* one's specific relationship to those others. These displays of "concernfully-being-with" are manifest mainly through subtle vocal tones, nuanced intonations and inflections, various levels of facial and visual inclusiveness, bodily posture, carriage, energy level, etc. Thus, face-to-face interactions are "overlaid" with a "bodily gloss" that expresses appropriate regard to those others with whom persons are comingling. Such performances provide meaningful shows of respect for current relation states as well as pay appropriate homage to the other's recognized "statuses." I can summarize this by suggesting that a self is expected to be "not merely a mechanical relay but someone to whom a relationship of sorts must be extended and expressively confirmed" (Goffman, 1974, p. 473).

Third and finally, throughout the duration of an encounter, interactants "give" and "give off" (Goffman, 1959) expressions which can be taken as ritualized statements on their own character. Self is always at least implicated in its involvements (i.e., that toward-which it is concernfully comported) and in the various accouterments implicated in those involvements (i.e., its with-whichs). And yet, the attribution of character to an interactant, within a given encounter, is often taken to be generalizable to other encounters with this interactant. That is, characteristics of personal selfhood therefore refer to those qualities which a given individual is taken to possess before the present engagement began and which are expected to be possessed after the current encounter terminates. Nevertheless, qualities such as poise, dignity, sangfroid, graciousness, and other "personal characteristics" are but subtle communicative accomplishments that draw upon historically sedimented and socially embodied enactments.

I must also stress that each of these three types of ritual displays can be analytically distinguished, and yet, in practice, they interact, overlap, and covary without achieving coincidence. Indeed, in the nettlesome density of concrete interactions they are deeply intertwined and are even implicates of each other. For example, in everyday life someone may be encountered as "rude," and yet, we might not be able to "know ultimately" whether this is a statement on the relationship between us, a "character" aspect of the other, or an expression of the current occasion/situation of the would-be offender. In general, in being-with-others-being-toward-world, lived-bodies maintain varying levels of ceremonial reverence for that toward which they are codirected as well as for the others with whom they are co-comported.

The general spirit of these three way laminations is well summarized by noting that the ritualistic institutions work to ratify the sacredness of humans and their dealings. They furnish the articulate texture of "communicative praxis" so that various aspects of character can be manifest, negotiated, and experienced. All in all, face-to-face engagements, as a being-with-others-being-toward-world, embody a dialogic structure whereby interactants laminate their situations within the "canons of self-modesty and self-respect." Goffman eloquently tells us how this ritualization of mutual involvements serves both personal and social functions:

> One way of mobilizing the individual for this purpose [to be a self-regulating social participant] is through ritual; [the individual] is taught to be perceptive, to have feelings attached to self and a self expressed through face, to have pride, honor, and dignity, to have considerateness, to have tact, and a certain amount of poise. . . . These rules, when followed, determine the evaluations he will make of himself and of his fellow participants in the encounter, the distribution of his feelings, and the kinds of practices he will employ to maintain a specified and obligatory kind of ritual equilibrium. (1967, pp. 44–45)

The ceremonial observances are a form of embodied expression that allows for self's concrete experience of character.

Negative and Positive Rituals of Selfhood   On many occasions it is inappropriate to initiate interactions with another to whom one is unacquainted, particularly if that person is already accompanied or is of a different social standing. Persons who are not ratified as participants in a state-of-engagement, that is "onlookers," will be expected to bodily—and especially by way of physiognomic comportments—display what Goffman (1963a, p. 156) aptly calls "civil inattention." Bystanders commonly give a ritualized show of not eavesdropping, or of being sustained and maintained in other involvements (having other toward-whichs). Thus, those who are not ratified participants are required to remain "tactfully inattentive" to the toward-which shared among the interactants. Such "negative ritual" observances sanctify the uniqueness of the relationship between the participants and also confirm a particular "for-whomness" to face-to-face involvements.

Should an encounter initiation be attempted, one must offer a gloss of ceremonial care, including "good reasons" for initiating, subtle displays that inappropriate advances on the other will not be taken, and a general show that one is of good intent and character. Also, there are many dialogic constraints which regulate the initiation of face-to-face interactions. Hence, interactants are required not only to have a good reason for engaging in contact, but they also must wait for proper ceremonial displays or distance is to be maintained. For example, the initiation of interaction is highly ritualized, Goffman tell us, "through the use of prognos-ticative expression. An open and friendly address conveys that overtures will be welcomed; a wary and stiff mien, that importunement will result in open rejection. Anyone wending his way through his daily round is guided not only by self-interest but also by these expressions" (1971, p. 375). To prevent an unwanted request for an encounter, particularly from a stranger, I strategically may avoid any "clearance signs" (e.g., eye contact) and may intentionally project purposeful or concernful looks elsewhere, thereby precluding the ritualized beginning of the interaction sequence. Note here that using such a strategy on certain occasions, or to particular acquaintances, could result in a demerit to one's own character or an insult to the others'. Relatedly, although one may be physically available to all interactants at a given occasion, one is normally ritually available to a much lesser degree. This should not be surprising, for the "analysis of how people manage the information they convey about themselves will have to consider how they deal with the contingencies of being seen 'with' particulars" (Goffman, 1963b, p. 48). That is, because questions regard-ing one's character often are drawn from the company one keeps, there is a ritualized concern over being seen "with" someone. In some cases, interactions of spies, paramours, or persons with social stigmas, the very act of being seen "with" a particular other can create self-conscious ten-sions as well as give rise to questions regarding relationship statuses and moral characters.

In addition to the sheer protection from unwanted encounters, there are many negative ritual constraints upon communicative conduct that might be described as partitioning practices. Goffman presents a host of terms and concepts such as "talk lines,"[22] "fugitive signs,"[23] "collusion,"[24] and "evidential boundaries,"[25] all of which recognize that our "being-with-being-toward" is ritually partitioned off so that self is concretely articulated according to who is "in the know" and, even more specifically, who is kept out. Ritual practices of modesty and tact enable interactants to speak differently, if not in content, then at least in tone and intonation, according to a particular person's presence or absence. Such observances express regard for moral character and "face," and additionally, implicate a ceremonial expression to the current relation statuses, relations not only to the absent, but to those with whom one talks about an absent someone. Indubitably, talk about an absent third person is a primary way that two persons can display the uniqueness of their relationship to each other. Given the underlying notion that the human self is sacred and must be treated with ceremonial care, this microtexture of commu-nicative praxis provides the conditions and space for appropriate handling and treating of such beings. In general, these communicative practices are the very fabric and texture in which character is meaningfully stitched.

Whereas negative ritual keeps separate those of foul or nonrelation, "positive ritual tends to be restricted to individuals in a personal relationship" (Goffman, 1971, p. 91). Within face-to-face involvements, ritual expressions regarding the occasion, other, and self are made manifest through varying levels of tonal expressiveness, vocalic intonations, bodily deportment, facial comportments, eye glance inclusiveness, eye expressions, etc. These subtle communicative practices operate as a concrete texture in which characteristics of selfhood are manifestly, though most often prereflectively, articulated and accomplished. That is, through this "body idiom," which inscripts various levels of respect for the occasion, for others, and for self, interactants meaningfully negotiate and experience various social dimensions of selfhood.

The institution of positive ritual is highly evident in that interactants commonly display an alignment with the prevailing "mood" of the encounter, which also carries the implication that contradictory (i.e., "personal") feelings and involvements are held in abeyance. Said simply, different involvements require different levels of ceremonial regard to that toward-which we are concernfully co-comported. Individuals commonly allocate a proper amount of attention to the occasion's main involvements, and thus, interactants, on many occasions, give the appearance of being "spontaneously involved" even when they are not (Goffman, 1967, pp. 113–136). Given these ritual practices, persons who anticipate an inability to appropriately meet these implied demands may tactfully avoid the gathering altogether. Such a person's absence may be taken as a rejection to the occasion and to its participants, and yet, such a rejection is likely to be less offensive than would be an unsustainable show of appreciation and regard for the others or the occasion.

The most commonly acknowledged ceremonial observances in everyday life are greetings and farewells, or "access rituals."[26] These are much more than an announcement which opens a mutual state-of-talk; it is not simply a report, or a "directional signal"[27] communicating that one is currently available for communicative exchanges. Greetings well include this function, but they more importantly involve a paying of appropriate "ritual dues." For example, when arriving to an occasion, interactants are expected to give some show of concernful regard to particular acquaintances. They accomplish this through displaying, by dramatic gloss, a level of appreciated worth for the other as well as making subtle shows that ratify the current relation status with that particular other. Acquaintances normally embody, in some way or other, just how intimate and close the relationship is and how pleased they both are to have this chance to talk. Also, the greetings and farewells can be ceremonially attenuated—through energy level and vocal and visual inclusiveness—to display the amount of time between the last or perhaps until the next face-to-face engagement. In general, when acquaintances come into contact some ritual homage must be offered, and thus, failure to perform various communicative practices is cause for a felt embarrassment or insult, and perhaps grounds for questioning the moral character or present situation of the would-be offender.

Widely known areas of Goffman's work on positive ritual are "remedial exchanges"[28] and "face-work,"[29] both of which correct or give appropriate remedy to minor and major "incidents." Employments of "accounts," "apologies," "explanations," "minimizations," "tactful blindness," all afford interactants with means to offer ritual remedy to offenses to the occasion, offenses to others, or to distance oneself from unwanted implications to self. Goffman maintains that the "combined rule of self-respect and the rule of considerateness is that a person tends to conduct himself during an encounter so as to maintain both his own face and the face of the other participants" (1967, p. 11). Thus, in "polite society" efforts at "saving-face" embody and display a certain reciprocity or dialogical character. We find here what Burke (1952; 1966) has called the "paradox of substance" whereby persons can become themselves only with the help of others.

Obviously then, on certain occasions (indeed, on many), interactants are not by any means simply interchangeable. Various ritual demands overlay our mutual dealings by specifically requiring that certain "being-withs" and certain "toward-whichs" are not equally for all others indiscriminately. This non-interchangeability leads Goffman to admonish that "the very forms of behavior employed to celebrate and affirm relationships—rituals such as greetings, enquiries after health, and love-making—are very close in character to what would be a violation of preserves if performed between wrongly related individuals" (1971, p. 58). Thus, ritual practices, both positive and negative, have concrete particularity as their basis for distinguishing ritually "appropriate" actions from "inappropriate" ones. The point here is that others are ritually encountered in their once-occurrent particularity, and thus selfhood unfolds in such a way that it is always open to meaningful social negotiation.

In concrete face-to-face involvements, where I see others' faces and they see mine, we engage in various communicative practices by which selfhood is maintained; it is here that selfhood, as Thayer (1987) might say, is "real-ized." Experiences of oneself or an other as rude, witty, courteous, reliable, honest, respectful, etc., are inseparable from the manner in which regard for self, regard for others, and regard for the occasion are concretely played out in our little ritual ceremonies. The pompous air that some persons maintain or the courteous deferentiality of others are not expressions of an inner self. They are ritual dimensions within the texture of communicative praxis. It is in concrete face-to-face interaction that the micropolitics of social identity are played out. This also means that the same comment can seem to be rude or polite, witty or unkind, depending on where (occasion) who (character) said it to whom (others).

"Who" someone is refers to the kind of treatment we can expect from them and the kind of treatment they can expect from us. As a commonplace example, if I am said to be "with" someone and out on the town, my very "being-with-this-other" subtly regulates the appropriateness and/or acceptability of "that toward which" I am to be comported as well as the kinds of concernful comportments I am to maintain thereby. I am not to attend continuously to others, or give deep meaningful looks to certain others. In fact, because I am being-with-being-toward, such behavior on my part could be seen as an insult to whom I am "with," and/or an incrimination to my character. Indeed, my gaze and facial directedness are fundamentally regulated and so operate within an understanding, even if only implicitly, of my particular being-with. In general, the microsocial order of selfhood is regulated and orchestrated so that our intentional comportments are meaningful in terms of their appropriateness and acceptability to institutions of ceremonial regard.

I am that being who cares over the there which is codisclosed along with the here of the lived-body. And so, it is really not surprising that many ritual practices regulate and orchestrate displays of regard for various lived-through world-experience configurations. Face-to-face encounters are saturated with ceremonial observances, dramaturgical displays through which reverence for the sacred is instantiated. These many little rituals that laminate and couch our concrete interactions comprise a well-articulated and comportmentally embodied texture in which social selfhood is negotiated and experienced. Goffman has said so much and said it so well that I cannot but, out of due respect and homage, let his words conclude this section's analysis:

> Many gods have been done away with, but the individual himself stubbornly remains as a deity of considerable importance. He walks with some dignity and is the recipient of many little offerings. He is jealous of the worship due him, yet, approached in the right spirit, he is ready to forgive those who may have offended him. Because of their status relative to his, some persons will find him contaminating while others will find they contaminate him, in either case finding that they must treat him with ritual care. Perhaps the individual is so viable a god because he can actually understand the ceremonial significance of the way he is treated, and quite on his own can respond dramatically to what is proffered him. In contacts between such deities there is no need for middlemen; each of these gods is able to serve as his own priest. (1967, p. 95)

Once-Occurrence as Sociality

I began this chapter by considering the largely anonymous sociality through which the world itself is socialized. I examined others' handling and handiwork to suggest that the world is already socialized through this mode of spatialization and temporalization. I also discussed how I am already being-with-others. This simply means that the lived-body assumes various comportments toward entities and concernfully makes them available for and relevant to projects and dealings already within the traditions of acceptability and appropriateness. Said simply, I am social in that my lived-body is able to concernfully co-comport-toward an already socialized world. Likewise, I can function interchangeably regarding the social roles I am able to fulfill through my being-with-being-toward. Clearly, a good deal of social meaning is maintained according to the interchangeability of persons (i.e., according to pre-decompressed lines of action and/or according to handmade artifacts).

But my examination regarding face-to-face encounters and the ritual order of communicative praxis revealed that, I, as a lived-body, am also fundamentally unique with regard to various layers of social meaning. That is, we found a basic interpersonal particularity to characterize concrete interactions. I bear a unique history (e.g., various previous and particular "growing-older-togethers"), a unique set opportunities (e.g., various "with-whichs" and "toward-whichs"), as well as a unique set of possibilities (e.g., various capacities of "being-toward"). All of this leads to my uniqueness. It is my once-occurrence that needs further, if only brief consideration.

Bakhtin provides a wealth of insight regarding the lived-body's once-occurrent participation in lived-through world-experience (also see Anton, in press A). He writes,

> If I abstract myself from the center that constitutes the starting point of my once-occurrent participation in Being, and I do so moreover, not only from the content determinateness of my participation (determinateness with respect to time, space, etc.) but also from its being actually, emotionally, and volitionally acknowledged and affirmed, then the concrete uniqueness and compellent actuality of the world will inevitably begin to decompose; it will disintegrate into abstractly universal, merely possible moments. (1993, p. 58)

This basically means that humans "in general," do not factually exist and that theoretical intentions (comportments of intellect and logical assertions) commonly posit a general or abstract human. They posit (and basically can grasp only) a "someone" who is actually no one, a someone who is not concretely and actually existing within a once-occurrent worlding. In this regard theoretical approaches to individuals (e.g., individuals as the intended objects of mathematical comportments) most easily posit that all persons are basically interchangeable or not nonreplaceable—not uniquely held by their place in existence. As Bakhtin suggests, the "theoretical world is obtained through an essential and fundamental abstraction from the fact of my unique being and from the moral sense of that fact—'as if I did not exist'" (1993, p. 9). This theoretical world can mislead our understanding because it commonly fails to address how one's absolute uniqueness is a vital part of sociality.

My lived-body never does not exist in my life; it is never unnecessary or irrelevant, and only theoretical positing (i.e., imaginative positing) can make this seem to be so. The world posited in such theoretical considerations, Bakhtin tells us, "has no center, it provides no principle for choice: everything that is, could also not be, could be different. . . . From the standpoint of sense or meaning, only the endlessness of valuation and absolute restlessness are possible" (1993, p. 43). Said simply, all possibilities, even those logically demonstrated to be justified and those that I agree are desirable, may still lack any sense of being emotionally or volitionally compelling. Said otherwise, theoretical intentions can create an imaginative sense in which we (i.e., you and I) are replaceable or that our lives "could have been" different. In reflecting back upon our lives, considering situations in which we "could have done otherwise," we imaginatively pretend that we were not there, or fancy that we were irrelevant.

These reflective considerations can seem to offer us an alibi. Clearly, the world and our place in it can be radically different in the future or in the present, but neither it nor we could have been different: both have become what they are in once-occurrent existence. What needs a deep appreciation is that it is the nontheoretical case, the absolute noncounterfactual conditional (i.e., this existence and *not* another) which provides us no alibi. At this level of lived involvement we are held uniquely, every single one of us. The once-occurrent and total throw that is my existence, including the unique historical and social traditions and institutions I bear, these ultimately noncounterfactual lived-experiences give us "no alibi in existence." Bakhtin provides a useful statement regarding this point of uniqueness:

> This fact of my non-alibi in Being, which underlies the concrete once-occurrent ought of the answerably performed act, is not something I come to know of and to cognize but is something I acknowledge and affirm in a unique or once-occurrent manner. The simple cognition of the fact is a reduction of it to the lowest emotional-volitional level of possibility. In cognizing it, I universalize it: everyone occupies a unique and never-repeatable place . . . [but] Nothing in Being, apart from myself, is an I for me. In all Being I experience only myself—my unique self—as an I. All other Is (theoretical ones) are not I for me, whereas my own unique (non-theoretical) I participates in once-occurrent Being . . . [in] what is

and what ought to be: I am actual and irreplaceable, and therefore must actualize my uniqueness. It is in relation to the whole actual unity that my unique ought arises from my unique place in Being. (1993, pp. 40–41)

Bakhtin maintains that my uniqueness is easily theoretically distorted, cognitively taken up, into the logical proposition "I am unique." Moreover, since everyone else can also say it, this becomes a vacuous theoretical assertion. Just because both you and I can equally, that is interchangeably, say, "you" and "I," this does not at all imply that we, you or I are interchangeable. To believe so would be like believing, as Korzybski might say, that one just as well can eat the menu as eat the meal.

Part of our sociality implies that we need to develop and to cultivate our otherness to others. We need to recognize that our outsidedness to others is part of what locates and specifies us as social beings. For this reason Bakhtin urges us to see that, "The productiveness of the event of a life does not consist in the merging of all into one. On the contrary, it consists into the intensification of one's own outsideness with respect to others, one's own distinctness from others: it consists in fully exploiting the privilege of one's own unique place outside other human beings" (1990, p. 88). But I must be very clear here, for the notion of my once-occurrence refers not simply to the fact that I am different from all other individuals. Rather, it stresses that I am once-occurrently bound and woven into a historically situated location which holds me uniquely in its thrownness; I am situated within concrete relations with particular others and am the bearer of a given historical tradition. This means that each person is the bearer of thrown and projected horizons of possibilities given their concrete dispersal in the socio-historical event of world.

Said quite otherwise, I may, in one sense, be simply one person among other persons in a world that goes on without me after my death. And yet, I am, for me, that person who is never not there, that person who somehow is always cogiven along with the world; I, for me, am never simply "a person" in "the world" nor can I not exist in my world. Therefore, one of the most important aspects of my sociality is my particular place and moment in lived-through world-experience. I am a non-interchangeable, nonrepeatable lived-through gravitational center, a concernful flight of valuation and action directed toward a uniquely unfolding event-horizon. In a word, I am uniquely held in the fateful throw out from Earth and this itself is an essential part of my social being.

SUMMARY: SELFHOOD [AND] SOCIALITY

In this chapter I have explored how lived-through world-experience is already social-experience. I suggested that sociality "is a given of the human condition, not a product of human making" (Stewart, 1995, p. 137). Moreover, the world that I discover, the there toward which I am concernfully comported according to various intentional threads, is a world already funded by the handy touch of others. This means that Earth's internal negations and continual upsurgings into world [and] self, move out along the pre-decompressed lines of force which are made manifest, even if only indirectly, by the intentional comportments of others and their correlative handled material conditions. Additionally, others orchestrate and regulate the lived-body's various intentional powers. They extend the negativity infecting Earth, and open world [and] self to socially meaningful comprehensions which, as modes of taking care, implicate others. In general, in concernfully being-toward-world, I already am being-with-others.

Sociality means that I am interchangeable with others in our world. But I considered others as more than a force of socialization to world [and] self. I examined how others, in the flesh, are living events of existential decompression by which I am made manifest in certain ways. Others constitute the condition by which I can be what I am as a thingly object. They are the existential condition for my having a seeable face, as I am that being through whom their faces come to seeableness. I also stressed that others not only objectify and alienate me, but also, they are able to consumate my life into an aesthetic whole.

A major consideration throughout the chapter, one slowly funneled into, was that of interpersonal particularity. Within the ongoing event of communicative praxis we find many ritual practices which sustain a sacredness to human existence. These practices institute appropriate levels of ceremonial regard according to exceedingly particular ontical contingencies (i.e., the concrete and specific with-whichs, toward-whichs, and with-whoms). I have closed this chapter by considering the significance of my non-interchangeability with others. That is, a most vital part of my sociality is my total once-occurence, my outsideness to all others, my otherness to all others.

I should also mention that just as with the previous chapter, I have concluded the present one by turning to theoretical intentions and the ways sociality and self can appear in cognitive considerations or theoretical assertions. And so, I again have been led to an explicit consideration of language practices per se. In the next chapter, Chapter 4, "The Lived-Body as a Sonorous Being," I return to Chapter 2 and take up where I left off. I explore the human as an intentional nexus, here focusing on our intentional powers of speech and language, our sonorous being. Speech, I hinted earlier, is one of the lived-body's intentional vectors, perhaps even a special power granted to (inflicted upon?) human existence. Indeed, speech is one of the most powerful intentional threads by which world [and] self come to be. It is one of the lived-body's most potent and fecund powers for spatialization and temporalizations (i.e., for existentially decompressing particular configurations of world-experience). Still, when we speak, we undeniably speak a language, and language is undeniably learned from others. Nevertheless, the power to speak is not bestowed by others. Such powers can have, ultimately, only an Earthly ground.

I now advance Chapter 2's discussion of the lived-body's intentional threads by moving out from the various modes of sociality as guiding features. In general, I explore how human selfhood, as both embodied and social, is equiprimordially sonorous.

CHAPTER 4

The Lived-Body as a Sonorous Being

Scholars and social theorists increasingly are interested in how communication enables, shapes, directs, and alters the manifestness of world and/or self. Moreover, when asked about the "peculiar proper" of human selfhood, contemporary theorists commonly appeal to speech, language, and/or symbolicity. And so it must be agreed that "the linguistic turn" is a distinguishing characteristic of social theorizing within the second half of the twentieth century (Ihde, 1986; Schrag, 1986; Taylor, 1995). The present chapter does not deny the depth of self's linguisticality or symbolicity (i.e., what I shall be calling "sonorousness"; Merleau-Ponty, 1968). Nevertheless, it does argue that the potency of sonorousness needs to be situated within Earth's fateful sending of itself out from its nonexistence. We must recover the rightful office of speech [and] language to humans, and ultimately, to world.

Many attempts to specify the interrelations among basic concepts such as speech, language, thought, embodiment, sociality, and temporality are plagued by difficulties, ambiguities, and shortcomings (Thayer, 1987; Stewart, 1995). Although a flurry of investigation and discussion surrounds the topics of language, communication, and symbolicity, there remains little agreement on fundamental issues (Derrida, 1977; Schrag, 1980; Taylor, 1995; Thayer, 1987). This chapter therefore discusses some issues that need to be addressed if the continued interest in sonorousness is to do justice to the phenomena in question.

Immediately, a deluge of unanswered questions flood upon us: What is the relationship between speech and world? Is there world without speech? Without any language speakers, how many things are there in "the world?" How can there be things independent of speech if "things" is a word? Could one say anything which would not be just that, one saying something? Are "the world" and "all 'things' therein" nothing but the product—the symptom—of language practices?

What is the relation between speech and selfhood? Is "selfhood" only (i.e., merely) a word? Does self use language? Does language use "self"? Who would say so? It was Alan Watts who has playfully observed that, "Trying to define yourself is like trying to bite your own teeth." So, we might ask, Am I on the side of the teeth biting or on the side of the teeth bit? Said otherwise, am I that which is talked about in the description (i.e., its sense-content) or am I the unsaid source of the description? Am I the said, the saying, or the sayableness?

Could anyone say what we could know without language? What are the differences between knowing "about" language and knowing with or by it? Is language or speech a set of things? How many things is language? Is it even possible to count, to analytically sort out and specify, how many words someone "knows?" What would it mean to know "a" word? Is knowing a word the ability to use it spontaneously in speech? Is it to understand "it" when others use it? Perhaps to recognize it—to be able to translate it—according to its context? And what of those who think they know a word's meaning and yet are mistaken? For example, what does the word "remedial" mean? Are you sure? What does it mean to say that we are sure of a word's meaning? If "people have meaning and words do not," how can we know that we have "made a speech error"? What does it mean to say there are rules to speech practices?

If eyes deliver the sense of sight, what is it that speech delivers? What is that which speech makes manifest? More specifically, what are the relationships among speech, language, and thought? Can we have thought without using speech or language? Does speech arise after thought? If speech is not an "after-thought" or a set of representations for a pre-existing mind and independently existing world, then what does "it" do?

Are there significant differences between speech and language? Is the ability to speak bestowed upon individuals, as fire can be passed from one tribe to another? What are the relationships among speech, language, and sociality? Is sociality separate from or dependent on the acquisition of language? Are the powers of language or speech at all related to my once-occurrent existence?

CLEARING THE WAY

The two previous chapters stressed the themes of embodiment and sociality, respectively. The reader might now wonder whether speech will be treated as part of the lived-body's intentional powers, or as an available and relevant "with-which" left behind through others' previous existential decompressions. I must make clear that the preceding two chapters were necessary first because speech is an embodied intentional power that is also "social" in a more profound way than the lived-body's other intentional vectors. It must be granted that to speak is to speak a language, a language learned from/with others. But this does not mean that the ability to speak is bestowed by others. On the contrary, it is human sonorousness per se (i.e., language [and] speech) that is the breathing proof of how far atomistic individualism is off the mark.

Therefore, before I head directly into an exposition of the positive characteristics of our sonorous being, two broad and generally opposing camps must be addressed and respectively tempered. First are those thinkers who, regardless of their careful attention, seem to understate the indigenous fecundity of speech. Second, and on the other hand, are those thinkers who appear to over-exaggerate speech's powers and office. Let me begin with the first.

The Understatement

To best articulate the difficulties related to those who would understate the case, I turn to the recent work of John Stewart. Of concern here are his *Language as Articulate Contact* (1995) and his edited *Beyond the Symbol Model* (1996). Stewart, showing formidable erudition, argues that several seminal theorists in the Western tradition (including K. Burke, E. Cassirer, J. Kristeva, S. Langer, C. S. Pierce) problematically subscribe to what he calls the "symbol model." This model roughly consists in holding that language is a tool-like system comprised of discrete "bits" (i.e., symbols) which are used instrumentally by preexisting individuals to represent nonlinguistic meanings, thoughts, or things. The symbol model persists in spite of the fact that "representing," according to Stewart, cannot adequately account for most everyday interpersonal conversation, the paradigmatic case of speech.

Further documenting the specifics of this underestimation, Stewart (1995) offers several commitments commonly associated with the symbol model. Generally, the world is taken as pregiven, and language, so it is assumed, works by representing it. In some form or another, a division is posited between two worlds: the world of things or ideas and the world of our representations for those things and ideas. Speech and language are thereby viewed as a kind of tool, a system of atomistic bits which represent preexisting things in the world, be this world an empirical one or one of ideas. In a word, the notion that speech is a collection of arbitrary noises which individuals use to encode thought, meanings, or things for social transmission remains prevalent throughout Western theorizing (Stewart, 1995).

This underestimation of the indigenous resources in speech perhaps arises because the other intentional threads (e.g., motility, perception, emotion, imagination), so it is presumed, are "natural" in a way that speech is not. Indeed, for many people—both lay and scholarly—speech seems to be something that was invented, or purposefully created. Language is historical rather than arbitrary (O. B. Hardison Jr., 1989), and therefore, it metaphorically can be said to have been created, as when one creates a tract, a verse, a poem, a word, etc. This cannot be denied, for even the *Oxford English Dictionary* is "based on historical principles." Still, my contention is that we must fight against the pervasive individualism that can lead us to conclude that because language is either learned with or acquired from others, then, it is a technological bestowal and somehow "not natural" (cf. Bookchin, 1995). Consider, for example, Cassirer's statement that

> Physical reality seems to recede in proportion as man's symbolic activity advances. Instead of dealing with things themselves man is in a sense of constantly conversing with himself. He has so enveloped himself in linguistic forms, in artistic images, in mythical symbols or religious rites that he cannot see or know anything except by the interposition of this artificial medium. (1944, p. 25)

Why does Cassirer, at the end of his otherwise insightful statement, call symbolic activity an "artificial" medium? Is speech some kind of alien (i.e., non-natural) presence? A good deal of modern scholarship has maintained this line of thinking. In describing what he calls "the received Idea," David Cort suggests that, "language is . . . artificial; it is not instinctive; it has to be learned" (1970, p. 1). George Steiner, as another example, remarked during an interview printed in *Psychology Today* that "Language is not a description of 'reality,' but an answer to it, an evasion from it" (February, 1973, p. 66). Moreover, Steiner elsewhere claimed that "Language is the main instrument of [the hu]man's refusal to accept the world as it is. . . . Ours is the ability, the need, to gainsay or 'un-say' the world, to image and speak it otherwise. . . . It is not, perhaps, 'a theory of information' that will serve us best in trying to clarify the nature of language, but a 'theory of misinformation" (1975, pp. 217–218). Throughout these considerations, we find well articulated a variety of what Stewart (1996) has forcefully indicted as the "two-world" hypothesis. This postulate, that of two worlds (one symbolic and the other nonsymbolic) is potently distilled in Korzybski's famous "law of non-identification": "Whatever I say a thing is, it is not" and in his much celebrated, "The map is not the territory."[30] The weakness of these positions is that speech is now exiled from its organic basis in the human condition. Speech, which is inseparable from us and our world, is now seen as somehow alien to both.

It may well be, as Geertz points out, that "man is an animal suspended in webs of significance he himself has spun" (1973, p. 5). Still, we have not created, have not invented, the capacity to spin webs of significance any more than bats have "invented" their bodily powers of echolocation. We must remember and stay with the claim that the human is the "talking animal" (Heidegger, 1962). There does appear to be great difficulty finding comparable powers in other species of animals. Nevertheless, sonorousness is indigenous to existence: speech is natural to worlded earth; we, as lived-bodies, have been blissfully, and perhaps cursefully, entrusted with (or sentenced to) its incredible powers (Herder, 1966).

As already suggested, a pivotal and most peculiar aspect of speech is that we speak a language learned with and from others. This is quite distinct, so says common sense, from the other empirical senses. The lived-body's other intentional powers seem to operate well before the child's speech activities commence. Still, common sense remains highly problematic. In the first case, we learn to listen and hear language well before our bodies leave the womb. Said otherwise, we learn language by listening to it, not simply by speaking it (Levin, 1989). Hence the idea of someone's "first word" already assumes a rather distorted and overly atomistic individualism. Second, and more importantly, language is not literally bestowed nor does language bestow sociality. The twin phenomena of speech [and] language are such that they seem to remain a mystery, but this is due mainly to unstated commitments to individualist prejudices. We seem to presuppose that if language is learned with and from others, then it is somehow an invention or not natural in the ways the other bodily powers are. This mysteriousness will undoubtedly persist if these individualist presuppositions are not seriously challenged. Said most simply, although language is learned, this does not necessarily imply that language is not natural. Rather, it means that overly rigid divisions between self [and] other can be quite problematic. Sonorousness (i.e., speech [and] language) is an exemplar of our being-with-others-being-in-the-world, and so, once the rigid divisions between self [and] others are broken down, and I am understood as having both being-for-me and being-for-others, then the mystery somewhat dissipates. Sonorousness is the bodily power which most clearly demonstrates the fact that we are social in our being.

The Overstatement

Let me now turn to those who overstate the case. There has been a tendency in later twentieth-century theorizing to overclaim the powers of speech practices, to overstate their capabilities to "construct" reality. Here we find what M. C. Dillon (1988; 1995) has aptly called, "semiological reductionism." Those who would overstate the case can be found engaging in linguistically reductive social constructionisms (e.g., Lyotard's [1984] postmodern reduction of Wittgenstein's "life-forms" to "language-games"). Some thinkers have suggested "There is nothing outside the text," (Derrida, 1974, p. 158) while others have argued that "Being that can be understood is language" (Gadamer, 1975, p. 474). Others still suggest that we now live in a "hyperreality," where "the real" is only that which can be "represented" (Baudrillard, 1983). Stewart (1996) too, for all his trenchant insights regarding those who understate the case, seems to fall into overstating it, as if all human meaning is furnished by and in language practices. His project thus underaddresses the ontological conditions of temporality and spatiality (reducing them to products of articulate contact) and moreover, seems to underplay the lived-body's other indigenous powers for understanding (Anton, 1999).

Those who overstate the case seem to suggest that speech provides nothing but reification *and* that this is reality. Embodiment, temporality, spatiality are but reified typifications and so are artifacts, products, of speech practices. This also can be said of all order and distinction: these are imposed by humans. The claim, then, is that "nature hath no joints nor seams of its own," but instead, language itself creates the divisions (Rorty, 1979; Bochner, 1985). Now, it may be somewhat true that speech "constitutes" reality,[31] and it is quite clear that talk can reify "things" as seemingly independent of us [and] our various intentional activities. But, it is also the case that "It's more complicated than that" (Burke, 1961, p. 227). In fact, the exact same reifying (or in my terms, existentially decompressing) tendencies can be found to characterize all of the lived-body's intentional powers. With regard to the phenomenal fields presenced by the various intentional threads, I already suggested that "nothing separates any object from its background." I will return to this later.

I suggested in Chapter 2 that to all intentional threads there is an intending, an intended, and an intendableness. For example, when I look to some object, say the pen in my right hand, there is an act of seeing, a thing seen, and the very seeableness of the pen. Or, closing my eyes, I can run my hand along the pen. Here we find the act of touching, the thing touched, and the touchableness of the pen. Notice that the thing seen and the thing touched are the same thing, only it is presenced or manifested differently according to the understanding given to the different manners of making contact. The different profiles, the different lived-through world-experiences, are differences in intendableness, and thus, in talking about the pen, we likewise find the same triadic structure: there is the speaking, the thing spoken of, and the speakableness. And, what must be made clear is that this "sayableness" of world [and] self cannot be reductively derived from either the world or the subject. It is, on the contrary, a dialogic constitution.

Overly linguistic social constructionisms, which commonly give to speech more than it deserves, subtly make purchases on the romantic idealisms from a century ago (Schrag, 1994, p. 119). The so called "arbitrariness" of language seems to imply that all sayableness is created by the subject, or that sayableness is nothing but a human attribution, a human way of organizing experience. Although there are different languages, radically divergent ones, this does not mean, as linguistic idealists would have it, that world is utterly devoid of its relation to sayableness. Still, sayableness should not be reduced to something the kin of a postitivism or a nominalist literalism nor a ethnocentric naturalism. We must learn to accommodate the claim that there are no things without speech, without, on the other hand, falling into the claim that speech makes it all up. Therefore, we must be as cautious of naively literal accounts as we are of overly individualist/humanist ones. Sayableness is not simply a human creation, and yet, it is not there independent of speakers, any more than visual fields are there without eyes. It comes as much from the world as from people. Only in a thrown-and-projected finitude, (i.e., only in a world [and] self) would sayableness even come to meaningful fruition.

SONOROUSNESS AS A PRIMARY INTENTIONAL VECTOR

Earthly worldings, I already stated, are localized sites of existential decompression, ongoing events of internally negating Earth. Existential decompression is carried out to "perfection," to use Burke's terminology, within our sonorous intentional powers. Sonorousness is a "gift" granted in the fateful sending of Earth out from its nonexistence (Levin, 1989, pp. 1–3). It is thus one of the lived-body's powers for existential decompression; it is the manner in which lived-bodies, as flights of transcendence, release and appropriate the sayableness of existence.

Human beings are naturally sonorous entities, caring for more than the here and now of their own bodies by releasing and appropriating the sayableness of existence. Unfortunately, speech and language are often conceived as inventions, tools, or as an "after-thought" to an otherwise natural being (Stewart, 1995; also see Bookchin, 1995). This means that "the world" is commonly "naturalized" and unified into that which is available to the empirical senses, while speech, on the contrary, is viewed as somehow not natural as the body's other powers are said to be. The belief that language is alien or not natural (perhaps humanly created) must be carefully scrutinized.

Sonorousness, I argue, is not a tag on, literally not an after-thought to the empirical senses. Merleau-Ponty points us in the right direction where he states: "If we were to make completely explicit the architectonics of the human body, its ontological framework, and how it sees itself and hears itself, we would see that all the possibilities of language are already given in it " (1968, p. 155). Speech is just as indigenous to self [and] world as our perceptual senses (i.e., sight, hearing, touch, smell, taste), or as our emotions and imaginations, or even as natural as our motility and movement.

I have made four general points regarding all of the intentional threads discussed in Chapter 2. Each of these now must be carried over and explicitly applied to sonorousness.

Preliminary Considerations

Early in Chapter 2 I suggested that to each of the various intentional activities (intentio) and their intended objects (intentum) belongs to a peculiar proper regarding the specific intendableness of the intended. This intendableness of the intended, I argue, is neither subjectively created nor objectively present. Said otherwise, there are the intending (intentio), the intended (intentum), and also the very intendableness, and, this intendableness cannot be reductively located in or isolated to either the subject or the object. We find, then, a dialogic or transactive nature to the intentio and the intentum. Most generally, a line of existential decompression—a line of force—centripetally moves back toward the embodied self while simultaneously moving centrifugally toward particular figure-background configurations (Schrag, 1968).

Second, I also argue that every intentional power of the lived-body maintains its own peculiar mode of "understanding" world [and] self, even if only prethematically. That is, each thread concernfully makes manifest in a way that is proper and peculiar to itself. I thus suggest that when we consider some object in the room (e.g., a chair), our interest is in the object "in the how of its intendedness." We are interested in it according to its peculiar disclosedness given by the different ways we meaningfully take it under concern (e.g., looking at it, sitting on it, calculating about it, speaking about it, etc.). Hence, each of the various bodily powers disclose worldly entities (e.g., objects, events, or persons) according to the understanding-of-being given to that mode of intending (e.g., perceiving, acting upon, or in speaking) and to the objects' dialogically respective intendableness.

Additionally, I maintain that each intentional disclosure always includes, as its existential correlate, a particularly implicated and configured comporting experiencer. For example, the different manners by which a chair manifests itself also thereby implicate differently comporting selves (i.e., a sitting self, a calculating self, a dreaming self, a speaking self, etc.). Speech, then, is not simply a means of caring for worldly entities, but also, it is a way we implicate ourselves as in-the-world, even if only implicitly (Heidegger, 1982; Schrag, 1969). In an astute and almost mystical statement, Jakob Boehme well captures the self-implicature of our speech activities when he states, "Whatever the self describes, describes the self." This means that selfhood is an intentional implicate to how things are talked about. As we come to terms with lived-through world-experience we accomplish selfhood; in our speaking, we concernfully speak about something and so disclose and inscribe a concerning self. This is what Heidegger means where he states, "In the manner in which Dasein in its world speaks about its ways of dealing with its world, a self-interpretation of Dasein is also given" (Heidegger, 1992, p. 8E). A memorable one-liner from Spinoza also expresses the self-implication involved in our sonorousness. He tells us: "Whatever Peter tells me about Paul, tells me more about Peter than Paul." Santayana too argues that, "other people's idea of man is apt to be a better expression of their nature than of his" (1956, p. v). The general point here is that sonorousness is an intentional tissue and so "reaches 'back' to a centered experiencer as it reaches 'out' toward figure and background" (Schrag, 1969, p. 86). Heidegger, once again, well summarizes this discussion of speech's intentional nature when he writes, "to intentionality belongs, not only a self-directing-toward and not only an understanding of the being of the being toward which it is directed, but also the associated unveiling of the self which is comporting itself" (1982, p. 158).

Recalling these preliminary remarks on intentionality, the task at hand is to describe the peculiar proper to the threads of speech. As already suggested, speech does not represent preexisting "things" in a preexisting world, nor does speech "socially translate" preexisting personal thought. That is, speech does not subrogate for physical or mental phenomena. But, if speech does not represent or signify, if it does not stand for something else, what does it do? Indeed, how is one to make evident that which sonorousness makes manifest? How are we to encounter sonorousness?

Stated most abstractly, sonorousness makes manifest certain configurations of world-experience. It releases and appropriates profiles of the human world, those peculiar possibilities that are indigenous to sonorously self-negating Earth. As intentional in character, sonorousness meaningfully endures its own completion, understandingly making-room for the sayable sense it accomplishes.

Sonorousness, I suggest, accomplishes the field of sayable sense, what is often called a "stream of thought" or a "flow of ideas." But what does it mean to say that sonorousness accomplishes "the field of sayable sense"? No one can say what sense is, for to do so, given that saying and sense are so close of kin, would be to presuppose an understanding of sense. But what does this mean? We inevitably come upon the central difficulty in trying to speak competently about speech. The problem is that one would have to possess speech in order to understand any explanation of it whatsoever. Moreover, only someone already possessing speech could even begin to question it. Therefore, when we ask a rather simple question, such as, "What is speech?," this already involves us in a comprehension of it, even if only prethematically or nonanalytically. That is, the question must have been comprehended, and this, then, demonstrates that we already understand speech (Anton, 1997). In this regard, we should ask ourselves: when someone inquires, "What is speech?," what would or could be made manifest in the answer which would not or cannot be made manifest in the question? Even more to the point, what is that which would have to be in both any question and any answer which also answers these questions?

But I must again ask, how shall we say what sayable sense is? We might say that sayable sense is a continuous taking-for-granted, an unceasing secretion of understanding from speaking's fecundity (Anton, 1997). Or perhaps, we might say that sense is part of the world, part of sayably organized lived-through world-experience. Or perhaps, it is that which is accomplished, released and appropriated, in events of speech; it is that peculiar order which is meaningfully undergone when one hears a tongue not as noises (Anton, 1997). When the noisiness is focally absent—and one is meaningfully stretching along within the room-making-gathering of articulate speech—one is, in a word, dwelling in sense.

We live-through different world-experience profiles, one of which is manifested through sonorousness. It might help, then, to contrast the phenomenal fields made manifest when someone sees an object, when someone is blindfolded and touches that object, and when someone merely imagines that same object. These differences are no more dramatic than the phenomenal differences between seeing something and talking about it. There is a rangy and already understood difference between the lived-body's various powers. Nevertheless we still might ask: Is the phenomenal field that speech makes manifest more similar to sight, or to hearing, or to touch, perhaps to movement? Is its peculiar proper at all similar to our affective intentionalities? Perhaps it is more like our imaginative powers? Our sonorousness might be viewed as similar to seeing in that many metaphors of speech refer to "seeing what someone means," and "bringing things to light," or perhaps, "getting clear on things." But Herder most astutely examines how "hearing . . . is the sense of language"(1966, pp. 139–147), and Stewart (1996) also lends an ear by calling our attention to the aural nature of sense. Does the claim that sense has an articulated sound not "ring true" to our experience? (also see Ong, 1967). Still, sayableness seems as much like touchableness as like seeableness or hearableness; it is a mode of anticipatingly acting on the world (Burke, 1966). Speech can "grasp," and by means of

it, we can "get a handle" on things (Malinowski, 1923). Speech, it could
be argued even further, is how lived-bodies make hands (either their own
or others') articulately move at a distance (e.g., "Stick 'em up!" or
"Would you pass the salt?"). And yet, speech is also quite like our affective and imaginative intentionalities as well. Emotional-volitional intonations ride in and throughout speech, and so, through speech's "liquid
tonalities" we can "dance attitudes" by way of "verbal choreography"
(Burke, 1957, p. 339). Speech too seems to make manifest, to bring into
view (into light), and so is strikingly similar to the ways our imaginative
powers operate (Collingwood, 1938, pp. 225–272; Dennett's [1991]
"Purple Cow"; also see Kearney, 1991, pp. 134–169). In the end and as
already suggested, we seem to retain the very comprehension that speech
is even while and though we raise so many unanswered questions about it.

Perhaps we can locate the peculiar proper to sonorousness by once
more examining negativity, for clearly speech does allow a saying of what
is not the case (Steiner, 1975). We are free to speak about persons, events,
and object as they are not. Kenneth Burke argues that such verbal powers
of negativity are gained first through the immersion in "tribal hortatory
don'ts." It is from the command "don't" that persons go on to develop a
sense for the "is not." As Burke maintains, "the human infant will learn
'thou shalt not' quite some time before the grasp of words is strong
enough to comprehend the 'it is not'" (1961, p. 279). But at the end of his
quite brilliant "Terministic Screens," Burke cites T. S. Eliot's doctoral
thesis, which quizzically states, "Our only way of showing that we are
attending to an object is to show that it and ourselves are independent
entities, and to do this we must have names. . . . We have no objects
without language" (1966, p. 61). This claim somewhat camps Eliot—
and perhaps Burke—with those who would overstate the powers of language, and, it simultaneously underaddresses the negativity that makes
possible all of the lived-body's intentional powers. While much may be
gained from Eliot's insight, there is reason to exercise a bit more caution. Let me first unpack what Eliot's insight implies, and then move on to
address its potential weakness. The overall goal, remember, is to seek
out the peculiar proper to sonorousness.

First, it must be made clear that there are no things without speech.
About this elementary fact Eliot and Burke are astute. Again, How many
things are there without language? None: "Things" is a word! There
should be little doubt that "things" is a word. In fact, nothing could be
said which is not just that, something said. Only where language is, are
there discrete entities of world. Said otherwise, where there are "re-cog-
nized" entities there already is speech (Heidegger, 1971, pp. 139–156).
This indeed leaves us, as Burke notes, with an inability to tell "What Are
the Signs of What?" (1966, pp. 358–379). World and all that therein are

inseparable from sonorousness. Why? Because all "entitative punctuation" is funded by sonorousness. It is undeniable. With the prowess of speech we can, in an orderly and intelligible way, articulate and maintain the specific boundaries and parameters of "worldly entities." Without such sayable sense we seem unable to isolate and sustain particular configurations of world-experience. There is, in fact, neither "you" nor "me," nor "I" nor "world." Without sonorousness, there is nothing that could be said, and, this is not simply a game of semantics or a play on words. Fortunately, we do speak. This, I believe, is a fair interpretation of Eliot's insight. But, what is its weakness?

As for Eliot's undersight, consider Daniel Dennett's *Consciousness Explained* (1991) where he tells us that

> we hear speech in our native tongue as a sequence of distinct words separated by tiny gaps of silence. That is, we have a clear sense of boundaries between words, which cannot be composed of color edges or lines, and do not seem to be marked by beeps or clicks, so what could the boundaries be but silent gaps of various duration. . . . But if one looks at the acoustical energy profile of the input signal, the lowest energy level (the moments closest to silence) do not line up at all well with the word boundaries. The segmentation of speech sounds is a process that imposes boundaries based on the grammatical structure of the language, not on the physical structure of the acoustical wave. (pp. 50–51)

So, the problem is to explain how it is that there are "no separate entities without language," and yet how language itself cannot be a collection of different words, for in that case, we would have to ask: How are the words themselves separated from one another? The problem of how we can be separate from world without the powers of language is therefore subtly reinscribed: the problems of how language is separate from both world [and] self, as well as how it is separated within itself also remain. Does not Burke, in the end, need recourse to a negativity deeper than language and the hortatory don't? Could it be that sonorousness issues separate entities, and yet, only because it, as a strand in the lived-body's network of intentional powers, is already infected with internal negation (i.e., room-making negativity)?

What is it that separates speech from world [and] self? Speech? How is it separate from these? Nothing separates speech [and] world [and] self. That is, nothing separates me from my speech, and nothing separates speech from world. What is it that separates one word from the next? Nothing. Nothing separates one word from another. This is partly why I began with self-negating Earth and the theme of embodiment. I wanted to show that nothing separates any entity from its background, and, that these internal negations fund the positive projects of concernful intentional relations "between" world [and] self.

Sonorous Meaning

The lived-body, I suggest in Chapter 2, does not reflectively and analytically think about all of the activities and involvements in which it commonly engages. Our dealings are largely prereflective or nonanalytical in character, and this applies both to disclosed objects-in-fields and to the comportments lived-bodies routinely maintain. Still, the lived-body does have the capacity to analytically and reflectively attend to its intentional powers. I need to explore, therefore, the intentionality of sonorousness by giving specific attention to its predominately prereflective character and to the transformations that occur during moments of reflection.

Prereflective Meaning   Speech enables us to "know about the world" rather than simply endure the engrossing immediacies of existence. But recall American philosopher John Dewey's insightful claim that, "Things are objects to be treated, used, acted upon and with, enjoyed and endured, even more than things to be known. They are things had before they are things cognized" (1925/1988, p. 28). He suggests that cognitive knowledge, knowledge about things, is only one type of meaningful relation humans maintain with their world, and it is a derivative one at that. Applied to speech, note that we commonly do not know that we are talking (i.e., we do not believe that we are; we do not thoughtfully attend to that fact). We routinely endure and undergo speech events without turning our attention toward them per se. The speech acts themselves receive no reflective consideration. Endured events of sonorousness may not—and often do not—come into explicit or thematic awareness (cf. Merleau-Ponty, 1973, pp. 115–129). Instead, they tacitly travel unregarded as we absorbedly endure sayable sense (Polanyi, 1962; 1968). Said quite otherwise, we can, at certain times, reflectively "know" that our speech is distinct from its meaning, and yet, while submersively engrossed in prereflective speech activities, the meaning is endured without "knowing about" the speaking. Dewey was bringing this to our concern when he wrote:

> Modern psychiatry as well as anthropology have demonstrated the enormous role of symbolism in human experience. The word symbolism however, is a product of reflection upon direct phenomena, not a description of what happens when so called symbols are potent. For the feature which characterizes symbolism is precisely that the thing which later reflection calls a symbol is not a symbol, but a direct vehicle, a concrete embodiment, a vital incarnation. (1925/1988, p. 72)

Why does he say that a symbol is also not a symbol? The key point here is that, "the word symbolism . . . is a product of reflection. . . . [Said otherwise] the thing which later reflection calls a symbol is not a symbol." In prereflective moments of speaking, speech [and] its sense (or the message [and] its meaning) are experiencably inseparable; as we are undergoing speech, we do not experience both messages and meaning. Rather, the messages are simply experienced as meaning; they are thought itself, though in the mode of not being it. This insight is expressed wonderfully in Madison's appropriation of Sartre's writings on consciousness: "a word is not what it is and is what it is not (i.e., it is not what it is, a material thing, but is what it means)" (1996, pp. 85–86).

Let me be clearer here: I have suggested earlier, in talking about embodiment, that a from-to structure characterizes our intentional powers, and that a type of disappearance (i.e., a mode of absence) is directly related to this. Leder termed this process "focal disappearance" (1991, p. 26). To say an intentional activity "focally disappears" is to claim that when it actively thematizes a phenomenal field, it is absent from that field. Thus, the lived-body's intentional powers are passed over and beyond—surpassed and forgotten—as they pre-thetically make room for items and events of concern. For example, although my eyes are necessary to my sight, they, nevertheless, need not manifest themselves in an act of seeing. As intentional in their very character, they most commonly do not posit themselves in addition to what they make room for. Stated otherwise, an explicit awareness or conscious knowledge that "my eyes see" need not accompany acts of seeing, and in fact, I much more routinely become oblivious to the fact that my eyes are doing the seeing.

Sonorousness, therefore, is not a listening "to" the sounds spoken, but rather, is a listening "from" them. As Leder thoughtfully suggests: "In employing a sign I do not thematize its sheer physical presence (the signifier) but attend from it to that which is signified. The signifier thus undergoes a focal disappearance as it is incorporated. . . . The body of the sign is thus self-effacing" (1991, pp. 121–22). When we speak we listen from language, and so, we do not first hear "the sounds" and then, later, go on to the sense. Words are not first presented as mere sounds in the hope that they might eventually lead us to thought. Rather, thought exists only if it has adequate room made for it. It depends upon speech's self-effacing transivity and "therein lies the virtue of language: it is language which propels us toward the things it signifies. In the way it works, language hides itself from us" (Merleau-Ponty, 1973, p. 10). As we speak, we do not hear the noisiness of our own tongue as we do a foreign tongue. Instead, the noisiness is focally absent and we live speech as thought. Thought, as what is heard in lieu of the noises, is maintained and inseparable from acts of speaking.

Thought, therefore, is not that which precedes and is "encoded into" acts of speaking, less still is speech a translation out of one's thinking. Merleau-Ponty's classic *Phenomenology of Perception* (1962) provides a highly provocative passage. I quote it at length:

The word, far from being the mere sign of objects and meanings, inhabits things and is the vehicle of meanings. Thus, speech, in the speaker, does not translate ready-made thought, but accomplishes it. . . . Word and speech must somehow cease to be a way of designating things or thoughts, and become the presence of that thought in the phenomenal world, and, moreover, not its clothing but its token or its body. . . . [T]he process of expression brings the meaning into being or makes it effective, and does not merely translate it. . . . Thought is no "internal" thing, and does not exist independently of the world and of words. What misleads us in this connection, and causes us to believe in a thought which exists for itself prior to expression, is thought already constituted and expressed, which we can silently recall to ourselves, and through which we acquire the illusion of an inner life. (pp. 178; 182–183)

These remarks fall directly in line with Dewey's astute observation that, "When the introspectionist thinks he has withdrawn into a wholly private realm of events disparate in kind from other events, made out of mental stuff, he is only turning his attention to his own soliloquy" (1925/1988, pp. 134–135). As speech is pre-thetically operative, there is not speech on one hand and thought on the other. On the contrary, thought [and] speech are two ways of thinking about (i.e., talking about) a single multi-dimensional phenomenon.[32] Merleau-Ponty helps to clarify this issue further where he writes, "Expressive operations take place between thinking language and speaking thought; not, as we thoughtlessly say, between thought and language" (1964, p. 18). Elsewhere (1999) I suggest that this distinction could be examined in terms of "context." Whereas "speaking thought" refers to the context of what I say to others, "thinking language" refers to the context of speaking which is "only to myself." Edward Hall's (1976; 1983) distinction between high- and low-context messages is suggestive here. Messages within the context of "speaking thought," as more often than not lower-context, often require greater amounts of articulation, precision, and depth. In relative contrast, "thinking language," as often exceedingly "high-context," can remain meaningful even in light of sparse, weak, and fragmented articulation. Most generally and in both contexts, we habitually forget the fact that we are speaking, and our attention moves from speech to that which it makes manifest (Anton, 1997).

Spontaneously emergent speech activities such as sharing narratives, or singing to ourselves, or telling jokes, or recounting events comprise a great deal of our everyday encounters.[33] At these times, and in fact during most of our everyday lives, we are not thematically advancing assertions. We routinely fail to regard the fact that we are speaking (that is, we only occasionally attend to this fact). Therefore, we certainly can agree that

"Asserting is one of the Dasein's intentional comportments " (Heidegger, 1982, p. 207), even if we still maintain that, "most statements in language, even if they have the character of assertion when taken literally, nevertheless also show a different structure" (p. 210). This implies, on the one hand, that activities of speech are best understood not as reflective thematic knowing about; they are not a symbolizing, a representing, or a signifying. In obliviously looking past and beyond our speech, we dwell in the thought which thereby has been provided for. On the other hand, sometimes a symbol is experienced as a symbol.

Non-Representational 'Aboutness'   We must not reduce speech to little more than a practical comportment. It is neither solely nor merely an "everyday coping" (Stewart, 1995, p. 109). Our sonorousness includes more layers than the operative intentionality so far discussed. As developed in thetic acts of judgment, speech displays what might be called "aboutness." Therefore, our pre-thetic speech comportments can be subject to reflective idealizations and theoretical inquiries through resources held in sonorousness. In fact, this "aboutness" is an important as well as an indigenous resource to our sonorous being. To detail further how reflective speech furnishes a "knowing about," I now examine the transformative role "reflection" plays: Knowledge "about" things primarily is based upon reflective relations between a state-of-affairs and a statement about that state-of-affairs (Heidegger, 1962, pp. 256–273). Assertions become thematic objects of reflection as we compare them to that which was asserted about. We direct our regard in this manner so that the veracity of the assertions can be assessed (Dewey, 1910/1991). But we must be careful here. We must safeguard against reinscribing one more variety of the two-world hypothesis.

As already suggested in Chapter 2, Merleau-Ponty provides much instruction on this issue when he states, "Reflection does not withdraw from the world . . . it slackens the intentional threads which attach us to the world and thus brings them to our notice" (1962, p. xiii). By a "slackening of intentional threads," he refers not to reflection back toward oneself. Rather, our concernful attention turns toward the idealities of various intentio/ intentum correlates. That is, reflection, as the requisite moment for acts of representation, does not turn back to an "independent" subject nor attempts to "mirror" an independently existing reality.[34] It explicitly and thematically presences our intentional activities themselves. This basically means that reflection transforms our prereflective speech undergoings, producing the manifestness of both messages and meanings, of both words and thought. Said a bit more subtly, "as soon as we distinguish thought from speaking absolutely we are already in the order of reflection" (Merleau-Ponty, 1968, p. 130). The experienced division between speech and sense, or language and meaning is not given in prereflectively undergoings, and yet it is indigenous to reflection. Reflection, therefore, generates a kind of apophantic split by which both speech and sense seem to come to presence, (or more accurately, seem to already have been present), the former apparently representing the latter.

Thetic acts of judgment, it must be underscored, do not provide epistemological foundations regarding an objectively present or preexisting world. Instead, they, as moments of "signitive meaning" (Schrag, 1986, pp. 53–55), thematically develop what was tacitly manifest in our prepredicative (i.e., pre-thetic) involvements. This further implies that our theoretical assertions do not first bring about our relations to beings. We always already have had something to do with that which we make meaningful (truthful) assertions about. This means that speech can represent, can be about the world, in the sense of reflectively talking about what is already disclosed by other intentional threads (e.g., motor, perceptual, emotive, imaginative).

In summary, we find an important distinction between speech as it operates implicitly and speech as it itself is an explicit object of reflection. First, we commonly engage in sonorous activities without giving that fact any direct or explicit regard. Indeed, we often are expressively speaking to ourselves while this fact passes "transparently" by our attention; there is simply an attending from the speech to that which it makes possible (Anton, 1995). In a word, we routinely dwell in the sayable sense provided by and through speech without in any way attending to the speech itself; it routinely undergoes a "focal disappearance" during the unfolding and ongoing accomplishment of "expressive meaning." Second, we, in many instances, consciously and directly attend "to" our sonorousness. It is explicitly reflected upon during moments of signification. That is, when speakers offer what is to be taken as an assertion about some aspect of world-experience, the words themselves become thematically present-at-hand. This allows the statement to be compared to the state-of-affairs about which it was made (Heidegger, 1962). Therefore, sonorousness, as a whole, is a complex and unifying nexus. Although our speech is predominantly a prereflective social practice (and hence is primarily undergone tacitly), it also maintains a kind of theoretical sight, and so, it has a peculiar manner of developing itself in reflection (Anton, 1998a).

Sonorousness as Spatializing and Temporalizing

The lived-body's intentional powers articulate and choreograph self-negating Earth's existential decompressions along ecstatically unfolding horizons of spatiality and temporality. Furthermore, every intentional thread, as a connective tissue of lived-through world-experience, spatializes spatiality and temporalizes temporality in its own peculiar way. Earlier, in Chapter 2, I have considered the specific differences between seeing something, hearing something, and touching something. I there suggested that the differences in the respective "intendablenesses" refer to differences in spatializations and temporalizations. That is, each intentional power and its correlative object-in-field is differentiated according to peculiar modes of existential decompression, according to the different spatializing and temporalizing powers through which entities are concernfully made manifest.[35]

Spatializing Spatiality   Speech is a tissue of world [and] self comprehension. It operates by spatializing spatiality. To say that "speech spatializes spatiality" is to suggest that speech spatially guides and directs our bodily powers for de-distancing, for bringing-near, and most generally, for care-taking. It is, most often, through speech that we are instructed on how to "go on from here" (Wittgenstein, 1953; also see Thayer, 1997). I have suggested in Chapter 3 that the intentional threads by which we inhere in the world are ratified and sanctified by societal impositions, mainly through a flurry of "hortatory dont's" (Burke, 1966). I considered early parenting, where parents direct and guide their children's exploration of worldly entities. I also have examined eating practices and how they are guided by socially issued negativity. In general, we are drenched by a deluge of verbal and actional negativity, and this negativity, then, regulates and orchestrates the way "one" is to comport toward various entities as well as the kinds of involvements entities, as with-whichs, are to be available for and relevant to. Thus, others regulate and orchestrate the lived-body's spatial powers for making available and relevant (i.e., powers for dwelling in nearness). This, then, is a first way speech spatializes the spatiality of lived-through world-experience.

The present discussion has already implied, then, that speech is a way of dwelling in nearness: I can speak of things forever absent to the other intentional powers, or I can speak of far away objects, events, and persons. In either case, to say that speech spatializes spatiality is to acknowledge that it is one of the lived-body's powers for "de-distancing" (Heidegger, 1962). Indeed, speech is a way of concernfully drawing near to and/or keeping a safe distance from worldly entities; it is a bodily comportment which provides concernful nearness and yet which also furnishes the security of distance. For example, instead of walking over to something and actually handling it, I might first speak about it. In this way I can make it available for and relevant to my projects and still maintain a distance from it. I can, in a certain sense, deal with and manipulate it. And, if others are "carrying out my request," I can acquire and hold something at a distance by speaking (e.g., "Can you pick up some bread on your way home?").

To say that speech spatializes spatiality furthermore means that configurations of world-experience congeal into analytically isolatable and temporally maintainable entities (Dewey, 1988/1925; James, 1977, pp. 258–266; Edie, 1987). Speech is that way of being-with-others-being-toward-world that punctuates a sayable sense of spatial organization within experience. It is by speech (i.e., accomplished sense) that isolatable things, relations, aspects, and properties come to sustain themselves "objectively" (i.e., to exist) within concrete lived-through world-experience. With speech, we gain a "digitalization of analogic relations" (Wilden, 1972, pp. 155–195). As a simple example, I look down to my body. We might say that "it" appears to be one whole thing (i.e., a separate and independent entity), and yet the concernful directedness made possible by the word "body" already separates "it" from the surroundings. Even more illustratively, consider the words "arm," "forearm," "elbow," "wrist," "palm," and "fingers." How, if not by sayable sense, are we to specify maintainable boundaries, identities and oppositions, which separate these things? Indeed, without any speech, where and how could one socially differentiate the "palm" from the "wrist" from the "forearm"? Would it even be possible for someone to mean "skin rather than body" without any of the entitative punctuation (i.e., the digitalization) that speech releases and appropriates?

Speech spatializes spatiality. Aristotle knew this well, for it was he who told us that it separates and unites (also see Burke's brilliant discussion of "merger" and "division" in *Grammar of Motives*, 1952, pp. 403–418). Speech takes apart and brings back together. This is the essential operation of predicating assertions and is exactly what Heidegger had in mind in his *The Metaphysical Foundations of Logic*, where he discusses "referential intentionality" (1984, p. 101). Let's walk through an example. Reflectively consider the following assertion: "This sentence is inked onto paper." Speech such as this, when reflectively assessed, analytically punctuates "entitative" boundaries. Taking the absolute fullness, the plenitude of lived-through world-experience (the utter and endless inexhaustible whole of existence), this statement isolates, delineates, directs and re-relates. Further, it displayingly re-relates what it first operated to isolate. The predicating sentence in this case makes manifest the entities of "sentence," "ink," and "paper." Not only that. It more specifically choreographed them by articulately displaying the particular way these isolatable aspects exhibit a relatedness manifested by other intentional threads (in this case, ocular intentionalities). Heidegger explains this process most astutely where he claims,

> predication is primarily a disparting of what is given, and in fact an *exhibitive disparting*. This disparting does not have the sense of a factual

taking apart of the given thing into thing-pieces but is apophantic: it displays the belonging-together of the manifold determinations of the being which is asserted about. In this disparting, that being is at the same time made visible, exhibited, in the unity of the belonging-together of its self-exhibitive determinations. (1982, p. 209)

By sonorously spatializing lived-though world-experience, predicative speech manifests the fields correlated to the lived-body's other intentional threads in an "exhibitive disparting." Therefore, the assertion, "This sentence is inked onto paper," analytically specifies various "aspects" of the total visual field, and then, in a showing, articulately unveils how these belong-together. In general, such acts of speech are conditional renunciations of the total event-horizon in favor of some definite, isolated, and explicitly characterized aspect of it.

This also makes clear that assertoric (i.e., truthful) speech does not simply make up the relations; truth is that possibility given to the manner of decompressing world-profiles in the spatialized and temporalized ways of speech. Speech activities such as predication, or reflective and thematically offered assertions, or believed and uttered truth claims do not create truth, do not "make 'it' up." It is to stress this point that Heidegger writes:

> To the Dasein as unveiling there belongs essentially something unveiled in its unveiledness, some entity to which the unveiling relates in conformity with its intentional structure. There belongs to unveiling, as to every other intentional comportment, an understanding of the being of that to which this comportment relates as such. In unveiling assertion the Dasein is directed toward something which it understands beforehand in that entity's unveiledness. (1982, p. 217)

Assertions are such that they operate by dispartively "being about" what already has been forehad by other intentional threads: (i.e., assertions do not disclose or verify some independent reality).

And so, we must fight off all varieties of the two-world hypothesis and yet still acknowledge the resources of predicative speech, the fact that speech is fundamentally "about" something. In the end, to say that sonorousness spatializes spatiality is to suggest that it existentially decompresses Earth's plenitude into sayable configurations of lived-through world-experience. Sonorousness entitatively punctuates world [and] self. It concernfully makes room for the sayableness of existence.

Temporalizing Temporality   Let me now discuss how sonorousness, in its own unique way, temporalizes temporality. To examine how speech temporalizes temporality, we, first, must once again observe that to speak is to speak language, both of which, speech and language, temporalize in conjunction with each other. But let me first head off a potential difficulty. In contemporary social theory, the term "speech" commonly is taken to be personal gesticulations of the organism in its concrete and once-occurrent situations. It is associated with personal and actual acts of utterance. "Language," on the other hand, is taken as a social code, or a set of rules by which "intersubjectivity" can be established. In distinction to these views, I want to suggest that "acts of speech are embodiments of our futuralness, whereas the sediments of language reveal us in our pastness" (Anton, 1999). Said simply, speech is no less social than language is. Both exist in a world that is fundamentally being-with-others. Let me try to elucidate these claims.

First, we are beings whose temporalizations allow us to call back to ourselves from the future, and so, speaking shows itself as a temporal project. It is a project that leaps ahead of itself and fulfills itself by reaching back from its forwardly-projected-and-backwardly-stretching leap. As an initial consideration, I recently sat with a friend in a Chinese restaurant, and at the table next to ours, several people were speaking Chinese. As I listened to their talk, I could hear only a flowing succession of noises. I could not tell when one word ended and another one began, and I certainly could not distinguish beginnings or endings to sentences. In general, various noises seemed to flow along in linear succession; they rapidly arose and just as quickly vanished. The main point is that the noises disappeared as evenly as they surfaced, and so, they seemed to ride a razor blade moment of now. Is this not drastically, radically, distinct from the way we experience our own speech activities? Carefully consider the temporal gathering by which sonorousness accomplishes meaning. Feel the stretching-along, the unfolding-along-from-within, for example, while reading a single line from Ralph Waldo Emerson's "Experience":

> Without any shadow of doubt amidst this vertigo of shows and politics, I settle myself ever firmer in the creed, that we should not postpone and refer and wish, but do broad justice where we are, by whomsoever we deal with, accepting our actual companions and circumstances, however humble or odious, as the mystic officials to whom the universe has delegated its whole pleasure for us. (1968, pp. 350–351)

When we listen from the language that we ourselves speak, we somehow hear more than evanescent noises. We hear, we dwell within, something else: we undergo and endure an order that understandingly stretches itself along. This sense of understanding tarries and unfolds in a gathering that gathers by retainingly awaiting its own completion (Heidegger, 1962). In our acts of speaking, we are stretching-along, dwelling within the room made by the unfolding of speech's choreographed stretch. Speech's meaning, then, is not summed by the linear and serial succession of words; it is not simply pieced together according to a unidirectional and sequential progress of one word's meaning added to the previous ones'. Rather, its meaning is accomplished by a backwardly-reaching leaping-ahead. As an act of speaking unfolds over lived-through experience its meaning seems to be retroactively specified by the act's completion. Speech is an ecstatical unity; it is a retaining-that-awaits (Heidegger, 1962). This means that the specific meaning of what was "earlier" becomes articulated and vitally concretized by what comes later. Therefore, a vital part of human means for futural projection is speech (Wilson, 1948, p. 160). To speak is to stretch-along in a time-gathering gesticulation, one that accomplishes sayable sense by awaitingly-running-ahead-of-itself.

Second, sentences are comprised of words which are, more often than not, already of the past; they are a repetition of it (Schrag, 1994, pp. 49–60). They are a gathering which, within the projected stretching along of our speech activities, gathers by way of repeatability. The words and phrases within a sentence (i.e., the reflectively and analytically assessed "parts" of it) are born of their capacity for reiteration (Derrida, 1977). Each "part" within a reflected upon utterance maintains a kind of "synchronic intentionality" to earlier involvements and employments (Anton, 1998b). We might define language, then, as: that past which, as already spoken, can be open to present and future appropriations. The languages we speak from are ancient, even if we fail to appreciate this. "For most people," Holquist points out, "the oldest thing they will ever encounter in their lives is the language they speak everyday" (1990, p. 147). Again, our projects of speech are funded by the past, a past meaningfully maintained through the repeatability we call "language."

Speech, a temporal project, accomplishes thought by recollecting the institution of language in an awaiting that retainingly stretches itself along. But perhaps I should discuss at this point, even if only briefly, the different temporalizations given to prereflective or "expressive" meaning and to thematically reflective or "signitive" meaning.

Expressive speech is characterized by an "already-begun-forgetful-ness" (Anton, 1999). Here, actual acts of speaking are mindlessly endured as implicit sense horizons. Expressive meaning thus refers to that layer of meaning which is localized to concrete participations and involvements. Its temporality seems vaguely absent; it is diffusely and tacitly spread into entities and events of concern. In our everyday speech, as already outside ourselves and with-others, we concernfully co-comport to that about which we are speaking. In these experiences we do not attend to the speaking itself, nor do we attend to the fact that the speaking is occurring "in" time. Rather, we holistically and implicitly understand speech as thought. As such, expressive speech is mainly a tacit articulation of temporality rather than an event which occurs "in" time. This means that sonorousness is constituted "in such a manner, indeed, that the making-present which arises from this, makes possible the characteristic absorption of concern" (Heidegger, 1962, p. 405). In general, because prereflective understanding implicitly holds its already-begunness and its not-yet, expressive meaning resists any complete and/or exhausted explication (Schrag, 1986).

Signitive meaning, on the other hand, is characterized by analysis and explicit segmentations. Temporality is mainly experienced as broken into given segments of time. Speech, qua signification, seems to present itself as occurring wholly "within" time, perhaps within an isolated moment of now. This reflective clearing makes room for critical assessments of utterances and assertions. Such assessments can exhibit speech's sense in a thematic and explicit manner (i.e., as items of language per se). Reflective analysis thus provides for the experience of semantic repeatability, and so "propositional content" can seem to be prepackaged. It seems to dwell outside of the unique context of present involvements. Relatedly, this repeatability of sense may give the illusion that the sayable aspects of an entity (i.e., reflectively predicated properties) are timeless essences rather than eventual outcomes of concrete life-world engagements (Dewey, 1925/1988, pp. 135–136). Merleau-Ponty underscores this point where he suggests that reflection transforms our prereflective experience, and so constitutes "a kind of original past, a past which never has been a present" (1962, p. 242). Note also that right here something like a transcendental ego may show itself. It appears as that which is transversally implicated as a continuing identity and unity across various reflective or thetic moments (Schrag, 1969, p. 128).

As a final related consideration, note that human speech is commonly said to be unique due to its capacities for "self-reflexivity" (Burke, 1966; Leeds-Hurwitz, 1989; Ricoeur, 1967). Speech, unlike a "signal" system, is "reflexive to itself." That is, humans can talk about their talk (Anton, 1998b). This insight should not be denied. But still, this needs to be situated appropriately within the lived-body's overall powers. The reflexivity of speech to itself is not all that surprising. In fact, this is not too different from our ability to reflect upon other intentional activities (e.g., perceptual, motor, affective, imaginative) and/or their correlates. This inter-intentional reflexivity readily accounts for the predominance of two-world theses (i.e., speech can reflect upon the various fields presenced by other intentional powers). We can speak about speech reflectively just as we can reflect upon other intentios and their intentums (Anton, 1998b).

SONOROUSLY-BEING-WITH-OTHERS-BEING-TOWARD

Sonorousness is one of the powers by which self-negating Earth haunts itself as an other. It is a way that we, as temporal and social lived-bodies, implicate ourselves in concernfully tending to objects, events, and persons; it is a primary means by which we maintain our concernful "being-with-others-being-toward-world." In Chapter 3, I have suggested that we commonly encounter other persons as mutual flights of transcendence toward the unfolding event-horizon to which we are concernfully co-comported. Thus, when persons gather together they commonly share in a mutual toward-which of intentional concern. With relative ease we can notice a that-toward-which we, at any given moment, are concernfully co-comported, even if the fact of our being-concernfully-directed-toward remains largely tacit. The toward-which of our concernful dealings is often some event or happening which is disclosed (i.e., made manifest) through our sonorous powers. In fact, we often tell others, as they tell us, of "something that happened." Perhaps it is a fictional story, or a recounting of an event that took place earlier, or maybe, plans for some future activity. In any case, we commonly co-comport toward a there which is made manifest through the "mutual incorporation" (Leder, 1990) of lived-bodies' sonorous intentional threads. In talking with one another we become directed toward what is made manifest or disclosed by the speaking; through sonorous comportments lived-bodies thoughtfully co-attend to common entities or events of concern. This means that in our speech practices, there is "a taking up of others' thought through speech, a reflection in others, an ability to think according to others" (Merleau-Ponty, 1962, p. 179). This further means that during moments of speech's "mutual incorporation," moments in which we are mutual flights toward common objects or events of concern, we "grow older together" (Schutz, 1967). Therefore, others often are encountered as fellow sites of existential decompression, other beings who spatialize and temporalize lived-through world-experience by sonorously co-animated gesticulations.

This additionally implies that speech, as funded by repeatability (i.e., the pastness that is language), can be moved by different conversation participants. Others participate in speech's leaping ahead toward meaning because they can be sonorously co-comported toward that about which we speak. Again, different people can complete, or extend, or redirect a conversation because we, each of us, are outside ourselves and temporally projected: speech, this implies, is not a transmission from one mind to another. It is, on the contrary, a concernful being-with-others-being-toward the event-horizon which is unfolding through and around us. As Heidegger suggests,

Communication is never anything like a conveying of experiences, such as opinions or wishes, from the interior of one subject into the interior of another. Dasein-with is already essentially manifest in a co-state-of-mind [i.e., pastness] and a co-understanding [i.e., futuralness]. . . . In talking Dasein expresses itself not because it has, in the first instance, been encapsulated as something 'internal' over against something outside, but because as Being-in-the-world it is already 'outside' when it understands. (1962, p. 205)

An overly rigid separation between outer and inner, therefore, fundamentally fails to grasp the intentional and temporal character of human existence. Additionally, one of the main contributions and promising strengths of "conversation analysis" is its attentiveness to the way speaking activities can be stretched along, furthered and continued, by different speech participants (Mandelbaum, 1989).

Regardless of what one says, it is, in Bakhtin's terms, "always half someone elses." In fact, when Bakhtin writes that "the word in language is always half someone elses" (1981, p. 293), he means that our sonorous utterances are dialogic by their very existence. First, I have already suggested that our sonorousness develops and maintains itself in response to common contextual situations and others' previous (i.e., past) utterances and actions (Levin, 1989). My speaking first emerged out of my "replies and responses" to others, and therefore, the speaking body always has begun as a listening one (Goffman's 1981, "Replies and Responses"). Second, speech, as one of the lived-body's most powerful means of being-directed-toward the future, always anticipates further reactions; in speaking, we always anticipate some kind of response or reply. This dialogic flow from-the-past-toward-the-future is nicely summed up by Holquist when he cites Bakhtin: "There is neither a first word nor a last word. . . . For nothing is absolutely dead: every meaning will someday have its homecoming festival" (1990, p. 39). In the time-gathering life of embodied speech, others are always implicated.

Sonorousness and Ontical Sociality

Speech not only centripetally reaches back to implicate oneself, but moreover, as funded by language, it diffusely implicates others. I have argued in Chapter 3 that human sociality is multitiered, scaffolded into several interpenetrating layers. Roughly summarizing, these range from "anonymous interchangeability" to "particular configurations of concrete face-to-face relations" to each person's "absolute and nonrepeatable once-occurrence." Let me now further delineate these different ontic constellations by laying bare how our sonorousness fundamentally implicates us as being-with.

Sonorousness and Interchangability   First, because language is an institution, our sonorousness provides a level of "interchangeable anonymity" in its "being-with-being-toward." This characteristic of language furnishes what I shall be calling the "fundamental interchangeability thesis." The fundamental interchangeability thesis holds that the meaning of spoken exchanges can be addressed in the abstract by positing interchangeable speakers and transcendent (i.e., repeatable) meanings. Said more simply, to the extent that two or more speakers "speak the same language," their meanings can seem to be "anonymously interchangeable" with regard to that fact. Consider the "locutionary meaning" or the "propositional content" at issue in logical statements or syllogisms. Here a given speaker says something, the meaning of which is not supposed to change and significantly differ if it would be said by someone else. The interchangeability of anonymously related speakers via language's iterability is undoubtedly Derrida's well argued main point in *Limited Inc* (1977). Again, with regard to the meaning at issue here, "anyone" speaking the language equally could have said it; the speakers become interchangeable as the meanings funded through the institution of language seem to be transcendent (Thayer, 1987, p. 224).

The fundamental interchangeability thesis suggests that our sonorousness diffusely implicates others beyond oneself: the language one uses co-implicates those others who have participated in it, or even, those who would be able to participate in it. One's speech, as in a language, implies or expresses an alliance with other speakers of that same language. It can be taken as a kind of uniform, or perhaps, a pledge of allegiance. In general, to speak any language at all is to be human, but the particular language(s) that one does speak makes one political (O'Neill, 1989). This fact was known well to the Gileadites who seized and killed forty-two thousand Ephraimites for being unable to pronounce the word "shibboleth" correctly (Judges 12: 6). In a slightly less drastic yet equally serious example, the recent Angliophone and Francophone debates in Quebec likewise demonstrate a concern over the particular being-with that is implicated in one's sonorously being-toward. Therefore, we never simply talk about things; we implicate particular others by speaking a particular language, that language from which we maintain our concernful being-toward.

Sonorousness and Particularity   Second, in our sonorous being-with-others-being-toward-world we release and appropriate meaning by more particularized, less interchangeable being-withs. This more particularized meaning must be kept distinct from the anonymous interchangeability that language furnishes. To observe such layers of meaning, we must closely attend to vocalics and bodily gestures that accompany and "gestalt-with" our utterances. Human speech, as a care-taking, holds emotional and volitional intonations. Particular relations of being-with are modulated and expressed by particular modes of being-toward (numerous research lines explore these relations: see Heider, 1958; Bateson, 1972, pp. 412–413; Watzlawick, Beavin, and Jackson, 1967, pp. 51–54). By breathing an emotional-volitional spirit into their speech, speakers share in concerned "evaluations" about mutually-comported-toward persons, objects, and/or events (Bakhtin and Medvedev, 1978, pp. 119–128).

As an everyday example, consider how differently one can gesticulate: "Hello. How are you?" Such a common greeting extends beyond a linguistic report that "we now can speak with each other." A spoken greeting does not merely open to an acquaintance an opportunity for a mutual state-of-talk. Greetings may include this function, but they mainly involve paying appropriate ritual dues. They show appropriate self-regard, regard for others, and regard for the occasion. Therefore, when arriving at an occasion, acquaintances are expected to give appropriate acknowledgement to each other. They display an appreciation for the other and are a show of self-respect as well. Rejoining after an absence, acquaintances embody, mainly through facial expressions, intonations, and affective gestures, just how close the relationship is and how pleased they both are to have a chance to talk. Interactants also attenuate greetings and farewells to display the amount of time between the last or until the next face-to-face engagement. Moreover, failure to perform adequate ritual due is cause for a felt embarrassment or insult, and perhaps, a ground for questioning the moral character or present situation of the would-be offender.

In face-to-face spoken interaction, particular others commonly give some show of appreciatively being-with. They embody and express some demonstration of mutual concern over that about which we speak. For example, if I come home and, in a distressed tone, tell of the rude treatment I recently received, I expect some sort of co-being-toward that about which I am speaking, at least from those who are "with me rather than against me." And so, within a state-of-talk, particularized meaning is accomplished through vocalic intonations, bodily deportment and carriage, facial expressions, etc. It is mainly through this "body idiom"[36] that the lived-body not only accents and clarifies messages (i.e., offers feedback), but, it ritually negotiates and accomplishes an inscription of self [and] other by expressively embodying various levels of respect for the occasion, for others, and for self (Goffman, 1967).

Sonorousness and Once-Occurrence   Third and finally, sonorousness accomplishes a layer of meaning that could be described as an existential concern over my own most possibilities. Meaning, at this level of speaking, pertains to my absolute and nonrepeatable once-occurrent existence. The phenomenon of world [and] self that each of us is (i.e., the there-here) has been uniquely thrown, situated, and projected. This further means that we, all of us, need to learn to articulate, to come to terms with, the unfolding event-horizon toward which we are concernfully comported.

We, each of us, unfortunately may be facing and undergoing experiences for which the institution of language is failing; it may lack adequate resources for coming to terms with once-occurrent conditions. O. B. Hardison Jr. in his wonderful *Disappearing Through the Skylight* (1989), describes what he calls a "lag in language." He argues that the modern cultural and social environment changes too rapidly for language, and further states, "language increasingly refers to a world that no longer exists" (p. 161). Therefore, the language that has been passed down, including typical ways of using it and typical things said may be inadequate; they may fail to articulate the unique situations and possibilities which comprise our ongoing existence.

Moreover, it is so much easier to speak in clichés or to say only what others already say (Thayer, 1997; Zijderveld, 1978). In such a thoughtless circulation of words and phrases, that which we speak about can become displaced and lost in the telling. Here things become passed over. That about which we speak remains covered over. We can lose authentic touch with things as we, on hearsay, uncritically take what is given in only the speech that anyone says. Ortega y Gasset thoughtfully acknowledges that, "With some shame we recognize that the greater part of the things we say we do not understand very well; and if we ask ourselves why we say them, why we think them, we will observe that we say them only for this reason: that we have heard them said, that other people say them" (1958, p. 92). We speak whether we have had any other intentional contact with that about which we speak or not. And so, we can reduce things to a limited and leveled average intelligibility of what anyone has to say about them (Heidegger, 1962).

Traditions of language use, things others already have said, may confuse and mislead. But still, they also become in turn, that which calls forth a needed response, perhaps a reprise. Gusdorf makes this quite clear where he states,

> the life of the mind ordinarily begins not with the acquisition of language, but with the revolt against language once it is acquired. The child discovers the world through the established language, which those around prescribe for him. The adolescent discovers values in the revolt against the language he had until then blindly trusted and which seems to him, in the light of the crisis, destitute of all authenticity. (1965, p. 40)

We find that others, wittingly or not, have lied to us about many things, or that things are not as so many others have said they would be. This gap between what "they" have said and one's own intentional disclosures warrants a demand to learn to speak from once-occurence. As the once-occurrent event of world [and] self unfolds, new demands for articulation perennially arise (Taylor, 1991). This again means that I cannot rely upon speech already spoken to speak on my behalf (Lanigan, 1988; 1992). Only I can be answerable. We need to learn to speak from our own most potential for being, to claim a voice for ourselves, to individuate ourselves with regard to "the they" by our speech.

Just as a person "seems to have a special license to accept mistreatment at his own hands that he does not have the right to accept from others" (Goffman, 1967, p. 32), so we likewise need to learn to say things to ourselves and about ourselves that no one else can say for or about us. We must speak up against the "Unspeakable State of Soliloquy" and to learn how to talk to ourselves (Gass, 1985, pp. 206–216). If it is at all true that we implicate ourselves by the way we come to terms with world, then there are many things that we must learn to say, and gain the courage to say, for and about ourselves (Foucault, 1993).

In significant contrast to the "fundamental interchangeability thesis," we cannot, for many projects and involvements, simply recirculate what has been said already (i.e., what "anyone" would or could say). This is not without concrete implications: an actual living person (i.e., this person and not another) cannot simply rely upon ethical maxims to answerably provide a "fitting response" (Schrag, 1986). Each person's shoulder bears the weight of having "no-alibi" in existence; there is no one else who can speak answerably on my behalf (Bakhtin, 1993; Anton, in press A). As Schrag further states, "The ethical question is no longer an inquiry guided by theories of the moral subject and an inventory of the peculiar properties that constitute moral character, but rather becomes a question of the fitting response of the decentered subject in its encounter with the discourse and social practices of the other against the backdrop of the delivered traditions" (1986, p. 202). This does not mean that my projects and involvements must serve my own interests as contrasted to the interests of others. On the contrary, it more specifically suggests that my participation in and contribution to a public "fitting response" would be "responsible or answerable" only provided my uniquely located position, my particular "transgredience" to all others (Bakhtin, 1990). It is true that some things can be said by anyone. Yet, some things, due to my unique history and unique possibilities, only I can say. In the end, such fitting responses cannot be said if I myself do not say them.

SUMMARY SELFHOOD [AND] SONOROUSNESS

In this chapter I explored the nature and character of human sonorousness, and most generally, I tried to situate it as a perfect gift of return within Earth's internal negations. Sonorousness is one of the powers by which self-negating Earth haunts itself as an other. Acts of speech are ongoing events of internal negation which surpass their emptiness by being (i.e., by existing) their intentional disclosures. As a tissue of existential decompression, sonorousness is one of the lived-body's powers for articulating and choreographing meaningful configurations of lived-through world-experience. Said otherwise, sonorousness is an intentional nexus by which aspects of world [and] self are concernfully manifest and thoughtfully taken under care.

Sonorousness is an exemplar of our being-with-others-being-in-the-world, and thus, it radically challenges rigid divisions between self and others. In a word, although language is learned from and with others, this does not mean that the power to speak is bestowed by others. Sonorousness comes to fruition in that being who becomes itself only with the existence of others. Moreover, speech itself commonly passes by our attention as we absorbedly dwell in sense. Nevertheless, as developed in reflection, speech enables a theoretical about-ness. Sonorousness is a nexus of intentional threads riding in and through out the lived-body's other intentional tissues, and so, by way of assertive speech, we can talk reflectively about that which is disclosed in and through those tissues.

I have concluded this chapter by arguing that sonorousness operates through various modes of meaning, each of which implicates various levels of sociality (i.e., being-with-being-toward). Although language is an institution, and therefore furnishes something like repeatable sense which stands independent of particular speakers, it also, in concrete performative utterances, articulates meaning according to more particular being-withs. Again, by way of vocalics and emotional intonations my speech subtly and pre-thetically expresses meaningful evaluations of persons, events, and objects. Finally, my speech bears upon our own most possibilities for being, and so one layer of meaning pertains to our absolute once-occurrence. Some things, given my unique background, situation, and possibilities, only I can say.

The next and final chapter of this part of the study seeks to complete the sketch of selfhood by delineating the final interlocking dimension: temporality. Temporality already has been referred to, and in fact, has been present all along, serving as a kind of guide for the exploration throughout the previous chapters. In Chapter 5, temporality becomes the focal topic of interrogation. I need to show that selfhood is temporality, and further that embodiment, sociality, and sonorousness, in their own regard, are co-implicates of the uniquely temporal entity: the human. We, as lived-bodies, are that being by whom self [and] world "have been" and "will be." And, even more importantly, we also are that being who can dwell in the "will-have-been."

CHAPTER 5

The Lived-Body as an Ecstatical Temporal Clearing

Of the four dimensions in this study of selfhood, the temporality of self stands farthest away from lucid comprehension in contemporary social theory. Temporality, as a key dimension of selfhood, seems to have been pushed to the periphery of scholarly concern. Indeed, many thinkers, deeming temporality to be too metaphysical, quickly come to the self as embodied or as social, and more recently, as constituted through communicative/symbolic practices. Moreover, each of these vectors does span an ineradicable depth of selfhood. And yet, only by carefully considering temporality can we approach a complete portrait of selfhood. Temporality—equiprimordial with embodiment, sociality, and sonorousness—has been alluded to all along. It now takes center stage.

We all seem to know what time is until we are asked to speak about it. Time is so omnipresent, so never not there, so much the fact of our existence, that it also is continuously forgotten; we, as concernfully absorbed within any involvement or dealing, always already have fallen into the spectacle of cosmos. But already I am getting ahead of myself. Let me pull back and first consider a series of questions regarding the character of time and its relations to selfhood. These may help to illustrate why Saint Augustine, in his *Confessions*, would state: "What then is time? If no one asks me, I know: If I wish to explain it to one that asketh, I know not" (1951, p. 224).

Is time a real thing (a substance?) which stands independent of change? Can there be change outside of time? Is there a (or what is the) difference between time and change? Is time nothing but the measurement of change? What is the relationship or the difference between movement and change? Can something move without denoting at least some change (e.g., in position, size, density)? How would time show itself if everything stood absolutely still? Is common sense on the right track if it holds that time is that wherein movement or change occurs?

What is the difference between time and temporality? Would such a distinction be merely verbal and thus wholly arbitrary? Are time and temporality objective or subjective? Is "clock time" somehow more objective than temporality? Time measured by the clock does seem to be more objective, and yet, how are we to account for the seemingly universal experiences of temporality which are deemed "subjective" (e.g., the fact that time drags in boredom [Heidegger, 1995], or that it flies during sleep)? What could the word "subjective" mean here?

How about the nature of the future and the past? Are the future and the past verbal fictions? Is the past simply memory, the future nothing more than imagination? Are both past and future inescapably subjective? Is it the case, as some people say, that there is always only the present moment of now? Is the present, the moment that is now, more objective or more real than the past and/or the future? Clearly it is never not now, but what, then, is the difference between those entities which have rested in the past, and those entities which are their pasts? Said otherwise, what are the differences between entities which are in time (e.g., stones or furniture) and entities who are their time (e.g., humans)?

How is my experience of others and their experiences of me related to temporality and time? Are both time and temporality social constructions? If not wholly, where and how are we to draw the distinction between the time which is and the time which is not socially constructed? What is the difference, if any, between the cultural creations which structure and regulate our reckoning with time and that time which is structured and made articulate within a culture's forms of life?

And finally, how are time and temporality related to sonorousness? Are both time and temporality little more than words, objectified typifications transmitted through cultural heritage? Are the grammatical tenses of language and temporal words such as "before," "earlier," or "later" that which constitutes temporality? That is, are we temporal beings only if we *say* so? Are we temporal because we have been acculturated into such ways of dwelling in time? Could it be the case that only beings who "are their time" could have meaningful use for sonorousness? Said otherwise, do we "become temporal" because we learn language or are we able to learn language because we already are temporal?

In this chapter, the final component of Part II, I address this series of difficult questions. I first want to show that world [and] selfhood are accomplished in an ecstatical temporal constitution, meaning that we are not simply things which, as approached by others, are wholly contained in time. I proceed through four main sections. First, I briefly examine some commonsense notions of time, and then, I draw a distinction between derived time (i.e., that time we are "conscious of") and lived-through temporality (i.e., that which makes any mode of being-toward possible). Second, I examine temporality as a basic fact of the lived-body and the human condition. Third, I carry out this discussion by hermeneutically tying it back to my earlier discussion of sociality. Fourth and finally, I likewise reconsider Chapter 4, showing how sonorousness is grounded in ecstatical temporality.

DERIVED TIME

To tease out some of the many issues at stake here, I first must provide some distinctions. I address, for starters, "cosmic time," "measured time," and "ecstatical temporality." All of these terms interrelate, and so, the task at hand is to differentiate them while showing how the first two are derived out of—yet indigenous to—ecstatical temporality (i.e., existence). A main difficulty is that both cosmic time and measured time are identified in common sense as fundamentally "objective," whereas lived-through temporality is assumed to be basically "subjective." This unfortunate inversion is profoundly misguided, and it easily obfuscates a more originary notion of time, a notion which is necessary if we are to demonstrate the weaknesses of the subject/object dichotomy.

Cosmic Time

The theory called the "big bang," questions regarding the origin of time, and arguments about the ultimate destination of the universe, all these pertain to cosmic time. "Cosmic time" refers to that wherein the raw what-is-going-on, as seamless and unpunctuated, does whatever it does. Without an experiencer such time remains deaf, blind, mute, and ultimately, unregarded. We might even argue that in-and-by-itself, cosmic time does not exist! It requires sites of existential transcendence, places and moments of Earth's self-negation which articulately stretch-along, in a word: temporal clearings.

Recall my initial mythological exposition in Chapter 2, where I suggested that Earth cannot be a "was" or a "will be" and certainly cannot be a "will-have-been." It simply is what it is. I also argued that the notion of Earth can be approximated not by considering "nature In-Itself" (i.e., nature independent of people), but rather, by carefully considering the lived-body while it is sleeping without dreaming. How would we want to express "the time" of this most common and fundamental uneventful event? Only when we are awake can we, through theoretical intentions, consider "sleeping without dreaming," and yet, on the other side, while sleeping without dreaming, we do not attend to the fact of our awake lives. Indeed, if I never woke up, how would I tell the amount of time that passed? Somewhat similar to theoretical inferences about the fact that we "were" sleeping without dreaming, cosmic time is that which can exist, can be that which we attend to thematically, only because we are ecstatically temporal entities (i.e., we are awake). Ultimately, why is it that being awake is literally synonymous with being in a situation?

Cosmic time, in a most peculiar sense, is derived out of lived-through world-experience. But this is not to suggest that humans are simply making it up, or that cosmic time is open to subjective caprice and fancy. Obviously, the universe did not come into being with my birth, even though it comes to meaningful existence through the lived-body's intentional powers. It may help to recall Chapter 2, where I have argued that Earth is an ungraspable limit concept regarding the abstractions of Space and Time devoid of any experiencer. Said inversely, only so long as "there is" a uniquely temporal entity (i.e., a clearing) can cosmic time exist. The lived-body, a self-negating place and moment, is the "who" Earth does to existentially decompress Space/Time, to spatialize and temporalize world [and] self. The lived-body, therefore, is that entity by whom past and future exist, and so, self [and] world "have been" and "will be" so long as it is (Heidegger, 1982, p. 266). Past and future are as "real" as the present moment of now. As sites of existence, we have been entrusted with and sentenced to ecstatical temporality. Said otherwise, in and through self-negating Earth's temporalizing of itself, lived-through world-experience (including theoretical intentions about "cosmic time") comes to concrete manifestation and endurance.

We, each of us, are moments of self-negating Earth. We are time in the mode of not being it. This means that nothing separates past from present; nothing comes between present and future, and likewise, nothing separates future from past (Sartre, 1956). The paradox of temporality is that the lived-body, which fundamentally is "of" time, can appear to be something that is simply "in" time. There is, relatedly, an old riddle which claims that if change were total, then that change would remain imperceptible. That is, if everything is changing, the actual change would travel un-noticed. The logic is as follows: there must be something which does not change—something which stays constant—if the changes are to be registered; there must be something which, unchanged, observes and meaningfully regards the changes. This line of thought, in the end, is way too pure, way too tight. It misses the fact that the existential up-surgence of world [and] self need not constancy but merely differing rates of change. Different rates of change, therefore, become clearings "of" time. Applied to the present discussion, this means that humans are places and moments who, through a host of intentional powers, temporalize the very temporality that they are. To exist is to be time, though in the mode of not being it. And, in this manner, world [and] self show themselves, primarily, as "in" it.

Measured Time

In distinction from the cosmic time which we find ourselves "in" (which nevertheless emerges out of ecstatical temporality), we must consider time that is measured systematically. Just as the notion of cosmic time convinces me that the universe did not begin with my own birth, measured time works to secure a time that is not subject to subjectivism. Said otherwise, measured time is organized and standardized so that our "subjective" experiences "of" time can be kept in check. Still, measured time, as with cosmic time, is not more objective than temporality, even if this is the common assumption. I need to show, therefore, how measured time is derived from and yet indigenous to the temporality that we are.

It was Aristotle, Heidegger tells us, who defined time as "something counted which shows itself in and for regard to the before and after in motion, or in short, something counted in connection with motion as encountered in the horizon of the earlier and later" (1982, p. 235). Consider the many ways people have of measuring time by counting movements with standardized units: we may look to the position of the sun in the sky. We may be counting days on a calendar, or the number of full moons since a particular occurrence. We can watch sand grains pour down an hourglass or a second hand rotate around a clock's face. We even may attend closely to a split-second display on a digital stopwatch. In all of these cases, measuring devices show themselves as frames for counting movements as a succession of changes in abstract time moments. This means that time, counted and regarded along with movement in terms of the earlier and later, is often viewed as a flowing succession of smaller moments of now. The concept of time as a linear sequence of nows, is more particularly defined as a uniform, unidirectional, and irreversible sequence of nows. Such a conception allows for an "objective" constancy in the measuring units. That is, when something begins a movement, there is a certain amount of time and when that movement terminates, the device displays a different amount. This change, we might say, not only began at one time and ended at another time, but moreover, the moving "occupied" time throughout. Take a simple example, a stone held in my right hand. I throw it high into the air and count the number of time moments it takes to reach the ground. Here we can see time's manifestation as a comparison between two movements: the movement that is the counting of specified intervals and the stone's movement from my hand to the ground. This is apparent in Aristotle's account: the counting itself is a kind of movement, whereby another movement can be framed in terms of the earlier and the later.

As a final consideration we must note that, almost the inverse of cosmic time, measured time is characterized by an explicit beginning point and a notable ending point. For example, we start counting at T1 with the entity beginning a movement, and when it halts or ceases, we mark the time of arrival as T2. This implies that we already "have time" before we begin the act of counting and we also "have time" after we cease counting. Consider, to help bring out this peculiar feature, the difference between the actual acts of measuring time and that time (movement) which is measured. The acts have a beginning point and an ending point, but there is always more than the time which is measured. There is time before the counting begins and after it ceases. Said otherwise, when we measure time we "are there" before we begin counting, and also, we "are there" after the counting ends. This basic fact about measured time may seem rather trivial, and yet, it will become highly significant as the discussion of ecstatical temporality and sociality comes under consideration.

TEMPORALITY AS THE MEANING OF EXISTENCE

We seem to have forgotten that beneath and beyond our accounts and descriptions and explanations and theories, the human condition is the fact of existence. It is the fact of living (i.e., existing) as finite temporality. As living and growing creatures, we undergo continuous change, and yet, we also endure. We stretch along. We age. Indeed, no living person is without an age. But let us be careful here, for someone's age can be determined "from the 'outside'" (i.e., by others). And, because I am the other for others, I can tell them about their ages, as when I speak of a two-week-old baby. A baby herself need not know about her age to have one. Additionally, in this outsider conception of aging, persons can appear to be only the age they are at that particular instant. This abstract understanding of age requires a balancing corrective, one which gives careful attention to the fact that humans exist with their pasts and their futures. We are a certain past and a certain future.

It is so easy to forget (or never even notice) that we are temporality. Why is this so? Perhaps because the lived-body perpetually falls into and is absorbed by items of concern; we are directed toward that which has been concernfully made-room-for in the stretched clearing we are. It is perhaps also due to the change-over in experience that occurs when we explicitly reflect on time: when we try to attend to temporality, it seems to slip away. It slides from view, is overshadowed, as measured time or cosmic time comes to attention. Just as speech can appear as both messages and meanings when reflectively attended to, so too, temporality is broken up into explicit time moments when it is considered in analytic reflection. In a word, reflection can leave temporality unnoticed and even covered over, while the time we are "conscious of" most readily appears in reflective considerations. This implies that, as already suggested, we prereflectively forget about temporality; we go about our business by being absorbed in the activities and involvements at hand. Temporality, which is intimately close to us (i.e., nearer than the nearest near), remains for the most part far and away. It is pushed to the periphery of awareness as our attention is directed to the involvements in and through which entities valuatively show themselves and are concernfully drawn near.

To make my exposition more clear, I need to mark off and remain vigilant over the distinction between "interworldly extants" (i.e., beings present "in" time), and "lived-bodies," who, although no doubt are seen as "in" time thanks to others, are fundamentally extratemporal beings (i.e., beings who "exist") (Bakhtin, 1993; Heidegger, 1982). Whereas extant entities are wholly contained "in" time, existing ones are temporal in their very character. Reconsider the stone I hold in my right hand. It is an extant. It is an interworldly entity subject to physical laws, and therefore, we can presuppose certain causal connections which can be measured "in" time. For example, I might, considering it as it is now (T2), remember back to the day I first found it (T1). I found it three years ago walking along the Western shores of Lake Michigan. Moreover, this stone, after I box it away into my collection and place it on the closet shelf (T1), will presumably still be there (or at least somewhere) at some future date (T2). Note that the stone seems to be wholly present at each moment of time. At each time, it wholly and simply is what it is. Nevertheless, although the stone maintains a constancy from past to present and presumably into future, we do not, properly speaking, say that it "has" a past nor that it "has" a future.

The lived-body, on the other hand, is a site of existential decompression: world [and] selves exist as a continuation of various pasts and a projection of various futures. The lived-body's intentional powers have retentions and protentions by which given figure-background configurations are thickly manifested, implying that the past, present, and future are co-constituted in an "ecstatical horizonal unity": these three "ecstasies" of temporality belong together intrinsically (Heidegger, 1962). Schrag therefore rightfully suggests, "The past is not a thing which was once real and has now ceased to be. Nor is the future a real thing which will become real during the 'course of time' at a later date. . . . In the time of existence the past and the future are interrelated and intersect the present" (1961, p. 127). This insight challenges over-empirically-minded realisms which claim that "there is only now." Clearly, for me [and] world, it is never not now. But this does not mean that the now includes or makes room for only itself. As a concernful flight of transcendence, I dwell not simply, narrowly, nor exclusively, in the now (Mead, 1932). Instead, the now is an elongated stretch, always saddlebagged, as James might say, with retentions of what was prior yet not gone-by and protentions of what is impendingly not-yet. This shift in characterization signifies a recognition of "longitudinal intentionalities" riding through the various intentional vectors of the lived-body (Husserl, 1964).

As a lived-body, I am not a wholly given thing, something which stands present inside another wholly given thing called "the world." To be a body is to be an ecstatical temporal clearing, a once-occurent interpenetration of future, present, and past. Merleau-Ponty continually stresses that temporality is not a mere feature of human experience. Rather, temporality, the clearing which gathers time and stretches itself along, is our very existence. He writes,

> We are not saying that time is *for* someone, which would once more be a case of arraying it out or immobilizing it. We are saying that time is someone, or that temporal dimensions, in so far as they perpetually overlap, bear each other out and ever confine themselves to making explicit what was implied in each, being collectively expressive of the one single explosion or thrust which is subjectivity itself. We must understand time as the subject and the subject as time. (1962, p. 422).

The human is more than extant, is not simply a body resting "in" time, (as if a given human's existence were limited to the way the body visually appears to others). World [and] self happen and are happening through Earth's internal negations and corresponding existential decompressions. Merleau-Ponty, once again suggestively discussing this temporal constitution of world [and] self, states,

> In every focusing movement my body unites present, past, and future, it secretes time, or rather, it becomes that location in nature where, for the first time, events, instead of pushing each other into the realm of being, project round the present a double horizon of past and future and acquire a historical orientation. . . . My body takes possession of time; it brings into existence a past and a future for a present; it is not a thing, but creates time instead of submitting to it. (1962, pp. 239–240)

We, as emergent events from self-negating Earth, open room for the dramas of existence. This means that the lived-body is an "existing" being, a site of transcendence who is cleared such that interworldly entities can show themselves. In a word, to be human is to be "concernfully-beside" interworldly extants "in" time (Heidegger, 1962, 1985). But obviously, this abstract beginning description requires much more elucidation and development.

More Than Now

World [and] self are not simply given things standing in extended space. They are never fully completed or wholly done, never depleted of their inexhaustible thickness. Therefore, we once again must avoid conceiving of time as an already measured out grid which the subject, a thing, is located in and physically wades through, as if time were merely space. Merleau-Ponty thoughtfully directs the present exploration where he writes:

> If the observer sits in a boat and is carried by the current, we may say that he is moving downstream towards his future, but the future lies in the landscapes which await him at the estuary, and the course of time is no longer the stream itself: it is the landscape as it rolls by for the moving observer. Time is, therefore, not a real process, not an actual succession that I am content to record. It arises from my relation to things. (1962, p. 412)

My body, as it is for-me, not my body as it is for-others, is always more than in the now; it, as the possibility for any relations at all, is fundamentally more than present.

Recall that in Chapter 2 I have argued that each lived-body is at a unique—a nonrepeatable and noninterchangeable—moment and place in the once-occurrent Space/Time event of self-negating Earth. I have argued that the lived-body does not simply "extend" in space as a non-ecstatical thing, but rather, it "occupies and inhabits" space. That is, my body occupies space by opening onto more than itself, by being concernfully outside of itself, by "being its there." I have suggested that we, as lived-bodies, are "the there-here." This rather awkard expression attempts to stress verbally that the lived-body is not limited to, not simply contained within, the boundaries of the skin. Thus, where I discussed how the lived-body occupies space, I fought against atomistic or overly restrictive "circumferences" of selfhood (Burke, 1952). So, to speak of concretely occupying and inhabiting one's moment in the once-occurrent event of Earth is already to speak of radiations emanating outward from the body, longitudinal intentionalities which are temporally decompressing the event-horizon into thickly endured world-experience profiles. As always more than now, world [and] self are maintained within ecstatical decompressions according to the lived-body's powers of temporalization.

That I am not wholly contained within an atomistic and isolated present is well addressed in existentialist thought by the notion of "thrownness" (Heidegger, 1962). In a discussion during a Graduate Seminar on Heidegger, Calvin Schrag well summarized the notion of thrownness. He stated: "Whenever you find yourself, you'll always find that you already have begun." This means that I, for-myself, am thrown into existence and emerge only after I already have-been. My emergence is situated in a particular history having sedimented traditions of discourse and action. But, and this should be underscored, in moving out of my thrown past, I do not so much leave behind my place of departure as I ecstatically stretch out from it. As Heidegger suggestively notes, "Dasein is stretched along and stretches itself along' (1962, p. 427). The past is not some thing which has "gone-by" and now is abandoned, as if it were a thing severed from the present. I carry out and continue—or react against and challenge—that past into which I already have been thrown.

As a lived-body, I grow by way of continuance, and so, the notion of "habit" also well characterizes the stretching along of the past "within" the present (Kestenbaum, 1977; James, 1958). Merleau-Ponty, discussing the anonymous personal history of the lived-body, writes, "I perceive with my body or my senses, since my body and my senses are precisely that familiarity with the world born of habit. . . . [T]he person who perceives . . . has historical density . . . takes up a perceptual tradition and is faced with a present" (1962, p. 238). Lived-through habits, as prereflective "I can do it agains," are traditions which fund and orient my present encounters. They exemplify the past's continuance and the way that I, as a gathering of time, am a concernful flight and a stretching along. This does not means that the persistence of the past is explicitly noticed or regarded. In fact, it suggests that the continuance per se is more likely strangely forgotten. Indeed, "Over time, that which is acted out, rehearsed, and repeated seeps into one's organismic ground. . . . Habits . . . simply disappear from view. They are enveloped within the structure of the taken-for-granted body from which I in*habit* the world" (Leder, 1990, p. 32). We are able to do what we do, whether we notice this or not, because of the temporal gathering, the stretching along, of that which we have done already.

But the lived-body opens world [and] self to "more than now" not simply by growing out from its thrown past. It also ecstatically dwells by being-toward the unfolding future. As a site of Earth's internal negation and correlative intentional upsurgings, the lived-body emotionally and volitionally relates to its "not-yet." The lived-body, thrown and stretching itself along, concernfully faces an unfolding horizon which mainly manifests itself as yet-to-be-accomplished relations, deeds, and meanings. So as long we are alive world [and] self remain a "project" having much that is still outstanding (Sartre, 1956; de Beauvoir, 1976). This is well captured in Bakhtin's notion of horizon:

> My relationship to each object within my horizon is never a consummated relationship; rather, it is a relationship which is imposed on me as a task-to-be-accomplished, for the event of being, taken as a whole, is an open event; my situation must change at every moment—I cannot tarry and come to rest. The object's standing over against me, in space and time, is what constitutes the principle of the *horizon*: objects do not *surround* me (my outer body) in their presently given makeup and their

presently given value, but rather—stand *over against* me as the objects of my own cognitive-ethical directedness in living my life within the open, still risk-fraught event of being, whose unity, meaning, and value are not *given* but imposed as a *task* still to be accomplished. (1990, p. 98)

Our lives move toward meanings and values which have not yet been secured. The fragility here is implicated, perhaps even deviously furthered, more by the dispersions inherent in failed and incompleted projects than by the deadpan insensitivity to what slowly fades from memory. Either way, it is an undeniable fact that the meaning of our lives remains in peril, always. Entered from the other side: if world [and] self were totally done, already completed and accomplished, our existence would not blaze up with the evaluative and emotional light that it does. The lived-body is a concernful being-with-being-toward whose intentional comportments, shot through with emotional and volitional intonations, evaluatively care-over the precariously unfolding event-horizon. This implies that the lived-body's concern over itself is accomplished mainly by concernfully being-toward that which is drawn near and lived-through in an articulated stretching-itself-along (e.g., the spatial and temporal routes embodied in various projects and involvements).

Understanding [and] Projection

Radical accounts in biology suggest ontologically distinct temporalities are given to different living organisms (von Uexküll, 1926; Bleibtreu, 1968). Although such explorations go well beyond the scope of the present discussion, they clearly support the claim that humans are temporal entities. We are not simply things caught in time; we are temporal clearings whose ecstatical character opens us beyond the here and now of the body. The lived-body, as a thrown and projected clearing, stretches itself along and concernfully dwells alongside that which is made room for. It, as a site of worlding, concretely relates interworldy extants by traversing and ecstatically gathering routes of decompression.

I suggested that we find around us, at all times, a horizon of action, a cropping up of possibilities. And, in concernfully comporting toward everyday tasks, I free up entities, making them available for and relevant to those tasks. Through handy touch, I have argued in Chapter 2, the lived-body comports an understanding of objects, meaningfully disclosing them, even if only prereflectively, according to the projects they have been made available for and relevant to. What was lacking in this discussion, although it was already implicit, was an adequate address of the temporal gathering underlying our haptic intentionalities. By carefully re-considering "handy-items" in light of temporal constitution, I elucidate how pre-thetic understanding is funded not by predicating deductions and logical assertions (or even spoken typifications), but rather, is funded through ecstatical temporality. The task yet-to-be-accomplished, then, is to explain clearly how ecstatical temporality makes possible our pre-thetic comprehensions.

I have maintained throughout this study that "operative intentionality" refers to pre-predicative understandings, those comprehensions which antedate an explicit division between inner and outer as well as the separation of intentio from intentum. Absorption characterizes the modes and moments of pre-thetic intentionality, and hence, they are well described in Stewart's terms as "mindless everyday coping" (1996, p. 33; also see Dreyfus, 1991). Nevertheless, absorption, rightly interpreted, elucidates ecstatical temporality as the key to undercutting the subject/object dichotomy (i.e., why we are not simply "extants" standing fully present to a collection of things standing present in extended space). As a point of strategic entry, I proceed by a comparison to Stewart's (1994) recent problematization of the subject /object dichotomy and to his interpretation of Heidegger's notion of understanding. Stewart writes:

> In other words, Heidegger noticed something that humans 'are' and 'do' prior to operating as subjects on objects. He observed that we are immersed in what might be called *everyday coping*: For the most part 'without thinking,' we make our way about, grooming and dressing, driving vehicles, telephoning, avoiding or connecting with people on the street, engaging in business and professional transactions. These are all examples of our being-in-the-world. . . . So from Heidegger's perspective, the person is not first and foremost an isolated cogito employing reason to connect and disconnect with objects around it; but rather, the person is first and foremost a situated interpreter, understander, or 'sense-maker' engaged in everyday coping. (1994, p. 137)

Stewart is quite correct to stress that we are not Cartesian cogitos neatly located inside our bodies. Moreover, we are not simply employing cognitive and theoretical rationality to wend our way through everyday encounters. Still, as an unfortunate reduction of Heidegger's contribution, Stewart's term "everyday coping" seems to underappreciate (even underestimate) Heidegger's emphasis on temporality. (Not surprisingly, Stewart's explication draws heavily upon Dreyfus's text *Being-in-the-World* (1991), which is an extended analysis of only Division 1 of *Being and Time*). Said most simply, Stewart still has not explained the weaknesses of the subject/object split. Instead, he transmutes the problem from a knowing subject to a doing one. Elsewhere I have criticized Stewart's failure to address the temporal nature of our speech (Anton, 1999). And earlier, in Chapter 4, I have suggested that his notion of "articulate contact" seems to underassess the meaning-bearing intentionalities pervading the whole of the lived-body. Here, then, I more fully and explicitly address why the lived-body is not a thing (i.e., a subject) inside another thing called the world (i.e., an object).

I am not a knowing subject over-against a known object. But neither am I simply a doing thing over against something mindlessly done. I am an ecstatical temporal clearing who understandingly projects possibilities upon interworldly entities, and in just such a way that this allows me to "be" those possibilities. This means that the subject/object dichotomy eclipses the distinction between time and temporality, and so seems to address human existence as an "atemporal" spatiality. That is, the subject is posited as simply present and rigidly standing before things which are likewise wholly given and splayed out. Stewart's claim that we are a "doing" before we are a "knowing" is misguided not because it is untrue, but rather, because, more fundamentally, "understanding" is a temporal word, and more specifically, one which stresses our futuralness. This is why Heidegger suggests that "Dasein is constantly 'more' than it factually is" (1962, p. 185). "Understanding," then, basically means the ability to project possibilities existingly.

Heidegger's well-known example is best brought to consideration with the question: How do I encounter a hammer "as" broken? That is, how does its "brokenness" manifest itself? How does it disclose its "unavailability" to me [and] my projects? We can "see" that the hammer will not work. This is not because we have cognitively deduced, through assertions or predicating statements, that is has "brokenness" as one of its qualities. Our "sight" of such facts has to do with our powers of temporal projection; understanding always includes a projection of possibilities. It is the basis by which the meaningfulness, the intelligibility, of the surrounding world maintains itself. A hammer can show itself "as" a hammer, and even likewise "as" a broken one, because we, as temporal flights, project possibilities upon interworldly entities.

It is the temporal projection of possibilities upon extants which makes them intelligible as "available for and relevant to" various involvements and dealings. When we encounter tools or utensils we do not cognitively and deductively (i.e., knowingly) consider them. Instead, to recognize something as "the tool it is" already implies appropriate and/or acceptable manners of making it available and relevant. Such entities are not first cognitively and thematically predicated; we routinely and quite mindlessly incorporate them as with-whichs in our concernfully-being-toward. Said more simply, when we use tools, we do not first gain our comportmental orientation by way of rational thought and cognitive deductions. Instead, tools are more commonly with-whichs that are mindlessly incorporated into our skillful hand movements, and which, are implicitly part of larger projects at-hand.

I have argued that one of the ways the lived-body choreographs world [and] self by making items available for and relevant to certain involvements and dealings. By powers of temporal projection, lived-bodies exist-ingly project possibilities and thereby understandingly encounter inter-worldy entities. As Heidegger suggestively states,

> Temporality is the condition of the possibility of the constitution of the Dasein's being. However, to this constitution there belongs under-standing of being, for the Dasein, as existent, comports itself toward beings which are not Daseins and beings which are. Accordingly, tem-porality must also be the condition of possibility of the understanding of being that belongs to Dasein. (1982, p. 274)

The understanding, the "fore-thought" operative in everyday dealings, then, is not a thematic and explicit cognitive consideration. It is a pro-jection of possibilities that is mindlessly lived-through.

My body, as it is concretely lived, is an unfolding of actions, pro-jects, and overall "things to do." These various being-towards are marked out by boundaries of beginnings, middles, and ends (Carr, 1986). They are characterized, even if only implicitly, by an articulacy which includes external demarcation and inner unity. In my mundane activities, I open and follow out the routes of spatial and temporal decompression by which world [and] self maintain their continuance. When I bring things together for various purposes, there is an ecstatical gathering of time, "a stretched and stretching when," in and through which the bringing occurs. Moreover, handy items, incorporated into bodily powers for projection, open up pathways for particular configu-rations of lived-through world-experience. A spatial route and progres-sion is choreographed in the skillful handling of tools and handmade items (e.g., a sidewalk, a doorknob, a wrench, or a piece of silverware). Indeed, whether I am bringing groceries home from the market, doing the dishes, or bringing a ball up the court, I traverse and am existentially inscripted into particular lines of spatial and temporal decompression. Said otherwise, when we touch things, changing them and/or using them, we gather and organize the spatial and temporal routes in which world [and] self exist.

This means that most of the lived-body's comprehensions are accomplished not in a calculus of theoretical propositions deduced in linear fashion, but rather, they are enabled by a "thrown projection" that articulately stretches itself along (Heidegger, 1962). We under-standingly go about our business not by cognitively analyzing all we encounter, nor simply by an "acculturation" into a "set of background practices" (Dreyfus, 1991). It is because we are temporal clearings who are thrown and who project themselves understandingly. But, this is not to say that our powers of temporal projection are themselves rec-ognized explicitly. The lived-body's powers for temporal gathering, on the contrary, most commonly travel unnoticed. They fall from awareness as our attention is turned concernfully toward that which they make possible.

The Moment of Decision

It is both problematic and misleading to reduce temporality to a splayed-out time "in" which the lived-body can be located and contained. Selves [and] world are always more than now. In our understandings, we project possibilities existingly. I now need, if only briefly, to round off this discussion by giving adequate attention to "the moment of decision" (Schrag, 1961; 1994).

We, every one of us, should never forget—nor flee from the fact—that we will die. My death is "certain," even though the day and hour remain "indeterminant" (Heidegger, 1962). As someone who exists, I cannot put off my decisions indefinitely. I must make decisions and commit to action. Even more pointedly stated, many decisions and actions have a "right moment," a time when decisive action is "called for." For example, there is a time for sowing seeds, and fruit ripening on the vine has its time to be harvested. At certain moments babies are born and must be attended to, and at other moments, the newly dead must be cared for appropriately. Still, the "moment of decision" must not be confused with "the now" as conceived in abstract thought (i.e., specific time moments which "pass by" linearly and uniformly).

As this chapter has maintained all along, we unfortunately, "inauthentically," may conceive of time as nothing but a linear succession of nows, a mere serial sequence of uniform and unidirectional instances. Equally, we mistakenly may collapse time to space, fundamentally covering over the temporality we are. Said otherwise, in abstract thought I might seem to be nothing more than an extended entity standing present "in" time, as if time were space. We may think that we are things inside another thing called the world. In this light, world and we are simply "in" a serial secession of "present nows" of which each is only and exclusively "now." The past then seems to have irrecoverably "gone-by," while the future shows itself as still "not-present." The moment of decision, in high contrast to this, is not at all an isolated and atomistic instance of now. It is not "a moment in time," but, more broadly, is the event which acknowledges the fact that we "exist." It is in the moment of decision that I, through my actions and doings, meaningfully interpenetrate (ecstatically gather and bring together) past and future with the present.

The lived-body gathers past, present, and future in the moment of decision, and so, acts by meaningfully unifying selfhood through time. The task for the moment of decision is to exist (i.e., to gather time, to existentially decompress) in such a way as to concernfully organize future, past and present, binding them together into a meaningful whole. Schrag offers much guidance when he writes,

> The past is never simply past. It holds future possibilities which can be repeated in the authentic moment. Past history becomes contemporaneous in the act of repetition and is never past in the sense of being a completed or finished series of nows. In its historical existence the self lives out of the past and into the future, for the past is always a future possibility. In this temporal and historical projectedness it unifies itself by appropriating its past and future possibilities in the moment of decision. (1994, p. 26)

This means that in existence the three ecstasies of temporality are unified in authentic choice. Therefore, in the moment of decision, events and actions, deeds and doings, have their time, a time when we are called to act so as to gather into a whole our future and past. During such moments, we authentically dwell in "the moment," meaning that we choose in light of the whole of our existence, and, in which, we commemoratively retain the past while resolutely anticipating the future (Schrag 1961; 1994).

TEMPORALITY AND SOCIALITY

Sociality, like embodiment and sonorousness, is a temporal phenomenon; it is grounded in temporality. Said inversely, time [and] temporality, in their own way, are further evidence of a nonisolated, nonatomistic individual. In Chapter 3, I have highlighted several layers and modes by which others manifest and implicate themselves. First, I examined the world as already socialized due to predecessors' and contemporaries' intentional powers (i.e., to their capacities for spatialization and temporalization). Second, I examined three general modes of concrete face-to-face engagements between consociates: being-with (Heidegger, 1962; Leder, 1990; Schutz, 1967), being-alienated (Sartre, 1956), and being-consummated (Bakhtin, 1990). What is needed at this juncture is a reinterpretation of these different modes and layers in light of their temporal constitution.

Temporality, Time, and Anonymous Sociality

Predecessors traced out lines of possibilities, and so, in addition to the temporal gathering of the lived-body's habits, a temporal gathering pervades the anonymous world. The world I encounter has been spatialized and temporalized by others' intentional powers, and therefore, my own existence, as thrown, emerges from the inertial traces left by others' previous involvements. This means that the past is not simply gone-by (discretely completed and disposed of), even when it is not cognitively nor thematically represented. The past (e.g., Greek and Roman culture, the Enlightenment, the Civil War), is here today in so far as we dwell in its legacy. I wade in and have taken up the pre-decompressed possibilities left in the wake of others' projects and involvements: I have become who I am through others.

Tools, utensils, and other already handled material conditions, these are the repeatable legacies of others' projects. Said otherwise, the concernful flight of human hands is a mode of existential decompression which, in handling things and leaving "handiwork," grasps toward the future by opening up a "will-have-been-past." World, therefore, is filled with praxial inertias which exhibit the "fore-thought of others." This "fore-thought" refers to the ways others, in their capacities to project possibilities, have fashioned and left as available and relevant various material conditions which open and enable my own possibilities. That an item can be encountered as an available with-which not only exemplifies the fore-thought of others in their dealings, but also reveals transpersonal gatherings of time. Others have saved time for me in that I encounter a world whose manifold possibilities are already funded by previous accomplishments. In summary, the "anonymization" of world [and] self is inseparable from the lived-body's powers of temporalization.

Still, each person's indebtedness to others seems underacknowledged in modern North American culture. Contemporary interests in psychological structures, cognitive and internal states, as well as the information handling capacities of the brain, have worked to lessen interest in history and the past, and have potentially reduced them to little more than individuals' memories and/or cognitive activities. That is, the past may be reduced to particular processes in the brain and nervous system: it is that which is cognitively represented, in a word, simply memory. In this manner, we, who are cleared like no other creature, seem to be losing recognition of the fact that we are the historical animal. Too much contemporary thought leaves this fact underaddressed. Past and history exist because of our powers of spatialization and temporalization. We are eventful eventings who have been entrusted with, perhaps sentenced to, historical existence. Said more precisely, it is not that we are historical beings rather than natural ones. It is more the case that, world [and] selves, existing as more than now, are naturally historical accomplishments (Heidegger, 1962; Bookchin, 1995).

Time, Temporality, and Face-to-Face Encounters

Others, predecessors, always already were here before me. This simple sentence expresses one way that temporality and sociality are inseparable.

I need to show that the existential relations between temporality and sociality are not limited to the fact that predecessors already enabled and facilitated selfhood. There are, in fact, also those others, concretely encountered consociates, who I am "in" time with and with whom I can "grow older." An immediate obstacle is that when we reflectively consider temporality and sociality among consociates, we may assume that the basic issue is the means by which persons are able to gather together at the same time. Here we mainly think of those persons with whom we co-comport-toward world. This is an obstacle because we can neglect the other ways that time [and] temporality co-constitute sociality. So, first let me review how measured time facilitates planned gatherings, and then, I turn to the way relations "between" other [and] self are, in themselves, inseparable from the relation "between" time [and] temporality.

Measured Time as Planned Being-With-Being-Toward   Temporality is gathered across individuals by way of transpersonal decompressions. This is quite distinct from the way measured time, especially clock time, allows individuals to gather together "at the same time" (Hall, 1976; 1983). To begin with, lived-through world-experience is shot through with temporal expansions and constrictions. Various temporal modulations such as lapses of memory, decisions which fade from consideration, projects left incomplete and forgotten, and overall, various temporal aporia are endemic to existence (Ricoeur, 1988, pp. 11–98). Moreover, in many everyday engagements time seems to speed up or slow down, and, in some involvements, it seems to drag. Whether we are asleep, or intoxicated, or bored these moments temporalize in their own way, and so, if we are to organize socially, if we are to accomplish a "planned coming together," we need a standardized means of measuring the passage of time. In a word, being-with-others-being-toward is accomplished through intersecting modes of measuring time and measured time. We socially reckon with the aporias inherent to our temporal condition by submitting to measured time (i.e., that time in which events and activities can commence and cease through social orchestration).

Clearly, clock time is a product of human interaction. It is a social construction used for reckoning with that most basic fact: existence. Earlier, I have discussed measuring devices for counting time as an accompaniment to movement with reference to the earlier and later. Still, we do not routinely use the clock in this counting way. The clock, as in "sync" with other clocks, is an intentional structure, a spatializing and temporalizing arc beyond itself. When we prereflectively take up clock time, we look not to the clock, but rather, we look from it. We look over and beyond it, intending an "other than here and now." Said otherwise, a clock, which only can tell us what time it is at that moment we look, is, nonetheless, that which facilitates our ability to concernfully imagine an other than now (Heidegger, 1984). That is, a clock only "tells" the time that it is at each moment, and yet, we mostly use the clock by taking the now as existentially related to an "other than now." Looking from the clock I say to myself, "I have to be there in half-an-hour," or "How much time is left in class?," or "Is it time to start dinner?" I even have seen persons look to their watches to imagine distant future events. For example, persons may suggest that they are looking for extra work this summer while simultaneously gazing down to their watches.

The coordination of temporality via adherence to measured clock time is vital to social regulation and orchestration. Jules Henry's *Pathways to Madness* (1965) enters this issue most provocatively when he writes, "Prick me and I bleed time." He is describing the emotional-volitional tensions that become grounded in temporal and social regulations. He documents the importance of being sensitive to culturally measured time, and further elucidates the ways that such measured time intersects with lived-through temporality: other's valuatively laden projects and involvements are intricately tied into my own projects (Hall, 1983). This basically means that the demands of "the moment of decision" increase as one's projects and dealings become more deeply tied into particular other persons' projects and dealings. For example, I cannot delay if I am to help my friend to the hospital. I cannot put off and decide later whether or not I will concernfully attend to my son's third birthday. Socially reckoning with measured time as such, we may have "lots of time," or perhaps we "do not have any time." We may feel as if "time is running out," or perhaps, as if we have "all the time in the world." In the end, our everyday submissions to socially measured time manifests itself as a time that we have in some quantifiable amount (de Grazia, 1964).

Time [and] Temporality as Other [and] Self   So far I have considered time as a social construction (i.e., the means by which persons plan and coordinate their interactions and involvements). Nevertheless I now must show how existential relations between consociates are much more than collective reckoning with the measured time in which we find ourselves. Because abstract thought takes world [and] self as mere entities in space/time, (and so eclipses the distinction between the worldly clearings we are and interworldly extants), we should not be surprised that the distinction between time and temporality, as it bears upon self/other relations, is likewise commonly passed over. In general, we must not reduce face-to-face dealings to the regulation of the time in and through which we plan and coordinate our concernful being-with-others-being-toward-world. Our collective capacities to accomplish and reckon with measured time are important, but there is much more at stake.

Concrete experiences of self [and] other in face-to-face interaction are grounded in different phenomenological organizations of time [and] temporality. I am a historical continuance whose existence remains projected, and yet, as concretely encountered by an other, only part of me is given in any time. Similarly, the other, a project and concernful transcendence, commonly is encountered as a present body cast against the background of an environment. Just as others can appear to be limited to their skin's boundaries, so likewise they can appear to be limited to occupying a given now. Bakhtin provides an excellent discussion of these issues where he suggestively writes:

> A phenomenological examination and description of my self-experience and my experience of the other makes evident the fundamental and essential difference in the significance of time in organizing these experiences. . . . The other, all of him, is totally *in* time, just as he is altogether in space; there is nothing in my experience of him that interrupts the continuous temporality of his existence. I myself am not, for myself, altogether in time—not *all* of myself . . . the other I place *in* time, whereas myself I experience *in the act* that encompasses time. As the *subjectum* of the act that postulates time, I am extratemporal. (1990, p. 109)

Bakhtin's term "extratemporal" refers to what I have been calling "temporality." Said simply, Bakhtin's point is that I am extratemporal in that I am more than in the time which others, as the clearings they are, place me. Therefore, face-to-face relations are phenomenologically constituted by a difference of time [and] temporality. In fact, it is not unlikely that the regularities in social science grasped under the terms "the fundamental attribution error" and "the actor-observer bias" have their genetic roots in the basic differences in time [and] temporal relations between self [and] others. But these issues are complex and subtle, and hence, they need further detailed attention.

Taking only a cross-section of others (i.e., others as in time), I commonly sum them up as a whole, thinking, "they always have been that way." Indeed, I seem to have great difficulty recognizing the complex and differentiated stretching along of others, at least those others with whom I have not spent time growing older. Unless we have "grown older together," I may simply place the other in time. But what does it mean to grow-older with someone? Schutz (1967) discusses the "we-moment" in which, as lived-bodies, persons concernfully co-comport toward mutual projects and involvements. When individuals care for common worldly dealings, they "grow older together" (Schutz, 1967). In such events, we encounter particular others as mutual flights toward the unfolding event-horizon to which we are concernfully co-comported. This implies that those particular others with whom we have grown older are increasingly manifest to us in their historically situated particularity, and hence, they become less and less isolated to the now. Those particular others whom I "have known for a long time," therefore, may be opened existentially in their temporal existence in ways that unknown others are not.

Indeed, when we first meet persons and they, appearing to be a certain way, claim to have been radically different in the past (that they've changed a great deal), we may experience some difficulty in grasping this. We seem to "see" others as "having been" the way they appear to be now. That is, they may appear with such facticity—even though we take only a slight cross-section—that we think they "must have been" as they now appear (Sartre, 1956). On the other hand but still similarly, people who meet me for the first time (those others who "do not know me"), may imagine me as having been a certain way, simply because I appear to them to be that way now. As an even richer example: I recently heard a senior professor tell about the death of a close friend. He said that the now deceased was the only person still living who knew and remembered him as a youngster. He further said that his friend, unlike all others who now look at him, saw him as "more than 'an old guy.'"

As a final consideration of how the time/temporality distinction pertains to existential other/self relations, I address, only briefly, the fact of death, for it is in death that the relations among sociality [and] time [and] temporality are clearly revealed. First, notice that at my death, I am no longer the there-here. I, as a lived-body, shall never touch, or see, or perceptually experience my own deceased body. Thus the temporal whole of my life is never given to me experientially. It is only others who will encounter me as a cadaver. Still, it might help to consider the distinction between the "aging" of a dead body and the aging of a living one. Considering my own body, I experience only the latter. But if I consider the other's body, then, in either case, it equally appears as a whole manifested fully in time. This mode of being in time does not at all change after the other's death. The person's whole body is still wholly given and continues to change. In this sense, one's body (e.g., hair and nails) will continue to age after death, but this "not done aging" is qualitatively distinct from the existential not-yet which characterizes lived-through world-experience. The not-yet which remains outstanding during my existence is an ecstatical not-yet (i.e., a not-yet that I am).

If I were completely and absolutely alone (permanently devoid of any concretely existing others), the distinction between time and temporality would be irrelevant. But this is not the case. I, in my for-others, seem to be a physical whole that is but in time, and, given that I am an other for others, I am the condition by which they are expressly manifest as in time.

SONOROUS TEMPORALITY

In Chapter 4, I have considered how sonorousness (speech [and] language) spatializes spatiality and temporalizes temporality. In my discussion, I have generally sought to elucidate how the sayableness of lived-through world-experience is neither objectively present nor subjectively created. In this final section of the chapter, I explore what it means to say that "we are temporal clearings." And, more specifically, I attempt to undercut the seemingly overly postmodern claim that temporality is merely the product of our sonorous activities.

First, I suggest that sonorousness is indeed that which allows us to make sense of our experiences; it is by speech that temporality, as a concept, comes to exist. Second, I show that there is, nevertheless, a temporality unfolding within any speech activities whatsoever. And so, as existing sites of Earth's existential decompression, we are as much the eventing of speech as we are that which is spoken about. Finally, I consider some weaknesses of literalized speech about temporality and time, and then, I suggest how our talk, temporally speaking, is intricately linked to our experience of freedom.

Temporality and Sonorousness

Through communicative practices human existence opens beyond, and thereby transcends, otherwise engrossing involvements. This means that within the stream of lived-through world-experience, acts of speech can "fix" the flow. They render meaningful objects where before there were but eventful immediacies. In this manner, sonorousness fundamentally modifies our submersive (i.e., prereflective) relationship to temporality. In *Experience and Nature*, Dewey succinctly cuts to the heart of the matter, "When communication occurs. . . . Events turn into objects, things with a meaning" (1925/1988, p. 132). One of Dewey's many examples is: "Fire burns and the burning is of moment. It enters experience, it is fascinating to watch swirling flames . . . when we name an event, calling it fire, we speak proleptically; we do not name an immediate event, that is impossible" (p. 150). We therefore overcome and deny the eventfulness by turning our attention toward events "as" phenomenal objects (i.e., as events-with-meaning). This clarifies why Dewey states, "When it is denied that we are conscious of events as such it is not meant that we are not aware of objects. Objects are precisely what we are aware of. For objects are events with meaning" (1925/1988, p. 240). Sonorousness thus meaningfully concretizes the eventfulness of world [and] self into discrete and persisting entities.

Consider some further, though somewhat simple, examples: Roll up and clench your fingers on one hand. While holding them clenched, say to yourself, "This is a fist." Now release your fingers and open up your palm, and, ask yourself where the fist went. How about your lap? Have you ever wondered where it goes when you stand up? These bordering on comical illustrations point out how events, through our sonorous powers, are transcended to meaningful objects. As I suggested in the previous chapter, it is in and through the lived-body's sonorous powers that eventings are "entitatively punctuated" as something. Furthermore, our sonorousness likewise allows world [and] self's flowing eventfulness to be turned into "the past" and "the future." Indeed, the future and the past, as meaningful categories of human concern, are objects of consideration only given the human prowess of sonorousness.

Granting these claims, we must be careful not to reduce human reality to what is said (i.e., to "things with meaning"). Human existence is just as much the eventing as the meaningful objects. In delayed response to Watts' playful question in Chapter 4, I would suggest that we are both the teeth that do the biting and the teeth that are bitten; we are the defining and the defined. Said quite otherwise, sonorousness is deeply misconstrued if we fail to recognize how it is rooted in and inseparable from temporality. Heidegger, once more, offers some helpful directions where he argues that, "The complete constitution of the logos includes from the very beginning word, signification, thinking, that which is thought, that which is. . . . It could be that starting with the logos as verbal sequence leads directly to the misinterpretation of the remaining constituents of logos" (1982, p. 206). Human existence, I have tried to show, is temporality (i.e., finitude, projected and stretching itself along).

And so, sonorousness is an intentional comportment by which being-in-the-world-with-others is maintained. Sonorousness (i.e., speech [and] language), like us, exists. The powers of sonorousness, I am suggesting, cannot constitute that temporality in which they themselves are grounded. Temporality, more primordially, refers to the depth and endurance characterizing all lived-through world-experience. Existence, then, refers to that fundamental temporality which is the human condition (i.e., that through which and in response to which all cultural meanings, values, and accomplishments take root). Therefore, to say that "we are temporal clearings," or that "sonorousness exists," is not to offer mere typifications, not simply to proffer pieces of social construction.

The difficulty here is that when we attempt to "talk about" that which constitutes the possibility of our talk (e.g., embodiment or sociality or temporality), aporias often abound. Why so? Because anyone can always and easily say "temporality" or "the body" or "sociality," are all simply words, and so, are only concepts made possible by speech's constitutive power (Stewart, 1995; Morot-Sir, 1993). This is no doubt true.

Still, should we distort phenomena simply to save the coherence of our theories? Heidegger, in discussing the existential relations between discourse and temporality, explicitly expresses concern about these difficulties:

> Tenses, like the other temporal phenomena of language—'kinds of action' and 'temporal stages'—do not originate from the fact that discourse 'also' speaks about temporal processes, namely processes that are encountered 'in time.' Nor does the reason for this lie in the fact that speaking occurs 'in psychical time.' Discourse is in itself temporal, since all speaking about . . . of . . . or to . . . is grounded in the ecstatic unity of temporality. (1996, p. 320)

Although "temporality" is a word, and although our inherited language possesses time-tenses, these facts by no means imply that sonorousness constitutes that temporality in which it itself is grounded. This means that we have the kinds of understanding that we do because we are temporality, not simply because we speak language. It also means that speech is no mere system of objects which, standing in time, works to represent other entities in time.

Understanding, then, is not simply, as Dreyfus (1991) suggests, a product of acculturation into a set of background practices (e.g., one's cultural language practices). Rather, we learn to take up mindlessly these practices, and hence fall into both language and history, only because we are the already temporally cleared being. Heidegger thoughtfully suggests that:

> Dasein must be called originally and fitly the temporal entity as such. It now becomes clear why we do not call a being like a stone temporal, even though it moves or is at rest in time. Its being is not determined by temporality. The Dasein, however, is not merely nor primarily intratemporal, occurring and extant in a world, but is intrinsically temporal in an original, fundamental way. (1982, p. 271)

Sonorousness does not simply constitute temporality. It is a mode by which we, uniquely temporal entities, make sense of our thrown and projected finitude. Better said, it is only because we are temporal that a typification (any one at all) would "make sense"; only in a world that has temporal continuity and regularity (i.e., thrown-projection, stretching itself along) could the primary structure of the "I can do it again" be manifest (Schutz, 1967; Merleau-Ponty, 1962).

Understanding depends upon the ability to project ahead of oneself, (i.e., to call back from the future), and so, only entities who are their time would have meaningful use for discursively spoken language (Heidegger, 1992). Sonorousness is therefore meaningful only for an entity who is temporality, only for an entity who exists as "being-with-others-being-toward-world." We can say this more precisely by suggesting that sonorousness is a primary intentional thread by which the uniquely temporal entity (the human lived-body) temporalizes world [and] self. It is an indigenous possibility for that organism who is its temporality in the mode of thrown projection (i.e., concernful-retaining-that-awaits).

Freedom and the "Will-Have-Been"

We must never forget that we are beings who sing of existence. We are sonorous beings, and yet, sometimes we take our songs too literally. We hear them as the devil would like it: as prose (Thayer, 1987). We trouble ourselves because we are too susceptible to our own linguistic legerdemain; we are left spellbound by our own word magic.

Consider, for example, the way we commonly talk about time: The past seems to be something beyond our control because it already happened; it is already the past and so we seem to be sentenced to its irrevocable unchangeability. The future also is beyond our control, but here because it remains too unpredictable. We can seem to ourselves to be victims of its unknowableness. And then there is the present. That infinitesimal razor slice of now where there is so little time that any control seems helplessly feeble. In contrast to this common sense, I wish to stress that "the past" and "the future" are words, concepts whose meaning need to be carefully scrutinized. Moreover, I must emphasize that grave consequences stem from the way we talk about time and temporality. We must learn to use speech more flexibly, and, by drawing on its own resources, show that our thinking about, and experience of, our own freedom is intricately bound up in the way we talk about time.

Elsewhere, I have argued that the past, as past, is already done, and as such it "could not have been otherwise" (Anton, in press A). This means that its reality is the fact that it already happened. Could the universe not have happened? Such a question overlooks the reality of the past as past, and therefore implicates someone who has not learned the lesson: "Don't cry over spilled milk." The past that already happened could not have been otherwise. That is what it means to say that it is past. The weight of such a claim is that, looking back on our own lives, we could not have done other than we did. If we try to suggest this is not so, we pretend that we were not there, or that we have an alibi who can answer for our acts. Of all the things I already have done in my life, none of them could I have not done. I did them. And, any other explanation lets me off the hook. But, I must stress that this does not make us victims; it should not be taken to endorse a predetermined fatalism.

We need to understand the powers we have of being-toward our certain-yet-indeterminate past (Heidegger, 1989). In our acts and deeds, we can move out toward accomplishments which, once performed, could not not have been achieved. Whether we like it or not, Aristotle could not have not written his *Poetics*, the Beatles could not have not made "Abbey Road," and the "Bill of Rights" could not have not been produced. As an example closer to home, let me explain how I have applied this notion in my teaching. In the classroom I tell my students to hand in final term papers in their sixth or seventh draft. I stress this from the very first day. I tell them that they are to give me their best shot, a real honest-to-goodness attempt to show me and themselves what they are actually capable of. I then further tell them that if I receive a paper that looks rushed, poorly thought out, is filled with typos and spelling errors, and has other signs of procrastination, I will not think that the paper was put off and frantically done the night before. Instead, I will think, and will actually believe, "this, in fact, was the best they were able to do."

O.K. Let's be honest. We cannot completely know and cannot fully control "all" of "the future." This is known too well by those who gamble or play the stock market. Still all of life's involvements are not of this logic. Even if we face various "coefficients of adversity" (Sartre, 1956), and even if we must reckon with times of "recalcitrance" (Burke, 1966), and even if we never escape the "conditions of finitude" (Heidegger, 1962), nevertheless, humans are essentially free beings. But what, the reader might ask, does it mean for humans to be free? To say that we are free is to make a statement regarding our relationship to time. We are not simply in time as a stone is. We are not merely pushed along from behind by a unidirectional flow of causal forces. Basic laws of causation (e.g., that the cause temporally precedes the effect)—laws which are described by and fit into entropic and linear notions of time—cannot account for or cannot explain concrete human action. The lived-body experiences its freedom in its ability to live out of its potentialities for being (Heidegger, 1962, Sartre, 1956; De Beauvoir, 1976). We are beings who are able to call back to ourselves from the future (Heidegger, 1962).

Once again: I am not, by any means, suggesting that we have total control over the future or over all the events that impact our lives. "It is," as Burke rightfully reminds us, "much more complicated than that" (1961, p. 287). But I am suggesting that our ways of talking need to be more flexible, more loose, if they are to make apparent the temporality which is our condition. We will need to tweak our conventional grammar if we are to disclose authentically the meaning of temporality and how it is related to freedom. As a specific example, we need to see that the past is not always completed. By this, I do not mean merely that the past remains open to reinterpretation, nor do I intend to suggest simply that the past changes its meaning according future outcomes. These points are not denied. But still, a more important insight demands our attention:

there is a past which has not yet become what it is, a past that we still have a bit of control over. Said simply, what we normally call the future is actually the past; it is that past which will-have-been.

Heidegger's recently translated *The Concept of Time* (1992), a 1924 lecture given at the Marburg Theological Society, discusses this futuralness as characteristic of human existence. He suggests that we are futural in our ability to run "ahead to the certain yet indeterminate past"(p. 20E). Think of it this way: Human are time as temporality, which means that the past remains a future possibility; this is the past we still are moving toward. The future is that past which is still possible: what we normally call "the future" is equally the "certain-but-indeterminant-past." I therefore can concernfully move out toward the past that "will-have-been."

Our concernful being-with-others-being-toward-world can be performed within the context of that past we are still moving toward. Thus, in my day-to-day existence I can perform my once-occurrent life in concernful realization that I have "no alibi in being" (Bakhtin, 1993). Although I am not fully culpable for all that occurs within the world, I am answerable for all my deeds and actions, and/or for my inaction. If I am reading this I am here and so I could not have not been. I exist, and, so long as I exist I can resolutely call back to myself, temporalizing myself out of the future (i.e., out of the 'certain-but-indeterminant-past'). To recognize this is to acknowledge our existential freedom. Moreover, it is to understand that, in the end, once our decisions or deeds are finally completed, we could not have done otherwise.

SUMMARY: SELFHOOD [AND] TEMPORALITY

I have stressed throughout this entire phenomenology of selfhood that the lived-body is not simply a thing among other things. It is not simply in time as one more extant item of the universe. As lived-bodies who fatefully are sent out from self-negating Earth, we are sites of concernful existence. Part of the slipperiness of this limit concept comes from the fact that the word "being" ambiguously signifies both the extantness of beings which are extant and the existence of beings who exist. Granting this qualification, my best attempt at a summary statement would go something like this: "before" the existential upsurgence of world [and] self, Earth does not *exist*; "after" the existential upsurgence of world [and] self, *Earth* does not exist. This means that Earth's relation to the existential correlates of world [and] self is one of logical priority rather than temporal priority (Burke, 1952). Said more playfully, we undoubtedly commit an anachronism if we suggest that Earth "was" temporally prior to world [and] self. World [and] selves are indigenous to time while remaining at a distance from it; they are time as temporality. This means that the lived-body is time in the mode of not being it, and therefore, world [and] self manifest themselves as always already in it.

I have continually maintained that the word "existence" means ecstatical temporality, whereas the word "extants" refers to entities which manifest themselves as "in" time. I further suggested that we, as human, are temporal gatherings who concernfully tend over interworldy extants, making them articulately manifest through our intentional comportments. By considering "handy-items" in light of their temporal constitution, this chapter has examined how our pre-predicative understanding is not a thematic and cognitive rationality, but rather, is an intelligibility maintained through ecstatical temporality. Understandingly projecting possibilities upon tools and utensils, I existingly disclose these entities as with-whichs for my various everyday involvements. In bringing things near and handling them, I temporally dwell in the trails of choreographed openings. That is, when we make entities available for and relevant to various projects and involvements, we not only articulately open a moment and a place for worldly dwelling in possibilities, we also existingly implicate and accomplish selfhood.

I have considered the "moment of decision" in which we must act so as to gather into a whole both future and past. Authentically dwelling in "the moment" means choosing in light of the whole of our existence, and, in which, we commemoratively retain the past while resolutely anticipating the future.

Also, I have explored the ways that time and temporality interpenetrate and are co-constitutive of sociality. I have suggested that social reckoning with measured time facilitates the capacity for planned ontical gatherings. By adhering to culturally measured time, we are systematically able to coordinate various events of being-with-being-toward. But, as much more than this, I also have argued that self/other relations are, in themselves, inseparable from the distinction between temporality [and] time. In fact, I am the who who places others "in" time, while others are the who by whom I, as a temporal clearing stretching itself along, am concretely placed as an extant entity "in" time.

In this chapter I also have attempted to challenge the overly postmodern claim that "temporality" is basically the product of our sonorous activities. I have maintained that sonorousness is indeed that which allows us to make sense of our experiences; it is by speech that "temporality," as a concept, comes to exist. Nevertheless, I have uncovered a temporality beneath any sonorous activities whatsoever. And so, I have argued that human existence is as much the eventing of sonorousness as it is a world of meaningful objects spoken about. Finally, I have discussed how, so long as we exist, we can call back to ourselves by temporalizing out of that past which will-have-been. To recognize this is to acknowledge existentially that we are futural, which basically means that when any of our actions are finally completed, we could not have done otherwise.

The human condition is a fall into worldly, social, and sonorous existence; it is a fateful sending out from Earthly nonexistence, one which "first 'returns'" by way of intentional ensnarement from within the throes of finitude. World [and] self are embodied, social, sonorous, and temporal accomplishments whose meaningful development and precarious continuance occupies most of our time. In the end, as an earthly worlding, the lived-body is sonorously being-with-others-being-toward-world in a finitude that is thrown and projected, stretching itself along.

PART III

Authenticity Reconsidered

In Chapter 1 I have considered authenticity as a distinguishing characteristic of modern culture, and also, I there have discussed the debate regarding its meaning. Because of the myriad practices and engagements which are and can be performed in the name of the quest for authenticity, I have been interested in exploring how authenticity is tied back to persons' understanding of selfhood. Two primary questions I have wanted to explore are: What is the basis and character of selfhood? And, how are we to understand selfhood so as to further the quest for authenticity? My goal has been to disclose selfhood in a way that reveals how and why certain modes of self-fulfillment or authenticity are limited or even self-defeating while others are richer and more fulfilling. Further guiding these concerns, I have asked the following five questions: What is the specifically embodied character of selfhood? What is the specifically social character of selfhood? What is the specifically symbolic character of selfhood? What is the specifically temporal character of selfhood? How are these characters related to each other?

In the four chapters that comprised Part II of this study, I have explored the first of these questions. Indeed, I have attempted to explicate and elucidate the necessary yet "empty ground" of selfhood. In this third and final part of the study, I accomplish one main task. I return to my second primary question: How are we to understand selfhood so as to further the quest for authenticity? Thus, in Chapter 6, "Selfhood as an Authentic Project," I take a synthetic inventory of Parts I and II and suggest how the quest for authenticity relates to the previously explored phenomenological dimensions of selfhood. That is, my task is to consider how the results of Part II can be strategically applied to the concerns and questions raised in Part I regarding the contemporary quest for authenticity.

CHAPTER 6

Selfhood as an Authentic Project

The quest for authenticity, I have suggested in Chapter 1, refers to changes in contemporary ethics. Increasingly, individuals place moral weight on their right to self-realize and to be personally fulfilled. Nevertheless, the wide diversity of conceptions of selfhood leads to numerous distinct practices and engagements, each of which can be performed under the name of the quest for authenticity. That is, we find many different modes and means by which persons take up the quest for personally meaningful existences. The present project, therefore, was begun with a concern over this contemporary quest for authenticity. Most generally, I have sought answers to the questions: What is the basis and character of selfhood? And, how are we to understand selfhood so as to further the quest for authenticity? Even more specifically, I have wanted to disclose the phenomenological dimensions of selfhood in such a way as to reveal how and why certain approaches toward self-fulfillment are limited, impoverished, or even self-defeating. Said otherwise, I have sought to develop a rigorous account of selfhood which, if thoroughly taken, would provide an anchor sheet against the lower and/or shallow forms of self-fulfillment and self-realization.

A main concern, then, has been to carve out a space between the boosters and the knockers, and to do so by considering the requisite, or "transcendental," features of selfhood (Taylor, 1995). In Part I of this study, I have maintained that the quest for authenticity is not simply a kind of egoism nor a species of moral laxity. And, I have argued that we must recognize the requirements for horizons of significance as well as the fundamentally relational nature of selfhood. Recall also Taylor's specific argument that we need to "show that modes that opt for self-fulfillment without regard (a) to the demands of our ties with others or (b) to demands of any kind emanating from something more or other than human desires or aspirations are self-defeating, that they destroy the conditions for realizing authenticity itself" (1991, p. 35).

To flesh out what is at issue here I recommend vigilance over Taylor's key distinction between the self-referential orientation of authenticity and the actual content of the pursuit, which need not be self-referential. As Taylor states,

> Only if I exist in a world in which history, or the demands of nature, or the needs of my fellow human beings, or the duties of citizenship, or the call of God, or something else of this order matters critically, can I define an identity for myself that is not trivial. Authenticity is not the enemy of demands that emanate from beyond the self; it supposes such demands. (1991, pp. 40–41)

This distinction straightforwardly suggests that individuals are caught up outside of their bodies' skin, concernfully comporting toward persons, events, and things that critically matter. Selfhood, I have tried to show in great detail, is not simply a self-contained system, and so, we cannot concern ourselves only with ourselves. Personal fulfillment cannot explicitly focus upon oneself, as if selfhood were best taken care of in a literal and direct manner. Self-fulfillment comes not from a focus upon one's self per se. Instead, we are concernfully absorbed by that with and in which we meaningfully weave our lives. It is these basic yet profound ideas which Part II, in its entirety, has sought to flesh out and elucidate.

In this chapter I take inventory of Part II and apply it to the questions and concerns of Part I. And, for further clarity, I organize my discussion around two main areas. First, I discuss how the quest for authenticity is not best served. That is, I address what Part II should tell us about the shallower forms of authenticity. Second, I explore some of the positive contributions to the quest for authenticity and discuss how Part II directs our attention to higher and/or richer forms of "selfhood within authentic existence."

CURTAILING SHALLOWER FORMS

Let me begin by suggesting what Part II has not intended to imply regarding the culture of and quest for authenticity. Various conceptual and practical difficulties arise from the fact that, within the twentieth century, we regard selfhood mainly by the capacity to make ourselves objects to and for ourselves. Describing Mead's pervasive influence on social thought, Blumer rightfully claims, "In asserting that the human being has a self, Mead simply meant than the human being is an object to himself. The human being may perceive himself, have conceptions of himself, communicate with himself, and act toward himself" (1967, p. 62). It is here that I can further clarify Taylor's distinction between our orientation from self and selfhood as a content of concern. We must grant that our ability to act toward ourselves, to comprehend ourselves reflectively as content—as a said—is a vital and necessary part of what we mean by selfhood. And yet, I have labored to demonstrate the many layers of selfhood. Moreover, I have attempted to illuminate those layers which commonly pass unregarded by introspectionist and/or overly self-reflective accounts.

In fact, a "turning back and inward" is perhaps a main difficulty for current conceptions of selfhood within the quest for authenticity, at least to the extent that selfhood is taken only to be a content that appears in moments of self-reflection. In each chapter of Part II I have carefully tracked the distinction between reflective and prereflective modes of lived-through world-experience. I have struggled to elucidate selfhood as a whole, how it is (i.e., how it exits) even before and beyond our reflective attention to it. Because both reflective and prereflective modes implicate and accomplish selfhood, a serious reduction in the quest for authenticity awaits those who would pursue self-fulfillment to that self whom appears only in reflection. In such a perspective, the self as a material object in time comes to the fore. Here, someone might be preoccupied by his or her own body, either in its "internality" or in its "being-for-others." Consider some examples: first, embodiment must not be taken to imply that, as bodies, we primarily should be concerned with how we "feel." That is, the culture of authenticity should fight against a kind of self-pandering "cult of feel good." Those who would make "ease," "comfort," or always "feeling good" the main goal of authenticity may miss the prereflective import of our affective powers. They may mistakenly assume that emotions or feelings, rather than a part of our valuative "being-with-being-toward," are objects to be pursued in their own right, a kind of content of self that we need to attend to and care over. A second example would be a foppish concern over the lived-body's social appearances (Veblen, 1899). The annual revenue of the cosmetics industry is a case in point, as is the rise in plastic surgery and other forms of strategic body manipulation. These modes of concern may, in some way or other, help people "feel better about themselves," but such concern is not at all what Part II suggests about the meaning of our embodiment, our affectivity, or our possibilities for higher forms of authenticity.

By and large the study in Part II suggests that human embodiment does not simply refer us back to the thingliness of our existence, to our biological facticity, to the body per se. To suggest that self is embodied is not simply an insight about the fact that I am flesh and bones, that I am material, or that chemical and biological processes are going on inside my skin. Clearly, selfhood is not simply a content, not merely a that-toward-which the lived-body concernfully comports itself. It is, more globally, the fact of concernful attending, the concernful orientation that is implicated in the lived-body's caring-over any object whatsoever, not simply the "body" per se. We are headless care-takers, entities who need not have faces for-ourselves, for we are mostly ourselves when we concernfully face others, events, and things.

My study, therefore, has turned away from the predominant contemporary modes of theorizing on selfhood. Broadly construed, I have avoided positing and/or subtly reinscribing an objective realism, a subjective idealism, or even a reductivistic relativism. World is not "already present" (i.e., does not exist) independent of lived-bodies. But, lived-bodies are not "making the world up"; they are not creating it by "subjective" nor even "social" powers. I have underscored that world [and] self are not pregivens, but rather, are decompressed existential correlates which upsurge out of Earth's internal negations. Also, I continually have employed brackets ([ ]) to signify entities that exist by being suspended in intentional relations. In this way I have tried to maintain a vigilant watch over the dialogical constitutions "between" world [and] self [and] others (James, 1971; Merleau-Ponty, 1968).

This notion of embodied selfhood works against unduly limiting selfhood to the skins' boundaries. Selfhood, as embodied, is inseparable from outwardly-projected-worldly-concern, and so, to explicate fully the meaning of embodiment is to delve into the deep and metaphysical meaning of existence, world, and cosmos. We are existential openings, valuative and finite clearings in and through whom worldly existence—cosmos—comes to meaningful manifestation. We are places and moments of Earth which, negating its very nonexistence, upsurge into that supremely meaningful care-taking called being-in-the-world.

My first caution leads directly to a second misreading that must be cut off as well. I have maintained that self, as embodied, is outside itself. Further, we maintain a concern for ourselves by being concernfully co-comported toward the there. My second caution addresses the notions of being-outside-myself and of concernfully-tending-over-the-there. The task is to safeguard against "overly socialized" accounts of the meaning of various and particular with-whoms, with-whichs, and toward-whichs.

I have stated many times that the lived-body occupies space as a concernful flight beyond its physical boundaries. But this too easily can be misunderstood as a suggestion that people establish their selfhood—and/or maintain it—by employing appropriate and/or acceptable material objects as "symbols" or "signs" of their social identities. Said otherwise, it might be interpreted reductively to imply that selfhood only unfolds and develops within those material conditions and artifacts that individuals can employ purposefully (or others can take) as social identifications or disidentifications (Riggins, 1990, pp. 341–368). Indeed, we, as the there-here, are concerned over various items and entities within our surroundings that operate as signifiers and symbols of our social identities. I am referring here to those others, objects, and events that are (or can be) taken as signs of socially recognizable differentiations within identity categories (e.g., student, plumber, spouse, artist, or affluent). Some obvious examples include pieces of clothing that can signify gender, the kind of silverware one uses or the car one drives that can be taken to signify one's class, tools and handy items that can signify social and/or work roles.[37] Moreover, it is by way of finely nuanced ontical particularity that social role identity (i.e., character) is articulated: one has this car and not another, one has this silverware set and not another, this occupation and not another, or these friends rather than others. This means that socially recognizable identities are manifest by their implication as correlates to particular with-whoms, toward-whichs, and with-whichs. But, I must emphasize that such social identity is only a fragment of the way the whole of selfhood maintains itself.

Additionally, we must not conflate the ontical particularity of social meanings (i.e., identity) with the existential particularity of the overall caring project which is existence. Thus, the discussion of selfhood in Chapter 3 is not limited to socially constructed character. In a word, authentic selfhood is not obtained by surrounding oneself with others, events, and objects that symbolically establish and/or socially construct identity, as if we could establish ourselves as authentic simply by meaningfully incorporating certain objects, or by being-with certain others. Authenticity cannot be reduced to a system of articulated signs. Self-realization, self-fulfillment, a personally meaningful life, these cannot be accomplished or obtained by merely surrounding oneself with artifacts which can be taken as signs of authentic selfhood. Even more to the point, there is nothing I could buy which would bestow or render authentic selfhood, even if I purchase the most particular and exclusive items. Authenticity cannot be bought with either symbolic or monetary capital because money, by its nature, works as a system of exchange and substitution (Burke, 1961, pp. 291–297). And substitution, we can recall, is counter to particularity and originality, hallmark characteristics of authenticity. The sticking point is that authenticity is not furnished or secured by obtaining or maintaining any particular with-whoms, with-whichs, or toward-whichs. It is, I make clearer in the next section, based in the quality of our concern.

Another potential misinterpretation, one highly related to the previous one, can come for those who want to stress authenticity as a creative originality. Modern art often epitomizes this act of taking what in the past would have been inappropriate or even unacceptable, and freeing it as available and relevant in new artistic ways. From such a perspective, the meanings of "appropriateness" and "acceptability" are too constraining to individuals' freedom, and so, the task of authenticity, these persons might argue, is the quest to invent new ways of making entities available and relevant, subverting the taken-for-granted boundaries of what is appropriate and/or acceptable. Said otherwise, because sociality establishes and maintains appropriate and/or acceptable modes of freeing up with-whichs as well as manners of concernfully being-toward, it is these meanings which must be challenged.

It is here that we might recall Taylor's (1991) rough outline regarding the character and nature of authenticity as an ideal. He suggested:

> Briefly, we can say that Authenticity (A) involves (i) creation and construction as well as discovery, (ii) originality, and frequently (iii) opposition to the rules of society and even potentially to what we recognize as morality. But it is also true, as we saw, that it (B) requires (i) openness to the horizons of significance (for otherwise the creation loses the background that can save it from insignificance) and (ii) a self-definition in dialogue. (p. 66)

Authenticity, I need to show, is not simply making things available and relevant in new ways. It is not originality for the sake of originality. Originality is much more than this, and it always includes horizons of significance. It is a measure of the quality of our concern within our once-occurrent existences. The originality and discovery at issue here refer to the concernful implication and inscription of selfhood into worldly items and events. These are the higher and richer modes of authenticity. More will be said about this in the next section.

Selfhood, as discussed here, is a naturally historical accomplishment; it is operative beneath and beyond—and yet always in conjunction with— the content of our socio-cultural creations. It might even be that authenticity has no direct being-for-others, but instead, refers to the quality of the how in our concernful being-with-others-being-toward-world. So, even if it is true that most of our reality is "socially constructed," we must not overlook the fact that those very possibilities of socially constructing are natural to our phenomenological constitutions.

SELFHOOD WITHIN AUTHENTIC EXISTENCE

To maintain recognition of the intentional (i.e., the existential) relations "between" world [and] self—to never forget that they are funded by Earth's internal negations—it might be more revealing to talk not of an "authentic self," but rather, to speak of "selfhood within authentic existence." In this section, I try to show that the meaning of selfhood within authentic existence can be approached most clearly only if we examine selfhood [and] world as they are concretely manifested according to the quality of concern.

In many different ways throughout Part II, I have emphasized care-taking as a central characteristic of the human condition. I have argued that we are selves even when that selfhood is only prereflectively and implicitly inscribed into the ongoing fabric of communicative praxis

(Schrag, 1986), or even when that selfhood flees from us because it is for-others (Sartre, 1956; Bakhtin, 1990). Moreover, because world [and] self are existential correlates, we are selves by the mere fact that a world of concern "is there." Heidegger makes this most explicit where he writes, "The Dasein does not need a special kind of observation, nor does it need to conduct a sort of espionage on the ego in order to have a self; rather, as the Dasein gives itself over immediately and passionately to the world itself, its own self is reflected to it from the things" (1982, p. 159). This basically means that we accomplish selfhood in caring for world and concerning ourselves with others, even when these are not tied back to "self-interests." As lived-bodies who "are" the world, we are not simply nor exclusively concerned with or for our own bodies per se. We continually, all day long, draw near to things and tend over them by incorporating them into a host of practices, projects, and engagements. Again, "embodiment" means that we concernfully care-over things which are "not us," but which nevertheless "critically matter" (Taylor, 1995). As lived-bodies, we occupy existential centers, and so, worldly things, moment-by-moment, light up with valuative tones in terms of the total participations which comprise the project that is existence.

In Chapter 2 I have suggested that this most generally implies that regardless of cultural variations regarding the ultimate objects of concern as well as differing levels of valuation, to be human, at all, is already to evaluate participatively (i.e., to be concerned over and reckon with the disclosed world). It is in recalling and reconsidering this that I best can enter the meaning of selfhood within authentic existence. I have already suggested that authenticity refers to the quality of concern within lived-through world-experience. To disclose even further the relatedness of concern to authenticity, I must clarify the distinction between our "concern for others" and our "caring-over things," both of which, though in their own manner, range from inauthentic to authentic in the quality of concern. For the sake of clarity and brevity, I discuss each mode in both forms.

Caring-Over the World At-Hand

Caring-over, as the basic "how" informing our intentional comportments, ranges from inauthentic to authentic. Said more specifically, the care that characterizes lived-though world-experience ranges in its quality from passionate responsibility to neglectful indifference. Selfhood within authentic existence is a passionate responsibility which, as lit by the light of my once-occurrence, refers to being-in-the-world in its "could not have not been" and in its "will-have-been." Selfhood within inauthentic existence, on the other hand, is a neglectful indifference which, as numbed by the feel of my ultimate substitutability, refers to being-in-the-world in its anonymity and in its sense that I just as well could have not been. To further clarify these claims, we must explore the range of the quality of care (from inauthentic to authentic) as it relates to creativity and/or originality as well as to time and temporality.

Authenticity, as I suggested earlier, must not be reduced to a social role; it must not be collapsed to a socially constructed and typified identity. Not by any specific with-which, nor by any specifically comported employments can selfhood be said to be "authentic." It is not constituted by incorporating socially recognizable "signs" of it. This means that it cannot be purchased, not even by buying the most exclusive set of with-whichs. Neither can it be secured by pursuing particular toward-whichs. Ultimately, there is no toward-which, no in-order to, and no for-the-sake-of-which that could render or bestow authentic existence. In this regard authenticity is radically distinct from a social role, or a typified sign of identity. By its very meaning, authenticity demands creativity and a sense of originality. But what do I mean by the words "creativity" and "originality"?

Selfhood within authentic existence is a creative and original accomplishment of spatialization and temporalization in which sacrifice is a gaining. By shedding the distinction between world [and] the body, it is a creation, a timeless birthing, of an original self. When we care-over things, for example, some handiwork, selfhood is that which is slowly "cultivated" in the continued struggle to shape and articulate world (Csikszentmihalyi and Rochberg-Halton, 1981). Such deeds take great amounts of practice and patience. They must be struggled through. This includes tasks which offer natural resistance such as disciplined skills, practices of craftsmanship, accomplished musical talents. It is by being-against coefficients of adversity and various modes of recalcitrance that authentic care over worldly entities emerges and sustains itself. Such resistance, it should be noted, is the phenomenological basis for many "horizons of significance." Therefore, world [and] self are "cultivated" accomplishments which arise out of my concernful responses to difficult tasks and projects.

The originality of authentic concern over things consists in concretely realizing that one has no alibi (i.e., recognizing that one is not in a world, but is the site of worlding). Others, therefore, need not agree whether or not I am authentic. Authentic existence is not to be judged by others according to social criteria of skillful competence. It refers, more broadly, to the quality of concern in lived-through world-experience. Creative originality is the passion of being-toward, the love of world as illuminated by the light of well-done-will-have-beens. It discloses itself as a quality of the how of existing, and not as a quality of the exister per se. Originality, in this view, is neither a goal to be pursued nor an accomplishment ultimately obtained. Rather, it is that which each person already is. Authenticity, then, refers to how that originality is taken up, to the quality of the how regarding that originality. Think of it this way: selfhood within authentic existence is not that which is original as opposed to that which is not; originality is inevitable because we, all of us, already are once-occurrent beings. This means that authenticity is not a measure of whether one is original or not. On the contrary, it is some measure of how passionately one takes the whole of one's participations in once-occurrent existence. Said quite otherwise, what could be less original, less authentic, than a job, any and every task, done with less than vital concern? What could epitomize an inauthentic self more clearly than the "good enough" attitude of someone doing a task in the leveled spirit of bored mediocrity?

To be derelict of duty and indifferent to this fact, these are the hallmarks of inauthentic existence. Selfhood within inauthentic existence, therefore, is characterized by a deprecated quality of concern. It fails to escape the leveling indifference of anonymous sociality. Personal struggles and strivings seem unworthy of the effort, too much of a cost for the immediately existing self. Such a mode of selfhood is characterized by an existential languor, by emotive and volitional disclosures of one's felt irrelevance to the world. In inauthenticity we may experience no ultimate significance to the sheer fact of worldly existence. We may experience ourselves as trivial and tangential to existence. Even more specifically characterizing the quality of concern here, we can say that we are volitionally-intonated by our fleeing from the fact that we are once-occurrent worldings. It reflects the everyday attitude of anyone, and so embodies a neglectful indifference to that which calls for response. Note also the lack of creative originality manifesting itself here. By such a lack I mean that persons can pretend that the world is there regardless of them, that they are basically irrelevant, and that they just as well could have not existed. Thus, they know not the origin of world, and they fail to hear how existence calls upon them.

Authentic care over worldly things, in contrast, is creative and original. It is an ongoing passionate response to worldly calls in light of the fact that we have no alibi in being (Bakhtin, 1993). Said otherwise, given our once-occurrent moment and place in existence, demands press upon us to provide fitting responses, and thus, creative originality refers to the concrete responses (i.e., these and not others) that we give to the calls from world and others. This does imply that authentic existence can call us to develop "new" ways of being-toward. But still, this "new" must not be limited to a perpetually fleeting new, as an aesthete who is in too limited of a now and is searching only for the latest pleasures and gratifications. Indeed, the newness at issue here is an eternally old new. It is the newness that the moment continuously offers: ever fresh possibilities and new calls for fitting action.

The quality of concern within authentic lived-through world-experience is aptly characterized by the "timelessness" of practice. Therefore, authenticity is not an occasional act that occurs in time. It is not, literally, a caring comportment, a simple being-toward which occurs in time and has a certain measurable duration. It is not, by any means, a feeling that comes and goes, not an occasional state which is or is not present. Said otherwise, we cannot be authentic every once and a while. I repeat, authentic care over worldly entities is not an action or event that occurs in time. Rather, it is the way that temporality concernfully opens itself to itself. It, as accomplished in and through the moment of decision, is a way, an existential how, of gathering time. To be creatively original, to be authentic in care-taking, is to dwell habitually in the moment of decision. It, as a responsive tarrying in the moment, exists at the level of a prereflectively called practice. It is a newness which can be repeated: it exists in the timeless newness of a diligent though long-forgotten practice. Authenticity, therefore, does not exist as a single act; it exists only as a habit.

Being-With-Others in Authentic Existence

In Part II of this study I have suggested that sociality is an essential dimension of human selfhood. Others are a condition of my being-in-the-world, not an occasional feature of my experience. As the particular beings we are, a concernful project of historical continuance, we are immeasurably indebted to innumerable others. They fund world and enable us to realize possibilities that we, if completely alone, would never have come upon. We become who we are through many anonymous others who creatively fashioned various material conditions. This means that world already has been decompressed by others' intentional powers, and so, selfhood emerges within the pre-decompressed lines of inertia others already established. But, we are not only immeasurably indebted to historical others (i.e., predecessors), we also are implicated by consociates (and especially those particular others with-whom we have grown older). We depend upon particular others to free us for our possibilities, to enable us to become who we are, and they depend on us for their projects and their self-becoming.

Still, others must not be reduced to entities which are there at-hand for me, and which, in their particularity, can be taken up to serve my concernful interests or not. Taken in this way, they would be encountered as entities in our horizons which we are at liberty to care over or not. Neglectfully indifferent, we thereby may feel no obligation to respond to others' calls. Additionally, even if and when we do respond, the quality of concern may be leveled to the "average" responses of what we believe "anyone" would do. Most generally then, others are not expendable items that can be reduced to objects cared-over within "my" projects and dealings. They, in their particularity, are the very condition by which selfhood, in its particularity, concernfully transcends itself in order to become itself. This has deep implications for the meaning of selfhood within authentic existence, the most significant of which is that the meaning of selfhood undergoes a modification when we move from considering our authentic caring-over objects or events to examining authentic concern in being-with-others.

Sociality (the fact of others), I have maintained, is a condition of my existence, and hence, I must stress that the creative originality previously discussed is not directly applicable to authentic being-with-others. Recall that I suggested earlier that when we gather together, we commonly share objects or events of mutual care, even if only tacitly. That is, when we are physically with others, there is almost always a that-toward-which we are concernfully co-comported by various intentional threads. As already suggested in Part II, we jointly eat food, participate in or watch an athletic competition. We may play music together, or mutually attend to a talk. In these and other events of concernful co-comporting to a mutual toward-which, others are encountered as fellow sites of existential decompression. As concernful co-transparencies, we supplement each others' intentional powers, form common intentios, and concernfully share in common intentums. The main implication is that when we speak of authentic concern in being-with-others, we must note that one does not literally care over other persons. Others, as mutual sites of existence, are not merely a reflection of my creative and original projects; they are not the products of my once-occurrent doings. That is, others, authentically encountered, are not simply entities which are created as an expression of my originality. Even those others whom we directly are concerned with are never to be reduced to mere implicates of our creative originality. This also means that others are not simply "coefficients of adversity" or "modes of recalcitrance" which we must struggle against in order to accomplish authentic existence. To encounter others authentically is to work to free them for their possibilities of caring.

An authentic concern in being-with-others, is, as Heidegger (1962) notes, a kind of solicitude. By solicitude, I refer to the recognition that others are not things to be taken care of, but are (i.e., exist as) concernful flights outside themselves. Following Heidegger, I need to distinguish between two kinds of solicitude, one that "leaps in and dominates," and another which "leaps forth and liberates." Clarifying the latter, Heidegger writes, "This kind of solicitude pertains essentially to authentic care—that is to the existence of the Other, not to a 'what' with which he is concerned; it helps the Other to become transparent in his care and to become free for it" (1962, p. 159). He suggests, then, that this kind of solicitude, authentic care, does not directly enable the "what" of the other's concern, but focuses on the other's enablement in existence per se. Clearly, authentic being-with-others is not merely caring-over others. It is not a concern which "leaps in and dominates" the other, and as Heidegger points out, it is not simply a way of entering others' involvements and freeing them from concern either.

The passionate responsibility of our being-with-others is not such that it removes the others' concerns for them, but rather, it enables others to be free for their possibilities. Authentic being-with-others in lived-through world-experience is a passionate responsibility that recognizes that nothing separates me from the other, and so, it works to liberate others in the how of their concern. It exists as a call of conscience (Heidegger, 1962). Therefore, authentic being-with-others does not refer to aggregates of authentic individuals resolutely struggling against the indifference of a totalized "they." Instead, it shows itself as snarled nests of particularly related yous and Is authentically negotiating their collective existences in light of the facts that they could not have not existed and that they are vital to the world's will-have-been.[38] To that end, I have maintained that dialogic relations with particular others have the capacity to help me enable my interests and my possibilities, and vice-versa. This is also what is at issue in Gusdorf's discussion of communicative ethics, "Our concrete freedom is established to the extent our capacity to foster at one and the same time expression and communication within the language that makes us manifest. . . . The highest freedom begins communally—no longer a freedom that separates, but a freedom that unites" (1965, pp. 58–59). Existential particularity and once-occurrence, understood as the opening of possibilities provided therein, are that which selfhood in authentic being-with-others acknowledges and seeks to liberate.

To further my discussion, I now need to underscore the key importance of sonorousness to selfhood as being-with in authentic existence. I have stressed in Chapter 4 that sonorousness is an embodied intentionality as well as inseparable from our being-with-others: the language I speak is learned with and from others. This means that sonorousness is a naturally historical intentionality, and so, is a living testament to the fact that nothing separates me from others. Language [and] speech are a key example of how, in authentic being-with others, I do not care-over others, but rather, I free them for their own most possibilities. Stated more precisely, sonorousness, in its own regard, is a central exemplar of the indigenous possibilities for authentic concern in being-with-others. Let me clarify this point: Language is learned from and with others. Nevertheless, my power to speak is not bestowed by others. That is, I must learn language from and with others, and yet, I cannot hold the language itself responsible for my sayings; I cannot rely upon speech already spoken (i.e., language) to be answerable for my sonorousness. Likewise, then, although particular others can and will "learn language from and with me," they must learn to articulate, to come to terms with world, from their own particular situatedness. In general, I cannot speak for others by providing them with answerable recipes or maxims, for only from their once-occurrence can they speak authentically. Ultimately, neither I nor any particular other (this one and not another) can rely upon what "anyone" says; given particularity, we, each of us, must learn to speak language from out of our once-occurrence.

It is this gap between what "anyone" says and the disclosures of one's own intentional powers that warrants a demand to learn to speak out of one's particular and once-occurrent moment and place in existence. Said otherwise, we must learn to speak from our own most potential for being, to claim a voice for ourselves by individuating ourselves out of "the they" through our speech. This means that as the once-occurrent eventings of world [and] self unfold, they always call forth new responses and demand new forms of articulacy (Taylor, 1991). A mutually authentic dialogue emerges when I encounter others and they encounter me, as once-occurrent sites of Earth's existential decompression. It is here that we speak with each other in personal encounters. Others [and] I, each of us, are here ready and willing to be called into "fear and trembling."

Other persons, as lived-bodies, are outside themselves. They care over entities and events which critically matter, and so, others must not be reduced to thingly objects to be cared-over. To encounter others authentically is to embody a passionate responsibility which does not simply take over the caring of others. Such a responsibility, on the contrary, operates by loosening others "from their 'they' selves" (from the inauthentic selfhood of "anyone") and thereby frees them for their own most peculiar possibilities of care. Selfhood within authentic existence fundamentally acknowledges its indebtedness to others, and, in turn, is called to free others for their own possibilities. It maintains itself in and through our "fitting responses." Authenticity, therefore, is, at root, "called" authenticity (Heidegger, 1968). This means that it is not simply "the face" of the other that, assuming my gaze is in that direction, manifests an authentic call for response (Levinas, 1974). More necessarily, it is the other's voice which, intrusively disrupting my dream world and awakening me out of slumber, first opens my eyes and calls me to fitting social action.

In summary, authenticity refers to the quality of the concern which characterizes our being-in-the-world-with-others. It refers to the passionate responsibility within our everyday tasks, to selfgaining-selflessness, to the eternal love for the sheer fact of worlding. An authentic "how of concern" could be summarized, although a bit reductively, as a vigilantly embodied participation in three existential facts: first, lived-through world-experience is funded by Earth's internal negations; nothing separates world [and] self [and] others. Second, as persons who are existing now, we could not have not been. Third, as implicates in the world's will-have-been, we can sonorously decide and resolutely act within the whole of our participations in once-occurrent existence.

SUMMARY: CALLED PROJECTS OF AUTHENTICITY

To conclude my discussion in a fitting way, let me recall some thoughts to which my thinking is indebted. First, Nietzsche's Zarathustra spoke thus: "Your nobility should be obedience. Your very commanding should be an obeying. To a good warrior 'thou shalt' sounds more agreeable than 'I will.' . . . man is something that shall be overcome" (1954, p. 48). And, second, Gibran's "Almustafa the Chosen and Beloved," when asked about the meaning of giving, told us:

> You often say, "I would give, but only to the deserving." The trees in the orchard say this is not so, nor the flock in your pasture. They give that they may live, for to withhold is to perish. Surely those who deserve to drink from the ocean of life deserve to fill their cups from your little stream. . . . See first that you yourself deserve to be a giver, and an instrument of giving. For in truth it is life that gives unto life—while you, who deem yourself a giver, are but a witness. (1923, pp. 21–22)

Authenticity, viewed in these lights, is not in any way a radical autonomy or a total freedom to "do 'one's own' thing." It is not an egotistical drive of personal ambitions nor is it a selfish profiteering. But neither is it a slavish compliance to environmental stimuli and situational impingments. The "middle-way" most rightly characterizes authenticity (Zimmerman, 1981, pp. 229–276; Watts, 1995). Thus, we must be ready to live with paradox, or else, we may drown of thirst in "the vast desert of the shoreless sea" (Zimmer, 1946, pp. 35–52).

As a habit of passionate responsibility, authenticity is the practice of openness by which we are called to fitting responses. Authenticity, therefore, reveals itself as a kind of play: it is an ordered request and a blissfully seduced obedience. More simply addressed, it is a dutiful autonomy, one liberated by indebtedness.

CONCLUDING REMARKS

It's sometimes suggested that the all-too-common difficulty is finding the right way to begin. This is said to be so because we find, when we attempt to begin, that we always already have begun. On the other hand, endings seem much less difficult because it is easy to reflect back and see the path already traveled. Still, the very ease of providing a summary can cut against the spirit and goals of a text. Oh sure, many people do seem to like "a sense of closure." But perhaps a lack of closure is a good thing, at least in some cases. If a scholarly work ends with a tight summation and we are led to a sense of completion, the work may be placed back on the shelf while we, on the other hand, go on operating as if the reading hardly took place. A closure, in this sense, can serve as an ending to, rather than an opening of, a continued discussion.

I close this book, then, by turning to a work that has significantly informed and grounded the present research, even though I cite it now for the first time. I refer to Antoine de Saint-Exupéry's marvelous *The Wisdom of the Sands* (1950). This profound masterpiece, in my opinion one of the most inspiring and insightful books ever written, provides, perhaps, the penultimate study in authenticity. All said, I cannot think of a more appropriate envoi than to quote at length a small piece of his exquisitely crafted work:

> . . . With trembling hands he continued perfecting his fretwork, which had become for him as an elixir, ever subtler and more potent. Thus, escaping by a miracle from his gnarled old flesh, he was growing ever happier, more and more invulnerable. More and more imperishable. And, dying, knew it not, his hands being full of stars.
>
> Thus toiled they all their lives, building up a treasure not for daily use and bartering themselves for things of beauty incorruptible; alloting only a small part of their toil to daily needs, and all the rest to their carvings, to the unusable virtue of chased gold or silver, the perfection of form, the grace of noble curves—all of which served no purpose save to absorb that part of themselves they bartered, and which outlasts mortality. . . .
>
> In my long night walks it was revealed to me that the quality of my empire's civilization rests not upon its material benefits but on men's obligations and the zeal they bring to their tasks. It derives not from owning but from giving. Civilized is that craftsman I have spoken of,

who remakes himself in the thing he works on, and, for his recompense, becomes eternal, no longer dreading death. . . . Well I know those tribes degenerate who no longer write their poems but only read them; who no longer till their fields, but have recourse to slaves. . . . No love have I for the sluggards, the sendentaries of the heart; for those who barter nothing *become* nothing. Life will not have served to ripen them. For them Time flows like a handful of sand and wears them down. . . . For grief is ever begotten of Time that, flowing, has not shaped its fruit. . . .

Going a little farther . . . I saw, too, my one-legged cobbler busy threading gold into his leathren slippers and, weak as was his voice, I guessed that he was singing.

"What is it, cobbler, that makes you so happy?"

But I heeded not the answer; for I knew that he would answer me amiss and prattle of money he had earned, or his meal, or the bed awaiting him—knowing not that his happiness came of his transfiguring himself into golden slippers. (pp. 29–33)

NOTES

1. I can exemplify this issue by considering Bakhtin as somewhat of a knocker of the neo-Nietzschean spirit. Bakhtin (1981) contrasts the high and low arts, arguing that there is a centralizing and authortative function within the poetic and epic genres. In contrast, the novel is more open to the dialogical character inherent to human experience. Contrasting poetic art with novelistic art most succinctly, Bakhtin tells us: "Even when speaking of alien things, the poet speaks in his own language. To shed light on an alien world, he never resorts to alien language. . . . Whereas the writer of prose . . . attempts to talk about even his *own* world in an alien language . . . he often measures his own world by alien linguistic standards" (p. 287).

2. For an excellent discussion the issue of "background" intelligibility, Heidegger is a primary source (Heidegger,1962; also Taylor, 1995).

3. See Dennis Wrong (1961).

4. Berger and Luckmann openly grant that they have drawn from Schutz. Moreover, only an introductory study of Schutz's writings reveals the amount of borrowing to be enormous. For an excellent review which also exemplifies this overlap see Gurwitsch (1974), pp. 113–131.

5. Schutz (1967) is quite critical of Weber but is exceedingly friendly to Husserl's work. Not surprisingly, Husserl invited Schutz to study with him after the production of this text. see Carr (1986).

6. These potentials, these movements of internal negativity, loosely defined, are a bit like the logic of what Sartre has called "being-for-itself." That is, the operative logic beneath the present discussion of Earth, world, and self, can also be seen in Sartre's (1956) discussion of "being-in-itself" and "being-for-itself." Sartre states,

> But while being in-itself is contingent, it recovers itself by degenerating into a for-itself. It is, in order to lose itself in a for-itself. In a word being is and can only be. But the peculiar possibility—that which is revealed in the nihilating act—is of being the foundation of itself as consciousness through the sacrificial act which nihilates being. The for-itself is the in-itself losing itself as in-itself in order to found itself as consciousness. . . . The appearance of the for-itself or absolute event refers indeed to the effort of an in-itself to found itself; it corresponds to an attempt on the part of being to remove contingency from its being. But this attempt results in the nihilation of the in-itself, because the in-itself can not found *itself* without introducing the *self* or a reflective, nihilating reference into the absolute identity of being and consequently degenerating into for-itself.

The for-itself corresponds then to an expanding de-structuring of the in-itself, and the in-itself is nihilated and absorbed in its attempt to found itself. (pp. 81–84)

7. In the next chapter, where I discuss sociality, I show how one's face is not simply an intentional absent, but is, as Sartre suggests, "for-others."

8. See Bakhtin's (1993) discussion of Pushkin's 'Parting'; and Sartre's (1993) discussion of "helping Peter."

9. Whatever that would mean! Again, phenomenology studies only *phenomena*.

10. Note here the underlying fact that all humans, not to mention innumerable other organisms, face forward and move in directions of concern.

11. For a discussion of the gendered body, see Iris Young (1980).

12. I am indebted to Scott Caplan who, during discussion about these issues, produced this well phrased phrase.

13. Donald Norman, in his *The Psychology of Everyday Things* (1988), offers much by way of getting engineers to design objects with the body's comportments as the basis for organizing.

14. But this bodily "disappearance," this absence for the sake of the world's presence, does not imply an inability of the lived-body to reflect upon itself. We have extended powers for objectifying ourselves in thematic analysis. Because the lived-body is a *network* of intentional arcs, we can attend to one sensorimotor power from another: we can use one hand to touch the other, thereby reflectively attending *to* what we had been attending *from*. In either case, the embodied self is implicated: it is either implicitly stitched within the line of force manifesting a phenomenal field (i.e., it is an unthematized, implied correlate), or, it is explicitly thematized as an object of concernful attention in its own regard.

15. Someone might ask: Underneath all that is given in scientific accounts of it, and beyond what persons in their "everyday talk" commonly suggest with regard to it, what is eating? What does it mean to eat? How are we to understand this mysterious fact that we must eat? Has it not been radically covered-over?

16. Consider an example that may help undercut the strong sense of subjectiveness and further illustrate the dialogical constitution of an entity's "taste-ableness." Let us imagine that strange creatures from outer space land on the plant. Further, imagine that their sole food source is a dull gray putty. This food putty, in-itself, is absolutely, thoroughly, without any taste. In fact, the food substance was technologically designed so that someone can roll it up in small amounts, and, prior to placing it in the mouth, imagine and/or desire a certain taste, a certain kind of food. The putty then, in its actual (experienceable) taste, manifests exactly the taste the person desired, even allowing the person to change the putty's taste at each and every new bite. This hypothetical example brings out a fictional sense in which taste, as a sensorimotor power, would be subjective. But clearly, no one means this by the claim that taste is subjective. In summary, we must conceptually distinguish the experience of taste from the emotional-volitional evaluations of it.

17. I am partially indebted here to Hayakawa's (1940) early discussions. Let me cite his cite of James H. Robinson: "Except for our animal outfit, practi-

cally all we have is handed to us gratis. Can the most complacent reactionary flatter himself that he invented the art of writing or the printing press, or discovered his religious, economic, and moral convictions, or any of the devices which supply him with meat and raiment or of any sources of such pleasure as he may derive from literature or the fine art? In short, civilization is little else than getting something for nothing" (1940, p. 15).

18. The notion of "feral" children is sometimes given as an argument that individuals "become" social and so live in a common cultural world. Note that the actual word "feral" specifically implies that the animal was "belonging to or forming a wild population ultimately descended from individuals which escaped from captivity or domestication."

19. Obviously, it is a bit ludicrous to assume that individually existing humans are any less indigenously interrelated to everything than everything else is. All entities share infinite and indefinite natural associations, and so everything is ultimately related to everything else (Bateson, 1972; Hardison Jr., 1989).

20. See Jean-Paul Sartre's (1993) claim that I am only more "Intimate."

21. The negative depths of these self/other relations have been worked out painstakingly by Ronald David Laing. In fact, Laing has taken up and further developed Sartre's discussion of being-for-others to a remarkable degree (see Laing, Phillipson, & Lee, 1966). His analyses include not only my view of another's view of me, but they even go beyond my view of their view of my view of their view of me viewing them (Laing's *Knots*, 1970).

22. Goffman (1963a, p. 161).

23. Goffman (1963b, p. 45).

24. Goffman (1959, pp. 177–187).

25. Goffman (1974, p. 215).

26. Goffman (1971, p. 83).

27. Goffman (1974, p. 210, esp. note 15 on Bateson's notion of metacommunication).

28. Goffman (1971, pp. 95–187).

29. Goffman (1967, pp. 5–45).

30. The deep-seated difficulties with such a position are well argued by Hilary Putnam (1990). He maintains that Korzybski's claims seem to leave us with a reality which is always one step away from lived-through experience; the position, ironically, seems to undercut the pervasive and indigenous presence of our sonorous experiences. We might more playfully suggest that even if "the map is not the territory," maps are not not part of the territory. In this rather simple regard, all is territory, maps included.

31. Within phenomenological inquiry, the word "constitutes" does not mean to "build up" or to construct subjectively or psychologically. Rather, it more specifically means, to "flesh out a phenomenon's adumbrations or world profiles" (Husserl, 1993).

32. Someone might want to object to the claim that speech and thought are interdependent. Indeed, many people would argue that there is much that could be called thought which is independent of speech and language. I would not, at all, want to deny that there are many different "mental" phenomena. Who has not experienced fleeting images, vague cognitions, internal visualizations, mental sen-

sations, memories recalled, dreams, etc.? Clearly, who would want to reduce all mental or "conscious" life to speech [and] language? Still, the critical question is, without speech [and] language, could we experience their differentiation from each others? Would we even be able to order and comprehend these as different mental phenomena?

33. Goffman's "Alienation from Interaction" astutely addresses how our inability to become prereflectively absorbed in certain social, and specifically verbal, interactions is experienced as "alienation" (1967, pp. 113–136). Also and more generally, he here explicates the ritual means by which spontaneous prereflective involvement in conversations can be enabled, and how such failure can be managed.

34. William James hints at such a position when he states, "Why may not thought's mission be to increase and elevate, rather than simply to imitate and reduplicate, existence? . . . The notion of a world complete in itself, to which thought comes as a passive mirror, adding nothing to fact, Lotze says, is irrational. Rather is thought itself a most momentous part of fact, and the whole mission of the pre-existing and insufficient world of matter may simply be to provoke thought to produce its far more precious supplement" (1963, p. 175).

35. Although well beyond the scope of the present project, future research might explore how all of the various technologies of communication are "mutually incorporated," each providing its own manner of comprehension, each a unique function of spatializing spatiality and temporalizing temporality. We might examine the spatializing and temporalizing differences between speaking and writing, or between tape-recordings and the telephone. Likewise, airplanes, email, satellite dishes, microscopes, telescopes, etc. could all be examined as intentional technologies taken up by "mutual incorporation" into our concernfully being-with-others-being-toward-world.

36. Goffman (1971, pp. 33–35).

37. Consider the fact that Saint-Genet found out that items such as a tube of Vaseline can implicate the identity of one's sexual orientation (Hebdidge, 1979).

38. Near the completion of this work, someone asked me what my project has to say about Adolf Hitler. This person wanted to know if, given my account of authenticity, Hitler could have been authentic, and/or how this work would safeguard against such an audacious claim. For the sake of further clarification I shall consider a simple question: Could Hitler have been authentic? To respond to this question as fruitfully as possible, I need to set much straight. I start with the question itself.

The main, and perhaps most significant point to raise is that we should never ask whether someone else is or is not authentic. Questions pertaining to authenticity can be raised only regarding oneself. Thus, we never want to ask, or attempt to determine, if others are in "authentic existence." Moreover, even with regard to ourselves, our concern should not be over "our authenticity," but with those persons, events, and items which critically matter.

Second, I was a bit concerned that someone would wish for me to provide a text which would offer a rationale by which Hitler could be condemned. That is, this text is not, in any way, offered as something that can tell people how they are to think and react to someone such as this. Said quite otherwise, we might want to ask why should a scholarly work be offered as a safeguard? Or, even better: Who wants to use this text as their basis for a critique? And moreover, Are they thereby seeking an alibi rather than passionately responding from their own unique place and moment in existence? But perhaps I am getting ahead of myself.

Granting these two precautionary notes, I might, for the sake of argument, consider this somewhat misguided question. The first thing I would want to say is that Hitler was quite concerned with renewing the economic conditions of Germany. In this very specific regard, his concern did seem to be to free persons for their pursuits. Also, he clearly seemed to have a passionate recognition that he was a participant in the world's will-have-been. By the light of these two aspects someone might try to argue that he was, in fact, authentic. Such a conclusion is undoubtedly too hasty. First, Hitler failed to recognize the once-occurrence of each individual (i.e., their existential particularity). By this, I mean that his actions embodied and so demonstrated a leveling of qualitative differences. Moving out of a biological determinism, he reduced the "Jews" and the "Aryans" into anonymously interchangeable sets of persons. This clearly is against the spirit of authenticity as I articulate it here. Moreover, encountering the other as an object in his own horizons of involvements is another fatal flaw of his tactics.

Perhaps the best way to illustrate my reaction to the question, then, is to turn our attention in the following direction. The question then and now is: How and in what concrete ways am I called into fitting responses? How am I answering the call for a fitting response to this legacy?

REFERENCES

Anton, C. (1995). "Transparency and Opacity: A Brief Phenomenology of Message Flesh." Paper presented to the Semiotic Society of America. San Antonio, Texas. November. [Also forthcoming in J. M. Martinez and L. R. Gordon (eds.), *Communicating Differences: Essays in Phenomenology and Communicative Praxis*. Savage, MD: Rowman and Littlefield.]

Anton, C. (1997). "On Speaking: A Phenomenological Recovering of a Forgotten Sense." *Philosophy and Rhetoric, 30,* 179–192.

Anton, C. (1998a). "Concerning Speech: Heidegger and Performative Intentionality," *Philosophy and Rhetoric, 31,* 131–144.

Anton, C. (1998b). "About Talk: The Category of Talk-Reflexive Words," *Semiotica, 121,* 193–212.

Anton, C. (1999). "Beyond the Constitutive/Representational Dichotomy: The Phenomenological Notion of Intentionality," *Communication Theory, 9,* 26–57.

Anton, C. (in press A). "Beyond Theoretical Ethics: Bakhtinian Anti-Theoreticism," *Human Studies.*

Aristotle. (1941). Nichomachean Ethics. (W. D. Ross, Trans.). In *The Basic Works of Aristotle.* New York: Random House.

Augustine, A. (1952). *The Confessions of Saint Augustine.* (E. B. Pusey, Trans.). New York: Pocket Books.

Bakhtin, M. M. (1981). *The Dialogic Imagination.* (C. Emerson and M. Holquist, Trans.). Austin, TX: The University of Texas Press.

Bakhtin, M. M. (1990). *Art and Answerability.* (V. Liapunov, Trans.). Austin, TX: University of Texas Press.

Bakhtin, M. M. (1993). *Toward a Philosophy of the Act.* (V. Liapunov, Trans.). Austin, TX: University of Texas Press.

Bakhtin, M. M., and Medvedev, P. N. (1978). *The Formal Method in Literary Scholarship.* (A. J. Wehrle, Trans.). Baltimore: The Johns Hopkins University Press.

Barthes, R. (1970). *The Empire of Signs.* Philadelphia: J. Benjamin Publishers.

Bateson, G. (1972). *Steps to an Ecology of Mind.* New York: Ballantine Books.

Bateson, G. (1979). *Mind and Nature: A Necessary Unity.* New York: Bantam Books.

Baudrillard, J. (1983). *Simulations.* New York: Semiotext(e), Inc.

Berger, P. L., and Luckmann, T. (1966). *The Social Construction of Reality.* New York: Doubleday.

Bleibtreu, J. N. (1968). *The Parable of the Beast.* New York: Macmillan.

Blumer, H. (1967). *Symbolic Interactionism.* Englewood Cliffs, NJ: Prentice-Hall.

Bochner, A. P. (1985). "Perspectives on Inquiry: Representation, Conversation and Reflection." In M. L. Knapp and G. R. Miller (eds.), *Handbook of Interpersonal Communication*. Beverly Hills, CA: Sage.

Bochner, A. P., Cissna, K. N., and Garko, M. G. (1991). "Optional Metaphors for Studying Interaction. In B. M. Montgomery and S. Duck (eds.), *Studying Interpersonal Interaction*. New York: Guilford Press.

Bookchin, M. (1995). *The Philosophy of Social Ecology*. New York: Black Rose Books.

Burke, K. (1952). *A Grammar of Motives*. New York: Prentice-Hall.

Burke, K. (1954). *Permanence and Change*. Indianapolis: The Bobbs-Merrill Company.

Burke, K. (1957). *The Philosophy of Literary Form*. Berkeley, CA: University of California Press.

Burke, K. (1961). *The Rhetoric of Religion*. Berkeley, CA: University of California Press.

Burke, K. (1966). *Language as Symbolic Action*. Berkeley, CA: University of California Press.

Campbell, J. (1949). *The Hero with a Thousand Faces*. Princeton: Princeton University Press.

Carr, D. (1986). *Time, Narrative, and History*. Bloomington: Indiana University Press.

Casey, E. (1976). *Imagining: A Phenomenological Study*. Bloomington: Indiana University Press.

Cassirer, E. (1944). *An Essay on Man*. New Haven: Yale University Press.

Collingwood, R. G. (1938). *The Principles of Art*. Oxford: Oxford University Press.

Cort, D. (1970). *Revolution by Cliché*. New York: Funk and Wangalls.

Csikszentmihalyi, M., and Rochberg-Halton, E. (1981). *The Meaning of Things: Domestic Symbols and the Self*. New York: Cambridge University Press.

de Beauvoir, S. (1976). *The Ethics of Ambiguity*. (B. Frechtman, Trans.). New York: Carol Publishing Group.

de Grazia, S. (1964). *Of Time, Work, and Leisure*. New York: Anchor Books.

Deetz, S. (1973). Words without Things: Toward a Social Phenomenology of Language. *Quarterly Journal of Speech, 59*, 41–51.

Dennett, D. C. (1991). *Consciousness Explained*. Boston: Little, Brown and Company.

Derrida, J. (1974). *Of Grammatology*. Baltimore: The Johns Hopkins University Press.

Derrida, J. (1977). *Limited, Inc*. Evanston: Northwestern University Press.

Dewey, J. (1988). *The Later Works of John Dewey, 1925–1953. Vol. 1: 1925. Experience and Nature*. Carbondale: Southern Illinois University Press.

Dewey, J. (1991). *How We Think*. New York: Prometheus Books. Originally published in 1910.

Dillon, M. C. (1988). *Merleau-Ponty's Ontology*. Bloomington: Indiana University Press.

Dillon, M. C. (1995). *Semiological Reductionism*. Albany, NY: State University of New York Press

Dreyfus, H. L. (1979). *What Computers Still Can't Do*. Cambridge: M.I.T. Press.

Dreyfus, H. L. (1991). *Being-in-the-World*. Cambridge: M.I.T. Press.

Dreyfus, H. L. (1996). "The Current Relevance of Merleau-Ponty's Phenomenology of Embodiment," *The Electronic Journal of Analytic Philosophy*, 4 Spring.

Edie, J. M. (1987). *William James and Phenomenology*. Bloomington: Indiana University Press.

Edie, J. M. (ed.), (1965). *An Invitation to Phenomenology*. Chicago: Quadrangle Books.

Emerson, R. W. (1968). *The Selected Writing of Ralph Waldo Emerson*. New York: Random House.

Foucault, M. (1993). "About the Beginning of the Hermeneutics of the Self," *Political Theory*, 2, 198–227.

Frazer, J. G. (1909). *The Golden Bough*. New York: Macmillan Company.

Gadamer, G. H. (1975). *Truth and Method*. New York: Seabury.

Gass, W. H. (1985). *Habitations of the Word*. New York: Simon & Schuster.

Geertz, C. (1973). *The Interpretation of Cultures*. New York: Basic Books.

Gergen, K. J., Gulerce, A., Lock, A., and Misra, G. (1996). "Psychological Science in Cultural Context." *American Psychologist*, May.

Gibran, K. (1923). *The Prophet*. New York: A. A. Knopf.

Goffman, E. (1959). *The Presentation of Self in Everyday Life*. New York: Doubleday Anchor Books.

Goffman, E. (1963a). *Behavior in Public Places: Notes on the Social Organization of Gatherings*. New York: The Free Press.

Goffman, E. (1963b). *Stigma: Notes on the Management of Spoiled Identity*. New York: Simon & Schuster.

Goffman, E. (1967). *Interaction Ritual: Essays on Face-to-Face Behavior*. New York: Pantheon Books.

Goffman, E. (1971). *Relations in Public: Microstudies of the Public Order*. New York: Basic Books.

Goffman, E. (1974). *Frame Analysis: An Essay on the Organization of Experience*. Boston: Northeastern University Press.

Goffman, E. (1981). *Forms of Talk*. Philadelphia: University of Pennsylvania Press.

Goodman, P. (1957). *Growing Up Absurd*. New York: Vintage Books.

Greene, J. O. (1984). "Speech Preparation Processes and Verbal Fluency," *Human Communication Research*, 11, 61–84.

Gurwitsch, A. (1974). *Phenomenology and the Theory of Science*. Evanston: Northwestern University Press.

Gurwitsch, A. (1979). *Human Encounters in the Social World*. Pittsburgh: Duquesne University Press.

Gusdorf, G. (1965). *Speaking*. (P. T. Brockelman, Trans.). Evanston: Northwestern University Press.

Hall, E. T. (1976). *Beyond Culture*. New York: Anchor Books.

Hall, E. T. (1983). *The Dance of Life*. New York: Anchor Books.

Harding, D. E. (1981). "On Having No Head," In D. R. Hofstadter & D. C. Dennett (eds.), *The Mind's I: Fantasies and Reflections on Self and Soul*. New York: Basic Books.

Hardison, O. B. (1989). *Disappearing Through the Skylight*. New York: Viking Books.

Hayakawa, S. I. (1940). *Language in Action*. New York: Harcourt, Brace, and Company.

Hebdige, D. (1979). *Subculture: The Meaning of Style*. New York: Routledge.

Heidegger, M. (1961). *An Introduction to Metaphysics*. (R. Manheim, Trans.). New York: Anchor Books.

Heidegger, M. (1962). *Being and Time*. (J. Macquarrie and E. Robinson, Trans.). San Francisco: Harper Collins Publishers.

Heidegger, M. (1967). *What is a Thing?* (W. B. Barton and V. Deutsch, Trans.). Chicago: Henry Regnery Company.

Heidegger, M. (1968). *What is Called Thinking?* (J. G. Gray, Trans.). New York: Harper & Row Publishers.

Heidegger, M. (1971). *On the Way to Language*. (P. D. Hertz, Trans.). New York: Harper & Row Publishers.

Heidegger, M. (1982). *The Basic Problems of Phenomenology*. (A. Hofstadter, Trans.). Bloomington: Indiana University Press.

Heidegger, M. (1984). *The Metaphysical Foundations of Logic*. (M. Heim, Trans.). Bloomington: Indiana University Press.

Heidegger, M. (1985). *The History of the Concept of Time*. (T. Kisiel, Trans.). Bloomington: Indiana University Press.

Heidegger, M. (1992). *The Concept of Time*. (W. McNeill, Trans.). Cambridge, MA: Blackwell Publishers.

Heidegger, M. (1993). *Basic Writings*. (D. F. Krell, Trans.). San Francisco: Harper Collins Publishers.

Heidegger, M. (1995). *The Fundamental Concepts of Metaphysics*. (W. McNeill and N. Walker, Trans.). Bloomington: Indiana University Press.

Heidegger, M. (1997). *Being and Time*. (J. Stambaugh, Trans.). Albany, NY: State University of New York Press.

Heider, F. (1958). *The Psychology of Interpersonal Relations*. New York: John Wiley and Sons.

Held, K. (1997). "World, Emptiness, Nothingness: A Phenomenological Approach to the Religious Traditions of Japan." *Human Studies, 20*, 153–167.

Henry, J. (1965). *Pathways to Madness*. New York: Vintage Books.

Herder, J. G. (1966). *Essay on the Origin of Language*. (A. Gode, Trans.). Chicago: University of Chicago Press.

Holquist, M. (1990). *Dialogism: Bakhtin and His World*. New York: Routledge.

Hudson, L. (1972). *The Cult of the Fact*. London: Cape.

Husserl, E. (1964). *The Phenomenology of Internal Time-Consciousness*. (J. S. Churchill, Trans.). Bloomington: Indiana University Press.

Husserl, E. (1993). *Cartesian Meditations*. (D. Cairns, Trans.). Boston: Kluwer Academic Publishers.

Ihde, D. (1986). *Consequences of Phenomenology*. Albany, NY: State University of New York Press.

James, W. (1958). "The Laws of Habit." In *Talks to Teachers on Psychology: and to Students on Some of Life's Ideals*. New York: W. W. Norton.

James, W. (1963). *Pragmatism and Other Essays*. New York: Washington Square Press.

James, W. (1971). *Essays in Radical Empiricism* and *A Pluralistic Universe*. New York: E. P. Dutton & Co.

James, W. (1977). "The One and The Many," In J. J. McDermott (ed.), *The Writings of William James: A Comprehensive Edition*. Chicago: The University of Chicago Press.

Jonas, H. (1966). "Immortality and the Modern Temper." In *The Phenomenon of Life*. Chicago: The University of Chicago Press.

Kearney, R. (1991). *Poetics of Imagining*. London: HarperCollins Press.

Kestenbaum, V. (1977). *The Phenomenological Sense of John Dewey: Habit and Meaning*. Atlantic Highlands, NJ: Humanities Press.

Laing, R. D., Phillipson, H., and Lee, A. R. (1966). *Interpersonal Perception*. New York: Springer Publishing Company.

Laing, R. D. (1970). *Knots*. New York: Vintage Books.

Lanigan, R. (1988). *Phenomenology of Communication*. Pittsburgh: Duquesne Press.

Lanigan, R. (1992). *The Human Science of Communicology*. Pittsburgh: Duquesne Press.

Lazarus, R. S. (1969). *Patterns of Adjustment and Human Effectiveness*. New York: McGraw-Hill.

Leder, D. (1990). *The Absent Body*. Chicago: The University of Chicago Press.

Leeds-Hurwitz, W. (1989). *Communication in Everyday Life*. Norwood, NJ: Ablex Publishing.

Levin, D. M. (1985). *The Body's Recollection of Being*. London: Routledge

Levin, D. M. (1989). *The Listening Self*. London: Routledge.

Levinas, E. (1974). *Otherwise Than Being*. (A. Lingis, Trans.). Dordrecht: Kluwer Academic Publishers.

Lévy-Bruhl, L. (1975). *The Notebooks on Primitive Mentality*. (P. Riviére, Trans.). New York: Harper & Row.

Lyotard, J-F. (1984). *The Postmodern Condition: A Report on Knowledge*. (G, Bennington and B. Massumi, Trans.). Minneapolis: University of Minnesota Press.

Madison, G. (1996). "Being and Speaking." In J. Stewart (ed.). *Beyond the Symbol Model*. Albany, NY: State University of New York Press.

Malinowski, B. (1923). "The Problem of Meaning in Primitive Languages." In C. K. Ogden and I. A. Richards, *The Meaning of Meaning*. New York: Harcourt, Brace, and World.

Mandelbaum, J. (1989). Interpersonal Activities in Conversational Storytelling. *Western Journal of Speech Communication, 53*, 114–126.

McLuhan, M. (1964). *Understanding Media*. Cambridge: The M.I.T. Press.

Mead, G. H. (1932). *The Philosophy of the Present*. Chicago: The University of Chicago Press.

Mead, G. H. (1934). *Mind, Self and Society*. Chicago: The University of Chicago Press.

Merleau-Ponty, M. (1962). *Phenomenology of Perception*. (C. Smith, Trans.). Atlantic Highlands, NJ: The Humanities Press.

Merleau-Ponty, M. (1964). *Signs*. (R. McCleary, Trans.). Evanston: Northwestern University Press.

Merleau-Ponty, M. (1968). *The Visible and the Invisible*. (A. Lingis, Trans.). Evanston: Northwestern University Press.

Merleau-Ponty, M. (1973). *The Prose of the World*. (J. O'Neill, Trans.). Evanston: Northwestern University Press.

Morot-Sir, E. (1993). *The Imagination of Reference*. Gainesville, FL: University Press of Florida.

Nietzsche, F. (1954). *Thus Spake Zarathustra*. (T. Common, Trans.). New York: The Modern Library.

Nietzsche, F. (1979). "On Truth and Lies in a Nonmoral Sense," In D. Breazeale (ed.), *Philosophy and Truth: Sections from Nietzsche's Notebooks of the Early 1870's*. Atlantic Highlands, NJ: The Humanities Press.

Norman, D. (1988). *The Psychology of Everyday Things*. New York: Basic Books.

O'Neill, J. (1989). *The Communicative Body: Studies in Communicative Philosophy Politics and Sociology*. Evanston: Northwestern University Press.

Ong, W. J. (1967). *The Presence of the Word*. New York: Simon & Schuster.

Ortega y Gasset, J. (1958). *Man and Crisis*. New York: W. W. Norton.

Polanyi, M. (1962). *Personal Knowledge*. London: Routledge & Kegan Paul.

Polanyi, M. (1966). *The Tacit Dimension*. Garden City, NY: Doubleday.

Putnam, H. (1990). *Realism with a Human Face*. Cambridge: Harvard University Press.

Reynolds, D. K. (1983). *Nakian Psychotherapy: Meditation for Self-Development*. Chicago: University of Chicago Press.

Ricoeur, P. (1967). "Husserl and Wittgenstein on Language." In *Phenomenology and Existentialism*, E. N. Lee and M. Mandelbaum (eds.), 207–217. Baltimore: The Johns Hopkins Press.

Ricoeur, P. (1988). *Time and Narrative*, Vol. III, (K. Blamey and D. Pellauer, Trans.). Chicago: University of Chicago Press.

Ricoeur, P. (1992). *Oneself as Another*. Chicago: University of Chicago Press.

Riggins, S. H. (1990). *Beyond Goffman*. New York: Mouton de Gruyter.

Rorty, R. (1979). *Philosophy and the Mirror of Nature*. Princeton: Princeton University Press.

Saint-Exupéry, A. (1950). *The Wisdom of the Sands*. (S. Gilberg, Trans.). New York: Harcourt, Brace and Company.

Santayana, G. (1956). *Character and Opinion in the United States*. New York: Doubleday Anchor Books.

Sartre, J-P. (1948). *The Emotions: Outline of a Theory*. (B. Frechtman, Trans.). New York: Philosophical Library.

Sartre, J-P. (1955). *No Exit and Three Other Plays*. New York: Vintage Books.

Sartre, J-P. (1956). *Being and Nothingness*. (H. E. Barnes, Trans.). New Jersey: Gramercy Books.

Sartre, J-P. (1966) "Faces, Preceded by Official Portraits" (A. P. Jones, Trans.). In M. Natanson (ed.), *Essays in Phenomenology*. The Hage: Martinus Hijhoff.

Sartre, J-P. (1991). *The Psychology of Imagination*. New York: Carol Publishing Group.

Sartre, J-P. (1993). *The Transcendence of the Ego*. New York: Hill and Wang.

Schrag, C. O. and Ramsey, R. E. (1994). "Method and Phenomenological Research: Humility and Commitment in Interpretation, *Human Studies, 17,* 131–137.

Schrag, C. O. (1961). *Existence and Freedom*. Evanston: Northwestern University Press.

Schrag, C. O. (1969). *Experience and Being: Prolegomena to a Future Ontology*. Evanston: Northwestern University Press.

Schrag, C. O. (1980). *Radical Reflection and The Origin of the Human Sciences*. West Lafayette: Purdue University Press.

Schrag, C. O. (1986). *Communicative Praxis and the Space of Subjectivity*. Bloomington: Indiana University Press.

Schrag, C. O. (1994). *Philosophical Papers*. Albany, NY: State University of New York Press.

Schrag, C. O. (1997). *The Self after Postmodernity*. New Haven: Yale University Press.

Schumacher, E. F. (1977). *A Guide for the Perplexed*. New York: Harper.

Schutz, A. (1967). *Phenomenolgy of the Social World*. (G. Walsh and F. Lehnert, Trans.). Evanston: Northwestern University Press.

Shotter, J. (1995). "Before Theory and After Representationalism: Understanding meaning 'from within' a Dialogical Practice." In J. Stewart (ed.), *Beyond the Symbol Model*. Albany, NY: State University of New York Press.

Steiner, G. (1973). *Psychology Today*, February.

Steiner, G. (1975). *After Babel: Apects of Language and Translation*. New York: Oxford University Press.

Steiner, G. (1989). *Real Presences*. Chicago: University of Chicago Press.

Stewart, J. (1994). "Structural Implications of the Symbol Model for Comunication Theory: Language as Constitutive Articulate Contact," In R. L. Conville (ed.), *Uses of "Structure" in Communication Studies*. New York: Praeger.

Stewart, J. (1995). *Language as Articulate Contact: Toward a Post-Semiotic Philosophy of Communication*. Albany, NY: State University of New York Press.

Stewart, J. (1996). *Beyond the Symbol Model: Reflections on the Representational Nature of Language*. Albany, NY: State University of New York Press.

Straus, E. (1963). *The Primary World of Senses*. New York: Free Press of Glencoe.

Straus, E. (1966). *Phenomenological Psychology*. New York: Basic Books.

Taylor, C. (1985). *Human Agency and Language*. Cambridge: Harvard University Press.

Taylor, C. (1991). *The Ethics of Authenticity*. Cambridge: Harvard University Press.

Taylor, C. (1995). *Philosophical Arguments*. Cambridge: Harvard University Press.

Thayer, L. (1987). *On Communication*. Norwood, NJ: Ablex Publishing.

Thayer, L. (1997). *Pieces: Toward a Revisioning of Communication/Life*. Norwood, NJ: Ablex Press.

Veblen, T. (1899). *The Theory of the Leisure Class*. New York: The Modern Library.

von Uexküll, J. (1926). *Theoretical Biology*. New York: Hardcourt, Brace and Co.

Watts, A. (1966). *The Book: On the Taboo Against Knowing Who You Are*. New York: Vintage Books.

Watts, A. (1995). *Buddhism: The Religion of No-Religion*. Boston: Tuttle Publishing

Watzlawick, P., Beavin, J. H., and Jackson, D. D. (1967). *Pragmatics of Human Communication*. New York: W. W. Norton.

Wilden, A. (1972). *System and Structure*. London: Tavistock Publications.

Wilson, R. A. (1948). *The Miraculous Birth of Language*. New York: Philosophical Library.

Wittgenstein, L. (1953). *Philosophical Investigations*. New York: Macmillian.

Wrong, D. (1961). "The Over Socialized Concept of Man in Sociology," *The American Sociological Review, 26*, 183–193.

Young, I. (1980). "Throwing like a Girl: A Phenomenology of Feminine Bodily Comportment, Motility and Spatiality," *Human Studies, 3*, 137–156.

Zijderveld, A. (1978). *On Clichés*. London: Routledge & Kegan Paul.

Zimmer, H. (1946). *Myths and Symbols in Indian Art and Civilization*. New York: Harper & Row.

Zimmerman, M. E. (1981). *Eclipse of the Self*. Athens: Ohio University Press.

INDEX